HG
540   Weintraub, Sidney
W44   Our stagflation malaise

85252

DATE DUE	DEC 1 1 1982		
JUN 2 9 1998			

LEARNING RESOURCES CENTER
MONTGOMERY COUNTY COMMUNITY COLLEGE
BLUE BELL, PENNSYLVANIA

OUR STAGFLATION MALAISE

NEW TITLES FROM QUORUM BOOKS

The Uses of Psychiatry in the Law: A Clinical View of Forensic
    Psychiatry
WALTER BROMBERG

Abuse on Wall Street: Conflicts of Interest in the Securities Market
TWENTIETH CENTURY FUND

The Politics of Taxation
THOMAS J. REESE

Modern Products Liability Law
RICHARD A. EPSTEIN

U.S Multinationals and Worker Participation in Management: The
    American Experience in the European Community
TON DEVOS

OUR
STAGFLATION
MALAISE

ENDING INFLATION AND UNEMPLOYMENT

SIDNEY WEINTRAUB

Quorum Books
Westport, Connecticut • London, England

Library of Congress Cataloging in Publication Data

Weintraub, Sidney, 1914-
    Our stagflation malaise.

    Includes index.
    1. Inflation (Finance)--United States. 2. Unemploy-
ment--United States--Effect of inflation on. I. Title.
HG540.W44   332.4'14'0973   80-39658
ISBN 0-89930-005-7

Library of Congress Catalog Card Number: 80-39658
ISBN: 0-89930-005-7

First published in 1981 by Quorum Books

Greenwood Press
A division of Congressional Information Service, Inc.
88 Post Road West, Westport, Connecticut 06881

Printed in the United States of America

10 9 8 7 6 5 4 3 2 1

CONTENTS

CHARTS

TABLES

PREFACE

As politics in the electronic age has come to imitate theater, President Reagan, in his first TV talk to the nation on February 5, 1981, evoked memories of Franklin D. Roosevelt's fireside chats in lamenting that the economy was in "the worst economic mess since the Great Depression." It is possible to agree—reservedly—with this assessment.

Unlike the bold early experimental Roosevelt zigzag which vastly extended government intervention, President Reagan has espoused an opposite ideology to dismantle the public economic arm. All of us who value the nation's stake will wish for the president to succeed handsomely. Our country, and much of the world, would then be relieved of its debilitating plight of relentless inflation and remorseless unemployment. The dual affliction has been a 13-year itch and a cruel ordeal.

It is premature to pronounce a convincing judgment on the backward political evolution in a convulsive and complex age which bears little resemblance to the upstart technological and elementary institutional forms of bygone history. What *is* manifest is that President Reagan, with his advisers, has from the outset confounded the financial size of government with the scope of the market economy inflation perplexity, and the attendant unemployment. The transparencies are not the same, nor do they entirely overlap nor completely intersect. The top layer confusion of the separate species bodes trouble ahead. Any success, I venture, will be short-lived. The fundamental flaw in the market economy has not been corrected, for the president perceives the enterprise sector with undeserved optimism despite its inherent capacity for unmitigated distortion in the operation of labor and income markets.

In concert with the presidential takeover, there has been a din of spurious sloganeering by the Reagan retinue which has invoked a mostly mystic "supply side" economics. Probing under the thick cover of the seductive rhetorical flourishes which promise economic miracles, there is a thinly disguised tax-cut fever, a deregulatory fervor, and the brandishment of a fitful budget axe. Shorn of its pretentious verbal wrappings, the inner content would have commended itself to President McKinley at the turn of the century. The Kemp-Roth bill has enjoyed an amazing sales pitch even as it has drawn a fanciful one-sided analogy to the Kennedy tax cut.

After the implementation of the Reagan program, and the commotion and back-and-side tracking subsides, inflation may be shaved by a whisker. But, at best, it will yield temporarily. The job predicament can worsen, so that any drop in the misery index will be elusive. Deferred once more by the Reaganites, our officialdom will have to confront the systemic imperative of gearing money incomes to the productivity tempo or we will never banish inflation without condemning labor and capital resources to the underemployment rack to rout the price blight. The chronic refusal to admit the mad assault of pay versus productivity on the laws of arithmetic denies our claims to economic maturity and acumen.

My work is preoccupied with examining how this connection can be accomplished in harmony with our market system and democratic traditions, with only minimal revision of our institutional practices. Labor market relations will not be ruptured, for they have long ceased to operate on the script of the mythical models. In this context I refer to the enactment of TIP, the acronym for a tax-based incomes policy, conceived as a supplement to Federal Reserve monetary and federal fiscal policy for securing a sane price-level course without unemployment jitters. TIP is the one serious idea to have surfaced from the copious diagnoses of the stagflation havoc; exposed to fairly wide professional and journalistic scrutiny, it is still not a household concept.

Economic affairs have changed. Yet our policies pretend that the clock has stood still. So they are sterile, futile, and archaic, serving to entrench the stagflation mess and to intensify the sullen anguish among our people victimized by the sordid outcome. They deserve better. After TIP, improved stabilization variants may evolve. Economists stand in the dock of public opinion suspected of having shut their eyes, and minds, for too long to the realities which compel fresh remedies to steady the modern economy.

Ironically, both the radical left and the extreme right reject novel proposals peremptorily, often without viewing the contents. The two wings embrace in an unwritten alliance. The radical group wants the market system to collapse, and spurns measures to salvage it. The cast-iron conservative bloc acts on the premise that what has consistently sputtered must surely triumph so long as it is ardently pursued. Unremitting stagflation, however, deprives the market system of committed adherents among the legions who suffer, and among the majority on the middle ground who are made skeptical of the system's soundness by the perceived imperfections in the enterprise mechanism. Politically, the economic turmoil sponsors a stale quadrennial game of musical chairs in the presidency, with one proven incompetent displaced by another potential misfit. A corresponding charade has been in progress in other countries. Meanwhile, all of us are infected by the rot which ramifies beyond economic and political perturbation and upheaval to social tension.

Individual well-being and rational living depend on our piercing the stagflation barrier. This conviction prompts this book of somewhat unconventional ideas, containing "orthodox heresy," to provoke thought within an audience concerned with profound issues and reasonable resolution. I am grateful to my gifted students, Susan F. Cline, Robert Pinkham, and Doris Robinson for aiding me in assembling data.

PART I

THE STAGFLATION DILEMMA

The initial chapters sketch the twin disaster of excessive and relentless inflation and heavy, remorseless unemployment that constitutes the modern *stagflation malaise*. The economic, political, and social mischief perpetrated by the pair in juxtaposition is elaborated in an account which conveys a sense of the magnitudes entailed and the frightful accelerating pace of our venture into economic madness.

President Reagan in his first months in office has recognized the chaos and has sought to cure our afflictions through the federal budget and by lifting some overzealous regulatory burdens. Even if some temporary respite is purchased, the deeper stagflation rot will endure. The neoconservative vision, in this respect, invokes an image of the military leader who prepares for a precipitate battle in a remote place at an inauspicious time with insufficient forces. Tax relief may be a weak consolation prize for deeper political, economic, and social mischief.

1

THE STAGFLATION MALAISE:
THE AMERICAN TRAGEDY

Our *stagflation malaise*, universally identified by the scar of excessive unemployment and the symptom of far too high inflation, has become a chronic ailment. The twin disorder has bedeviled our economy for over 12 years now and without signs of abating. It has led to acute social distress and sullen political turmoil, while damaging our world credibility and diluting our power and influence in international councils. A cruel and wanton debilitation lingers amid prognoses of continued economic impairment.

The malady is awesome to contemplate. It occurs in an age when Nobel prizes are awarded to economists for scientific achievement, so the starry citations inform us. Mathematical techniques lend an aura of precision to the precious doctrines. Piles of data are assembled, organized, sifted, and the marvels of the computer are enlisted to speed econometric processing. Withal, our highly publicized economic luminaries have only been able to accomplish what no previous generation of unsophisticated and unsung economists could do, namely, to generate *simultaneous* inflation and unemployment!

This juxtaposition of a twin disorder is our stagflation malaise. One can only view this dazzling "triumph" of modern economics as an artful and extraordinary hoax, or a not bemusing low-wire trick. When economic events get so badly out of whack it must be that there are cracks and crumbling in the foundations of the edifice of dominant ideas. For practical policies rest on the fundamentals; the prescriptions extracted from them by economists are transmitted to the public and the politicians.

Sooner or later political leaders yield to professional expertise in framing legislative designs to cope with unruly economic phenomena.

Something must be inherently wrong in conception when the United States, the most mature and stable democracy, and by far the strongest economic power, displays the chaos that formerly confounded only Latin-American "banana-republics," or provided hilarious scenes for comic opera fantasies where everything would fly apart on cue. In one unpremeditated swoop, in a plunge out of our former affluent age, mirthful farce has become ensconced as a grim reality. For example, to signal the historical break, in the business cycle of our longer past the recovery and prosperity phase would report *rising* prices and production, and *falling* unemployment. A recession downswing would reveal *falling* prices and output, and rising unemployment.

One disaster, one at a time, was the inexorable bygone rule. Now, under the stagflation sway, an undeviating double trouble besets us, a double jeopardy in rising prices *and* rising (or too high) unemployment rates. Under recession, there is an added complication involving a triple evil as receding output is thrown in to form the *slumpflation* word-twister, or the ultimate in seamy comic opera plots.

Internationally, our stagflation malaise provokes scorn and derision. Our economic follies have supplanted the British Sickness as a synonym for a bankrupt economic policy. Over most of the post-World War II era, while its erstwhile foes were steaming ahead, England was tagged as the "sick man of Europe," what with its laggard productivity tied to wildcat work-stoppages and jurisdictional strikes, intermittent tea breaks, long weekends, and an archaic industrial plant. Our own ineptitude and the decline of American economic power with the onset of our stagflation meanderings can be traced back to the Nixon days of economic mis-government. Later on, the deplorable Carter economic crew accomplished a remarkable feat in accenting the Nixon bumbling, in an incumbency unmatched in our economic annals for sheer ineptitude. The gross Carter incompetence is grotesque enough to expunge memories of Herbert Hoover's floundering at the onset of the Great Depression.

STAGFLATION AND SLUMPFLATION

Stagflation and slumpflation are the new entries in the economic lexicon, with both words recently coined to denote the new phenomena. Since 1969 stagflation has been commonplace in the United States; slump-flation was present in the 1974 and the 1980 recessions. England, too, has been victimized by the same disease in the 1970s; Canada, Australia, and other countries reveal varying degrees of infection.

Prior to the 1970s our economy was free of these ignominies except for a very mild and brief stagflation fever in 1957-1958, which recorded a small trace in a price creep of under 3 percent and unemployment growing by about 2.5 percentage points. Some of us, at the time, were aghast and alarmed at what, in retrospect, was a feeble price breakout; it was pounced on at the time as "inflationary!" Now we are conditioned by the modern bunglers to face double-digit price bulges with equanimity, almost as a natural outcome, such as the 13.3 percent surge in the consumer price index in 1979 or the 18+ percent zoom reported for the first quarter of 1980. Gone are the glory days of that economic wizard, President "Ike" Eisenhower, who commanded our economic destinies casually, from the vantage point of the golf course; missing short putts he guided our economic affairs so miraculously, by inattention and inadvertence! In contrast, the inept members of the Carter economic crew adopted the bluff that the price disaster was preordained, and reflected acts of God rather than their own weird and monumental derelictions.

It is a dour commentary on the progress of Western civilization that the primary references in the sorry stagflation context are to the United States and the United Kingdom. Manifestly, it is even more frightful to contemplate the woes in much of the rest of the world where populations are less literate, governments more unstable, and technology far less advanced. Obviously, our great nation has hardly offered a luminous and inspiring lesson in economic management. Worse still, despite the self-serving pieties of our leaders, very little of our stagflation plight can be blamed on OPEC price exactions. (This point will be developed later.)

PRESIDENTS AND PRICES

Just to set some sights, Table 1.1 ties the price move, unemployment rate, and correlated *misery index* to each presidential incumbent since Harry Truman, where the misery index combines both the annual average price jump and unemployment rate. Obviously, an administration can neither be wholly praised for a good performance nor chided for a bad outing; many could plead mitigating circumstances on the grounds that in their early tenure they were inevitably locked into programs initiated by their predecessor. Nonetheless, even the crude computations impart some perception of our dismal economic retrogression.

Clearly, the Carter bunglers handily win the laurels for incompetence; with incontestable flair they have distinguished themselves from even the abysmal Nixon and Ford fiascos. To the present generation the Carter sojourn must surely eclipse the memories of the hapless and infamous Herbert Hoover, who was a Democratic campaign symbol of vitriolic partisan invective for a quarter-century. Republicans can rejoice, free at last to invoke in election rhetoric the Carter tragi-comedy. Unfortunately,

TABLE 1.1

Inflation, Unemployment Rates, and Misery Index, by Presidential Incumbent

	AVERAGE ANNUAL CONSUMER PRICE RISE (1)	AVERAGE ANNUAL UNEMPLOYMENT RATE (2)	MISERY INDEX (1 + 2)
Harry S. Truman (1948-1952)	2.5%	4.4%	6.9
Dwight D. Eisenhower (1953-1960)	1.4	4.9	6.3
John F. Kennedy (1961-1963)	1.2	5.8	7.0
Lyndon B. Johnson (1964-1968)	2.7	4.2	6.9
Richard M. Nixon (1969-1974)	6.9	5.1	12.0
Gerald Ford (1974-1976)	7.7	8.1	15.8
Jimmy Carter (1977-1980)	14.4	6.5	20.9

SOURCE: *Economic Report of the President* (1981), Council of Economic Advisers, Washington, D.C.: U.S. Government Printing Office, 1981. Hereafter cited as *Economic Report*.

the Nixon-Ford record is unlikely to inspire nostalgia for the "good old days."

For subsequent reference, Chart 1.1 plots the course of consumer prices since 1929. Most striking and pertinent for us is the price surge of the 1970s, after the practically flat price trend in the 1960s. Quixotically, the 2 percent annual price creep of the 1950s turns out be a mild jog indeed, in retrospect. Modern disasters revise older survivor judgments.

MUGGING IN THE MARKETPLACE

As the terms stagflation and slumpflation confirm, new times bring new words. Likewise, whereas once we spoke of urban street crime, the word "mugging" has now become the commonplace expression to "enrich" our language.

Mugging has a two-step connotation: (1) the violent and generally senseless assault on a defenseless victim and (2) the purposive lifting of the aggrieved person's purse or wallet.

Overlooking the pernicious force attached to (1), in relieving the victim of the money, the net effect is what economists call a "redistribution of income," from the molested and humbled "muggee" to the anti-social "mugger." The former reluctantly relinquishes wealth and the latter acquires the pelf. A one-sided income transfer is consummated, analogous to an inheritance, gift, or welfare payment, albeit under illegal and violent circumstances. Unlike the fabled chronicles of Robin Hood, mugging hardly classes as a condoned charitable act whereby evil souls are coerced to contribute to the well-being of "good" people. Instead, mugging is roundly, and rightly, condemned as an abhorrent, uncivilized crime.

A good and civil society can hardly condone violence; nor can it tolerate arbitrary coercive wealth transfers under circumstances not decreed by the civil authority, as the state through legitimate due process enforced mainly through the taxing and spending powers that reflect our civilized modes of imposing a democratic consensus in acts of redistributive justice. Most of us would be appalled by a society which approved of mugging; any acquiescence would succumb to the laws of the jungle where individuals took matters into their own hands, in a pandering to the merciless and ruthless members of society.

Ironically, in tolerating inflation we end up accepting a mugging process. Surely, inflation has a stream of redistributive consequences very much unlike the chivalrous and idyllic portrayals of the equities of Sherwood Forest.

Inflation has its keenest analogy in nonviolent mugging. At the 1970s pace it roars ahead as a vast engine of indiscriminate wealth and income redistribution. For an individual who had $100,000 in bonds or in a

CHART 1.1. The Consumer Price Index, 1929-1980

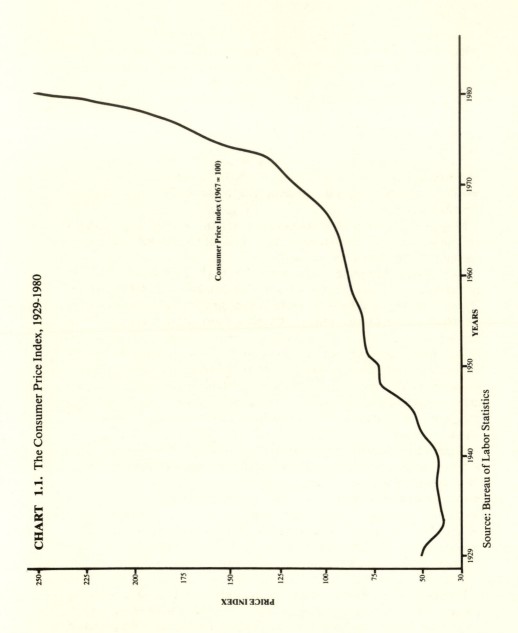

Consumer Price Index (1967 = 100)

PRICE INDEX

250 225 200 175 150 125 100 75 50 30

1929 1940 1950 1960 1970 1980

YEARS

Source: Bureau of Labor Statistics

savings account in 1967, and perhaps retired on its promise of embodied purchasing power, the untapped capital accumulation would be worth about $40,000, in terms of 1967 purchasing power, when confronted with the market prices of 1980. Without consent, the owner has been "mugged" of $60,000 of market goods. It would be as if a pickpocket, in 1967, gingerly relieved his quarry of this sum when the individual was about to make a market purchase. To add institutional insult to economic injury, there is no court in which to lodge a protest, no police precinct to register the crime, and a slim or no chance of future recovery. At best, there is only the ballot box on which to vent fulminations and rage on Election Day.

Politicians have been deaf so far to the complaints despite their messages of ritualistic solicitude and solemnity in opposition to inflation, filling the air with platitutdes while regurgitating sadistic monetary and fiscal remedies which have been notoriously ineffective against inflation. To rub salt into the price wounds their support generally has been for the same policies which add unemployment frustrations and compound the inflation anguish. Minds have been closed to any new initiative as we rock from disaster to debacle to catastrophe. Nero fiddled. Congress and the president dawdle, doodle, and purvey stale and solemn speeches.

By default of effective correctives, the government is a witting bystander in the inflation crime, abetting the mugging and only a legalistic hair away from being an active accomplice. Yet there *are* the means available to stop the illicit transfers which the expert advisers and the responsible officialdom have chosen to ignore as blind and paralyzed to the heinous events that take place under their eyes. Piously, they profess their virtue in public declarations while they abdicate to the vice of inflation mugging by futile nondeterrent policies. At bottom, their remedies are tantamount to a policeman turning his back on a crime, guided by a philosophic predisposition to see, hear, and speak no evil. Feasible preventatives are spurned.

Mugging is a cancer in the life of a civilized society. Preying indiscriminately on weak and strong, it shocks our intuitive sense of justice and offends our conscious moral code. Our people should be similarly appalled by inflation; except in violence it has, over the last 12 years, lifted more wallets and mulcted more souls out of vastly larger sums than all the street muggers combined. It is the ultimate economic outrage, mocking all pretense of fairness in market transactions. It is sheer institutional irony, with a measure of hypocrisy for prosecuting attorneys to plead with judges to mete out heavy sentences in instances of nonviolent mugging, theft, or burglary, and then to relax, in complacent conscience, because they lack constitutional authority to indict lawmakers who have become acquiescent by their evasion of preventive action to the colossal inflation larceny. While we clamor that our streets are unsafe, and demand more police protection, we fail to discern the urgency of organizing public safety battalions to "arrest" inflation. Yet the economic devastation of inflation far transcends that of street crime.

THE POLITICAL CHARADE

Not least among the sordid aspects of inflation is that our political dialogue and campaign oratory have become wispy, inflamed, recriminatory, and almost invariably irrelevant. Every legislative issue carries an inflation twist, every program has an inflation dimension; normal dissent becomes acrimonious as price woes poison the air. Political sounds proliferate almost without reason, and give vent mostly to frustration, reciting the vexatious position without leading us closer to resolution. The emotional bath is noteworthy mostly in blocking out reason and action.

While our political parties vie with one another over which can do a better job in controlling inflation, the indomitable facts are that the ordeal has been remarkably nonpartisan; the Carter price binge has been only, in degree, more horrendous than the Nixon-Ford horrors. *Both* parties have shown a hardening of the arteries in espousal and rationalization of obsolete doctrines. Neither can be accused of excessive imagination or immoderate innovation, or undue alertness to the approach of the 21st century. Each takes comfort in being out of touch or tune with fresh ideas. The Reagan administration in its brief span is unique only in hushing up its McKinley or Coolidge doctrines under a publicist's cover of "supply-side" economics.

That inflation and unemployment, or unemployment and inflation—depending on the year—occupy such a prominent place in our political dialogue, or rather the vacuous noisy rhetoric, impels a distraction from other serious, novel, and potentially ominous features of our age. The limited public attention span is absorbed in the bread-and-butter inflation and unemployment facets, and other heady and complex subjects suffer the fate of deferral and neglect. The implications of living with the nuclear bomb—the many issues associated with United States competition in the arms splurge—get short-changed, compared to the mutterings over pay, jobs, gas prices, autos, and so on. The disposal of nuclear wastes and the proliferation of the bomb to Third World countries, whether Iraq, Brazil, Korea, Pakistan, Israel, India, get the equivalent of the TV "two minutes in-depth" treatment, despite the complexity and severity of the subjects. Beyond their compelling immediacy, these become matters that are left to the experts who, unfortunately, have proven to be pillars of vulnerability.

Effective ways to cope with the barbarities of international terrorism, how exactly to break the energy deadlock, or to meet pressing health issues, or to combat urban decay, and to deal with the assorted 101 challenges of ecology, pollution, safety, and environment, fall by the wayside in our immersion in inflation and unemployment contexts where we interminably traverse well-trampled ground.

In former days where gold and silver coins served as money, Gresham's Law was frequently invoked to explain that when coins were clipped and debased, holders of coins sought to pass on the underweight coins, reserving for their personal hoard the full-bodied pieces. "Bad money drives out good" from circulation, according to the theory. There is an analogous principle at work in our political life where easy, familiar, and frivolous topics provide escape conversational pieces rather than hard or serious thought. There is no other way to interpret the commotion stirred by such "fresh" themes as the overriding preoccupation in 1980-1981 with a tax cut, and to present this as an original and vital idea whose time has come. Howard Jarvis in California on the property tax, and Congressman Jack Kemp in Washington on income taxes, have catapulted to instant fame on the easy and self-serving subject where, in the nature of things, opposition is practically nil. They have even gulled us into a belief that nobody has ever thought of a tax cut previously. Do we need the historical reminder that our country was born in a tax revolt? Who likes taxes anyway?

Inflation is a danger not least because it makes us backward in an economic, social, and political sense, impeding our preparation in unraveling the host of obstacles that must be surmounted as a prerequisite for life in the 21st century. Wherever we turn we now face problems where once we saw confident solutions. In education, health, social security, crime, prison reform, military defense, foreign relations and world influence, energy, environment, steps to cope with the needs or distress stumble over program costs, and thereupon the inflation impasse. *Without* inflation there would be more concurrence and fewer disruptive dissents over prospective action to attend the gnawing disintegration.

Because of inflation facts and fears our political campaigns center on the price blitz, and more often than not spread confusion and obfuscation by slogan and catchword, rather than eliciting in clarity some tentative plans to subdue the monster. For example, John F. Kennedy ran against the Eisenhower inflation; the figures averaged out to some 2 percent per annum: some of us thought those figures were excessive in those days! Kennedy, to his credit, imposed the Guideposts under the economic counsel of Walter Heller; they were adequate then, but they would lack bite now that the price thrust has become more painful. In

1968 Nixon railed at the Democrat inflation even though it had stuck well below the Eisenhower pace—at least until 1968, when prices started to poke toward the 4 percent mark. Under Nixon, and his handpicked successor, Gerald Ford, the two-term average closed in at about 8 percent.

Carter had his fun as he assailed the Nixon-Ford fiasco. Under his blighted stewardship his 4-year term will reveal a consumer price thrust that tops 12 percent per annum. And yet, despite the many years of TV deceptive imagery, we still cheer candidates who announce their opposition to inflation and equate their denunciation as a signal program to abolish it, despite the chary or, more generally, archaic specifics which add up to a submission. There is largely the same old hokum, differing only in nuance, depending on who peddles the horse medicine. There is always a 4-square stand belaying government spending—while screaming for a stronger defense force—and the usual diatribes at "waste," or the other fellow's military spending. President Reagan was only the most recent example in a long line of candidates to follow the empty script.* Castigating waste even transcends a commitment to motherhood as a ritualistic vow in seeking office. Routinely, and naively crafted to show the candidates' deep grasp even as it exposes their ignorance of the money process, there is an imperious injunction to the Federal Reserve to stop creating money.

The more shallow and banal the approach, the higher the chance of electoral success. Specificity dims the election process in the "in-depth, no-depth" TV age.

Measured in an inflation context, the quality of presidential campaign speeches shows no telltale signs of progress since the 1920s but ample indication of deterioration; unfortunately, Barnum the circus impresario, who spoke of the sucker born every minute, has become the more nearly correct prophet of the march of democracy. We have "advanced" to a 2-minute litmus test of a candidate's learning in the TV presidential debate spectaculars. Even prize fights, which are also media events, run their rounds for a full 3 minutes. On projected economic planks, especially on the facts and analysis of inflation, the audience is treated as the despised boobery that the cynical H. L. Mencken lampooned. The major 1980 presidential aspirants made no breach in the almost uninterrupted string of empty inflation expositions posing as informed economic education for our highest political office.

*To be sure, at this writing President Reagan seems to be preparing to act it out. But so did President Carter initially—and Franklin D. Roosevelt, and his predecessors. In any event, as our subsequent analysis will make plain, the adventure is misdirected in an inflation context however much we cheer it in other aspects.

The situation is no better in other countries. In the United Kingdom, Labour's Harold Wilson went out of office on his mishandling of the inflation mess and Tory Ted Heath assumed the seals of office. Heath out, Callaghan in for Labour. Callaghan out, and it was the Tory turn again, with Margaret Thatcher. Each Tory invoked the budget deity and deferred to the monetary gods. Inflation meanwhile lunged on in defiance of political identity, for all seem to follow, where it counts, much the same legislative attitude. Inflation rages and the public roils, now deceived by one political party and then hoodwinked by the other. Tweedledee and Tweedledum ride the price waves in the English-speaking world, in our own country, in England, in Canada where Pierre Trudeau plays musical chairs, or in Australia where one party is booted out to usher in a clone to earn discredit in mauling the price numbers.

France, Germany, Spain, Portugal, India, Israel, and elsewhere—Latin and South America certainly—the story of price mugging or inflation gouging is nearly the same, with only the stakes different, with varying corrosive inroads on economic viability and political and social sanity. Politicians take up sticks for a frivolous economic shuffleboard, and mostly wait their moment to strike when the price numbers become too precarious for public tolerance. The truly formidable problems of per capita income standards, of income division, of energy, and of peace and the arms race, are squeezed out with less than rapt attention, relegated to a place for occasional soliloquies and future repair in the universal immersion in inflation bumbling.

Those who aspire to a better day for freedom and democracy must, on this telling, first complete the most urgent task of all, namely, devising new initiatives against inflation. Otherwise the economic and institutional gains that have been laboriously won over the ages will be frittered away as we insist on surrendering ourselves as compliant prisoners of the same old monetarist theological and budget-balancing nostrums.

STRATEGIES: GAME PLANS AND GRADUALISM

GAME PLANS

In the modern idiom, governments no longer develop plans, programs, or principles to unlock problems, but instead, they are forever concocting "strategies." Behind the high-sounding euphemism the package tied in the fancy ribbon to deal with inflation contains nary a new idea; the originality runs to the belief that what has consistently failed in terms of monetary or fiscal policy will ultimately succeed, if pursued ardently and adamantly enough. This has been the grand delusion in our inflation orgy.

Nixon, the impeachable president, always talked of a "game plan" to lick inflation; the clumsy man usually used the macho reference during the football season to titillate the sports afficionados with a "strategy" of irresistable gradualism to unwind inflation, to drop it to 3 percent during 1969 and to walk the road to price stability. Defiantly, the Promised Land retreated as a distant mirage. In mid-1971, the inflation rate threatened to zoom to 8 percent in those remote and, in retrospect, calm pre-Carter years when 8 percent numbers sounded ominous. Scanning the horizons, the politically astute Treasury Secretary John Connolly reminded Nixon that his reelection could be jeopardized by the double thrust of inflation and unemployment. Nixon, who had often vowed never to impose price and wage controls, waived his flexible "principles" and ordered the price stops. After the election was safely won in 1972 the controls were hastily dismantled, beginning in January 1973. While they were in effect, especially for the first 3 months after Nixon's histrionic August 14 TV performance announcing a price freeze, they were successful enough despite predictable public flak over the economic straitjacket.

Ironically, and indefensibly, the controls were monitored by a staff that frowned on their use: the fox was appointed sentinel over the chicken coop; in deep-think, they would declare that the "suppressed" inflation would lead to a rash of inflation breakouts when the controls were removed. The obvious idea of perpetuating controls to fend off the eruption struck a repulsive chord. The controls were an election palliative, and were contrived as such. The controls were completely dismembered by the spring of 1973, and our subsequent inflation has been the most virulent price orgy in our history, though not necessarily correlated to the abolition of controls.* Blame for the ensuing fiasco will be attached, in our later analysis, to the porous refuge to monetary policy to man the price ramparts.

After President Ford assumed office the summons was for tax hikes in 1974 to fight inflation; not only did the price path explode but unemployment grew. With almost each passing day his economic advisers emitted cheery tidbits "proving" that the economy was "bottoming out": it was the fate of the Ford "experts" to midwife our biggest postwar bottom! By January 1975 President Ford, dauntless old football player, reversed field and issued a call for a tax cut; he was actually piqued that Congress did not respond with alacrity even though his

*To clarify my position at this point, I am not an advocate of controls. The critique is directed at their mode of imposition in 1971 and their dismantlement in 1973.

previous Spartan requests for a tax rise were still warm.* This must be one of the sorriest episodes of economic policy in exhibiting how Congress saved the day by its lumbering response to the prior urgent message on tax hikes. Charitably, the situation can be described as misjudged. But it indicates that some disasters are averted by inaction.

Nonetheless, under Ford in 1976 the scorching inflation rate abated, dropping to about a "mere" 4 percent annual pace in the last quarter, just prior to the Carter inaugural, and fresh from his election triumph on a promise "never to lie to the American people" and to institute "a government as good as our people." Mae West, the late sex symbol, often declared that goodness had nothing to do with her triumphs. Many of us would have likewise opted for a leadership that surpassed the average intelligence, discernment, and integrity.

Over his first year, in a revealing early lapse from his pursuit of excellence, President Carter savored the overdraft economic advice of his longtime banker friend, good "ole" Bert Lance. Rumblings of budget-balancing and businesslike government were rife. Yet the price index rose from 169 in January 1977 to 184 in April 1978. After the several seamy revelations led to Lance's ouster the president named his political chief Robert Strauss as inflation czar, presumably on the basis of as unimpressive a set of credentials as any person ever to hold a top economic advisory post. For his egregious flop Strauss was destined to be promoted to Mid-East peace negotiator, though foreign policy was not a notorious forte of his; but expertise by presidential appointment did preoccupy him until he was assigned to return to the Carter campaign chores in 1980.

On October 24, 1978, President Carter again revealed his intermittent concern with inflation by replacing Strauss with Alfred Kahn, fresh from deregulating air fares. In eagerly and innocently accepting the post Kahn explained that he would have to make a "study" of the inflation issue: this always attests to the "open" mind in the top positions; quizzes by TV public affairs "information" panels view unpreparedness as a signal virtue whose message deserves instant transmittal. (There is a strange principle at work: the lower the content, the more urgent the TV message.)

Despite the fanfare, the package handed Kahn by the president was not seriously designed to *stop* inflation; it was planned to *perpetuate* it! The "plan" called for a retention of wage and salary increases at about 7 percent per annum and prices about ½ percent lower. At best, inflation

---

*I can claim better prevision on that occasion. In an article written in November 1973, I had advised a tax cut as a quid pro quo for pay restraint to taper inflation. See "A Tax Cut to Avert Stagflation," *Challenge*, January 1974.

would roll at its past unruly rate and, if events went awry, the only margin for error was topside. Mainly, in the weeks following his appointment Kahn busied himself in ritualistic speeches equating the inflation struggle to a "moral equivalent of war." (Russell Baker has labeled—not libeled—such crusades as a MEOW.)

Over his entire term Carter's Council of Economic Advisers, easily the most unsuccessful in our annals, made it a practice, when asked about inflation, to explain how well they were combatting unemployment. The *Economic Report of the President* (1980) bravely declared that it would take until 1988 to slice the inflation rate down to 3 percent.

Evasions of this sort are dignified to masquerade under the "inspiring" word "strategy." In 1988, if the remarkably inept Carter crew were somehow still in office, the effective date would surely be shoved ahead to 1995—until another flip of the calendar at that time. Not to be outdone in absurdities, the Carter Treasury Secretary Miller pontificated in mid-1979 that the recession was already "half over." Perversely, it did not begin until 1980. It is too early to discern whether the Reagan team has a faster calendar. But it is possible to retain some doubts.

The amassed Carter-blundering conglomerate would be hard to duplicate. Fortunately, the opportunity to do so has been denied them. Media specialists nevertheless continue to assign fresh credence to their every utterance—even when out of office. To parody the Winston Churchill tribute in a far more heroic context: "Never in human history has so much economic damage been perpetrated on so many by so few." The weird record will be hard to emulate.

Inflation *can* be stopped. And well before 1988. Not tomorrow but over about a quarter-year it can be slashed sharply, and mostly eliminated in a year. But this will require new policies, with new people, with new insights, and new attitudes. President Reagan has new people, but it is doubtful that they possess new attitudes, other than in a shift in emphasis on the components of fiscal policy.

GRADUALISM

Timid souls who engage in the public relations ploys of "game plans" are also prone to advocate a leisurely countdown on inflation, decelerating it from, say, 10 percent per year to 9 percent, 8, 7 . . . and so on. Intended is a lingering and calculated slow knockout.

The premise is that many private decisions have been geared to the *expectation* of inflation, so that to stop the price blitz cold-turkey would imply disappointments and losses, and some severe economic handicaps.

This also amounts to a thinly disguised plea to continue ravaging only those people who have been ravished already. There are always losses—

and gains—and always disappointments and fortuitous happy tidings in the economy. Surely nobody has received an irrevocable ironclad agreement from government that inflation will endure; the gradualists pretend that there is.

Given the roughly 10 percent inflation pace, to clip off 1 percent per annum would require 10 years of a persistent policy to establish what Franklin D. Roosevelt called a "price level that will not change from generation to generation." There is no clear reason to prolong the therapeutic treatment, for, if we pursued the damping objective successfully, it would be the equivalent of a stable price level pursued consistently, and with the same effect on expectations. Only by a showing, say, that the "poor" would be affected adversely by a cessation of inflation, would the argument for a gradual down-drift be defensible. It is doubtful indeed that such an inference is valid.

BANNING THE FEZ

Kemal Ataturk (1880-1938), credited as the dictator responsible for dragging Turkey into the modern age after World War I, pursued a law to abolish the fez against the wishes of the traditionalists. Superstitious illiterates almost feared that God would smite them dead the instant modern headgear was worn. Queried on why he attached such importance to so trivial a matter, Ataturk was said to reply that by changing what was on the outside of the head, new ideas might percolate inside the head.

Likewise, we will have to yield some precious doctrines equally steeped in theology, and defying logic, to stop inflation and to maintain fairly full employment permanently. None of the practices to be abandoned, nor the new institutions that will have to be erected, will constitute a steep departure from our past modes of conduct; all of the transformations can be accomplished within our bounds of freedom and the mechanics of the market economy. But there will have to be *some* change. The switch in patterns of thought and in market restraints will be quite minor compared to the economic prizes at stake; the measures are easily within the capacity of an enterprise system to absorb, and to venture on in the higher freedom of ample job choice, and of savings commitments unhampered by the dollar erosion of inflation.

THE MENACE TO THE MARKET ECONOMY

Failure to make the imperative "small" modifications may well lead us to more serious crises ahead. For each frustration over jobs and the anguish of inflation arouses fresh skepticism over the ethics and the viability of a market economy, and the survival of capitalism. A system perceived as unjust can hardly win friends and attract devoted legions of adherents. Conservatives who resist any reform court the danger of greater turmoil and more far-reaching transformation.

Considered with a reasonably open mind, the constructive proposals to be advanced subsequently are inherently conservative in nature even though they foster the liberal vision of job opportunities for all. The proposals are concerned with salvaging the market economy, with making it work better, and not with replacing it with some brand of collectivism which is an anathema to our people. Only in some intentional deception can the revisions that our economy will have to make be condemned as a scheme to alter or erode the market economy.

Just as the proposals to be vented later have a conservative tinge, inflation itself, which the prescriptions seek to allay, has been the scourge of those who manifest a more liberal credo of an activist government. Inflation has been the bane of liberalism; still, it has been the hard knot which liberals have never sought to unravel beyond muttering some misguided platitudes pleading for price and wage controls, or for the former without the latter. Inflation has led to conservative success at the polls and has tolled the death knell for liberal programs. The priority of repairing the price surge has been a blind spot in liberal thinking, obstructing their agenda for a more humane future.*

Restoring our economic well-being is neither a unique liberal nor conservative prerogative. Both share the objective. It is an overlapping and vital mandate for *both* ideologies to install a steady price level, and to provide jobs for all, as an indisputable imperative for maintaining democracy and freedom as an ideal and as a pragmatic mode of solving commonplace, daily and contingent, occasionally convulsive, economic affairs.

*See my article entitled "The Liberal Blind Spot on Inflation," *New Leader*, July 14, 1980.

2

INFLATION HAVOC

As a prefatory step it is well to look at the inflation damage and the havoc wrought by the conventional measures instituted to block the price rot. Typically, the prophylaxis has been worse than the disease. Yet economists and "practical" men—often the most impractical of all—have persisted even as the therapy has plunged our economy from small inflation and minuscule unemployment to explosive price leaps and shocking miscarriages.

Noted earlier were the mugging inequities and pickpocket antics, and the inflation distractions from other vital topical festers, not least the overriding concern of war and peace. More, however, remains to be said on ramifications too often shunned by economists' symbolic caricatures of real-life behavior relieved of behavioral spillovers.

ANTICIPATED INFLATION

Modern analyses of inflation often stress the quixotic point that there would be no doleful quirks attached to a price rise if it was "fully anticipated." This is a calculated and remarkably irrelevant myth despite the disarming air with which it is entered.

The proposition is a weird dissimulation posing as a profound verity. Perfect foresight is a stultifying assumption guaranteed to block thought no matter how frequently it is invoked by eminent analysts. Years ago, it prompted Oscar Morgenstern, in conjunction with the great John Von Neumann, to reach out and pioneer the theory of games to cover episodes where the crucial variables were elusive. Consider the stalemate that must ensue if Sherlock Holmes knows that Dr. Moriarty will be at Euston Station at 8 o'clock, and that Moriarty knows that Sherlock Holmes knows this.* What will ensue? Probably nothing: the "full knowledge" game cannot come off: an encounter can come only via *imperfect* information on the part of one or the other participant *mis*calculating chances of victory. It is not perfect information that makes stock market trades, but the opposite: buyers expect rising prices and sellers see falling prices. At least one party must be mistaken. Horse races, political contests, or most daily acts which look to a future result depend on *some* informational gap about emerging events. If we *knew* the ultimate incompatibilities of marriage we could act—excluding perhaps Zsa-Zsa Gabor or Mickey Rooney—to forestall them so that fewer would be dissolved in divorce. With prescience of our careers we could take precise educational steps; internationally, we could sign the peace treaties without the awful barbarity of war. Insurance policies would be replaced by individuals amassing offsetting chest funds; illness might be fended off by preventive action.

There is no need to pursue the sheer fantasy implicit in the perfect foresight premise. Having prevision of our future life, with all its joys, loves, sorrows, disappointments, sickness—why live it? It could all be lived in anticipation, and with no need to loll about in a time void which would only spell boredom.

So it is with inflation. Contracts written today to cover rental agreements, or for borrowing through a bond issue to run for 20 years, or to undertake employment in a particular occupation, can *not* be based on perfect anticipation. The concept exorcises the uncertainty which is the very essence of the human condition. On a mundane ground, what economist predicted, as late as 1970, the price scourge for the decade? Who predicted it a decade earlier? (We exclude professional fortune tellers or prophets of doom who survive by preying on the gullible who find catharsis in fearing the worst.) Which econometric model has accurately enlightened us on price predictions over a meaningful price span? Notoriously, the price projections have been the weakest part of the models whose validity mostly extends over a quarter-year ahead— in an economy where only limited perturbations can transpire over the brief interval. (The "predictions" often are analogous to a "forecast" that a perfectly healthy person will feel fine tomorrow.)

---

*My memory ascribes this small paradox to Oscar Morgenstern.

There is just no way to know the tomorrows until we get there and on to the day after. Some may *guess* the events more nearly right than others. But to declare that inflation is not a problem if it is "perfectly anticipated" is a circumlocution for declaring it *is* a problem, although uttered with an air of scientific profundity to muddle the discussion in a meaningless digression.

Short of nuclear war, or an analogous natural catastrophe, inflation tops the list of institutional afflictions in our society. Specifically, it is "the one in many"; if we solve the inflation riddle we can inherit the better economic, social, and political day. Succumb on the price front, and we will remain plagued and mired in a host of evils. "Anticipated inflation," as if we have prevision on this matter, tosses a red herring into the pond, impeding our concentration on banishing the excrescence.

THE INFLATION DIMENSION

The often cited hyperinflations of the 1920s in continental Europe were human nightmares which devastated lives and destroyed arduously acquired large and small fortunes, and on a frightful scale. In Germany in 1923, prices rose by astronomical, scarcely conceivable, trillions and trillions of percentage points. Economic calculation covering the most elemental household budgeting for the next hour's shopping, let alone the next day, became ensnarled in gigantic confusion; foresighted behavior extending beyond the immediate moment was rendered virtually impossible; perversely, barter transactions, where possible, simplified exchange for the participants. The price chaos meant a gross step backward for a social economy for, with the price chains severed, the most routine transactions of a stable system imposed deliberate strains which required time to execute, and tested ingenuity in unraveling the exchanges. Ordinary conduct was disrupted by a focus on normally trifling matters. Unwieldy stresses were thrust on the exchange network which is critically dependent on the smooth efficiency of specialization and the division of labor. Absorbed in the intricacies of transactions under the vexing market circumstances, individual productivity was bound to suffer a relapse.

It is possible to recite lurid, absurd, and pathetic tales in the wake of the lightning hyperinflation disaster that struck suddenly. However, the recital would grossly exaggerate our own future fate; the analogy would be artificial. Our own problem has been one of mincing and nibbling inflation persisting over the last dozen years, with a marked acceleration recently. Our situation has progressed from a weak jog to a canter, to a gallop recently, but not remotely to the mad 1920s supersonic pace of hyperinflation in continental Europe.

During the 1950s, as noted, there was about an annual 2 percent creep, slackening to near 1 percent up to 1967, then picking up closer to 4 percent in 1968. Thereafter, the tale became sorrier under Nixon and Ford and abominable under Carter. At the 1980 double-digit 12 + percent rates, prices will double again by about 1986, and once more by early 1990—unless arrested. There is still time to abort the dread calamity. Otherwise, an accumulation of $100,000 in 1980 will dwindle to the buying power of $25,000 today after only 10 years elapse.

INFLATION DAMAGE

Granted that double-digit inflation, rather than hyperinflation, is our nemesis, how precisely does this torment us beyond the mugging characteristic? Although some may contend that this is already a harsh penalty, we can bypass the fact that it has made political campaigns banal and vapid, an insult to our intelligence in denouncing higher prices without a scintilla of a clue to its cessation. A fuller evaluation sets up a stronger condemnation.

POLITICAL AND SOCIOLOGICAL IMPLICATIONS

Once politicians are discerned to be foolish windbags uttering stale and sterile nostrums, the inflation presence must be apprehended as pernicious for democracy and the body politic, despoiling the whole systemic process as each candidate vies to stand as a carbon copy of past ineffectual incumbents. An electorate with serious concerns must view the hoopla as an elaborate sequence of fun and games, or a diversionary Roman circus designed to distract and mislead, rather than to govern and to exhilarate the human spirit to beckoning horizons. Deception becomes political fodder, and bombast is its staple.

Intellectually, the persistence of inflation siphons off a vast amount of highly trained, animated, and capable but pseudo-scientific resources to diagnose and dissect a subject that should by this time be as dead as the proverbial dodo. Instead of resolving the problem, it seems that economists prefer to live with the issue permanently alive! Successive generations of young students and old scholars are made to perform technical tricks while traversing well-trod surfaces. Writings on inflation pile up, to stock huge library warehouses, while the number of *original* and valid ideas are pathetically limited, to be counted on the fingers of one hand and leaving some unused. Perhaps the only merit in this repetitious exercise in parroting stale notions is that it provides busy work which, at best, brings the illustrative data up-to-date. A cynic might contend that it keeps the involved intellectual resources from venting more harm in other social studies where the conclusions are apt to be taken more seriously. In deflecting the vistas of aspiring students, and the electorate in the political process, the "studies" and the campaign "dialogue" must weaken the national psyche, political will, and patriotic resolve. The net effect of the political and educational blinders is incalculable, the certainly not inconsiderable.

Not least in the litany of political distortions is that the ongoing price climb wins no new and devoted friends for the market economy. Those who are ravaged by inflation *know* that the system that condones it is unfair. They are apt to be a more receptive audience for charlatans and demagogues of varying political coloration.

These add up as a menace to the future of democracy and durability of the economic system. Persistent inflation promotes cumulative cynicism and common despair over the morality and ethics of the market mechanism.

THE VISION OF PROGRESS

Inflation has been posited as the overriding economic blemish, the "one in many." It is time to document this thesis, for it touches both the liberal and conservative side of the spectrum regardless of exactly where the labels are pasted. Each has visions of a more ideal state. Each finds its image blotted by inflation.

Conservatives generally need no urging on the subject. Committed by reflex to a defense of property and income positions, including personal savings and fiscal prudence, they are congenitally opposed to inflation and lobby for measures to stop it; their error consists in a misguided perception of effective policies so they commit themselves to futile and even perverse remedies.

Liberals, on the other hand, have a quaint belief that their agenda for human progress can be compartmentalized as dwelling apart from the price escalation; they generally betray a blind spot on the inflation subject, thinking it less important in human terms. Yet it disfigures their dreams and thwarts their hopes of attaining prized goals.

Consider the outstanding issues of our age. Both political sects will usually affirm that we must restore our cities to a respectable, if not enviable place for living, rather than have them stay as tough and ragged as a battlefield. Why not arrest the decay and reverse the spreading devastation? Inflation is the roadblock. Every program or proposal is watered down or opposed because of its presumed cost and inflation toll. Why not embark on a crash program of $100 or $200 billion per annum—which would be about 5 percent of our GNP—to relieve our energy dependence on the Mid-East? Answer: too inflationary. Improve our system of health care, regardless of the precise form we favor? Inflationary. Purify our streams and waterways, and safeguard our ecological and environmental balance? Go slow, think small, fear inflation. Modernize mass transport, including the rehabilitation of the railroads to simulate even backwards countries, and conserve energy? Inflationary. More police to fight crime? More humane penal facilities? Inflationary.

Wherever we turn, whatever vision we conjure or image we conjecture, we are beaten by the same line of defense, namely, because of the inflationary impacts the reforms must be mothballed. And in postponement, the dilapidation compounds future misery. Progress held in abeyance because of the active inflation volcano pushes improved economic well-being out in time and maybe forever beyond reach. So long as inflation is unchecked, it provides a handy rationalization for inertia, thereby holding our economic and social system hostage. By piling up defects and decay, too many become too willing to supplant the market system, either out of idealistic impulse or with misjudgment in not identifying the supreme inflationary defect. Capitalism loses friends by exposing its communal shortcomings, rather than repairing them to relieve what John Kenneth Galbraith once characterized as "private affluence amid public squalor."

ECONOMIC FALLOUT IN RESOURCE MISALLOCATION

Economists, in some innate "scientific" aversion to new ideas which portend unfamiliar policies, are prone to deplore measures that impel some deviation from a mythical state of optimal resource utilization. In assessing any novel anti-inflation plan they will inject some imaginary outcome achieved in a perfectly competitive order operating at full employment with perfect foresight to compare to some shortcomings of intervention. The deck is stacked; the contrast is really not between what is and what might be, but between an unattainable ideal and an improved state within reach by deft policy revision. On the latter vision the actual economy is discerned as *not* in an optimal state, and unlikely ever to get there; the reality is never confused with the mirage. Inflation and unemployment survive, chronically; the stagflation malaise was surely never part of the idealized Pareto optimum parcel which is too often invoked by economists as their model criterion.

Injecting a fragment of realism destroys most of the standard economic objections to new policy designs to escape the stagflation straitjacket.

THE INFLATION DISTORTIONS

We consider some more strictly economic distortions of inflation, examining how the economic rather than the political and social texture is undermined by the protracted malaise of the last dozen years.

1. Personal buying decisions are rendered partially irrational. In a stable price-level environment there would be no need to hasten the purchase of a house, auto, furniture, appliance, or big ticket items generally. Actions which would otherwise be irrational and costly suddenly become the epitome of wisdom in the inflationary world where delay in acquiring material goods will erode living scales.

Young people thus become hoarders of house space, acquiring homes and house chores that are superfluous in the early marital years. Individuals whose incomes tend to lag behind the price flow are under pressure to moonlight, to work at multiple jobs to escape some distress: life patterns are rearranged to evade the price inroads, with undoubted implications for specialization in careers and in social living, perhaps contributing to divorce rates and marital disenchantment. Family formation is affected, and long-term economic trends deflected. Economic imperatives come to dominate lifestyles, and the quality of life is bound to reflect the inflation facts.

Superficially, the urge to take two jobs and to make hurried purchases might seem to carry a lesson in discipline and the cultivation of the work ethic. But, more certainly, it involves an interference in choice and entails wasteful economic commitments, in goods acquisition or in use of house space. The point is that the entire economic outcome is distorted, compared to the configuration that would emerge under a stable price level. Rather than *save* for future acquisitions, longer-range patterns are subjugated to favor the present.

In addition, the higher interest rates engendered by inflation have led to a reluctance to place savings in banks catering historically to the small saver, with the pool of funds directed to mortgage financing. There has been a marked diversion to various money market instruments promising higher rates of interest, with predictable consequences for the housing market, thereby altering the allocation of resources. As against decisions in a calmer price climate, inflation thus impinges on action in manifold ways. Not least, the high interest rates have made "overbanking" profitable by making this sector of our economy a uniquely attractive enterprise area. Financial power and finance capitalism have become more firmly entrenched.

2. The compression of savings may be glimpsed in Table 2.1. Since 1970, personal savings have tended to trend down, from 8.02 percent of dis-

TABLE 2.1
Personal Savings as a Percentage of Disposable Personal Income, 1970-1980

YEAR	%	YEAR	%
1970	8.02	1976	6.91
1971	8.07	1977	5.65
1972	6.49	1978	5.22
1973	8.64	1979	5.25
1974	8.52	1980	5.72
1975	8.60		

SOURCE: *Economic Report* (1981).

posable (after tax) personal income to about 5.7 percent in 1980. This suggests a feedback pattern that "inflation begets inflation" when the pervasive expectation of rising prices leads to spending behavior that keeps puffing up the price balloon by fostering a belief that it is foolish to place sums in the conventional thrift institutions.

It would be going too far to assign the dimmed saving behavior as a theory of inflation; the abnormal saving actions are a (mild) *aggravating* feature which complicates the price story by nudging the consumer price level higher; but it is not the important price elevator that some make it out to be. For without higher *money* incomes to begin with, the higher money sums could hardly be lavished on purchases. The savings percentage represents a *ratio*; the absolute sums that give an absolute dimension to the price level are to be found in the size of money income.

Longer series would show flux in this ratio, from double-digit figures of about 25 percent during World War II, and not infrequently thereafter to 4.5 percent and to 7.0 percent. A full analysis would entail a digression; the important point is the down-drift which conveys a tale of the response to inflation.

3. There is a deferral of investment in plant and equipment, and a consequent retardation in productivity growth. Some of the debasement in our technological capacity is undoubtedly attributable to inflation and to the high interest rate monetary maneuvers to check the price upheaval.

Inflation incontrovertibly eats away the real value of depreciation funds amassed to replace equipment. Machinery purchased in 1970 at $100,000 and depreciated over a 10-year interval on the straight-line method, may now face a replacement cost of $250,000. A firm will thus be compelled to dip into its capital, or borrow in the financial markets, merely to stand in the same physical asset condition as at the earlier date.

Reason abounds, therefore, to make old equipment run longer, rather than to replace it with superior technology. Similarly, firms which have reasonably good *old* equipment will enjoy a strong advantage against new competitors contemplating entry into the production field, but having to pay inflated capital charges to start production. For old equipment must merely meet running expenses while the new items must cover heavy annual amortization costs and historic high interest charges. Good reason, therefore, for less intense competition among small and medium-sized firms where inflation confers an enormous advantage to going concerns. Implications for productivity retardation are abundant.

Decisions to install new equipment, in the technical lexicon, depend on the "marginal efficiency of capital," meaning a comparison of annual net earnings as against the capital-cost of the equipment. Thus if an asset promises to earn $20,000 per annum over time, and costs $100,000 to put in place, the rate of return figures at 20 percent. Inflation swells the earnings prospects—unless there is a cost squeeze diminishing annual earnings. Simultaneously, inflation boosts the capital price of the equipment. Assuming that both elements of the rate of return equation rise roughly in tandem, the influence of inflation on earnings projections should be neutral. However, the rate of return comparisons are made with interest rate phenomena. As interest charges have skyrocketed to 15 percent or above, inevitably there are tendencies to defer investment decisions.

The higher interest rates that ensue as lenders seek to cope with inflation, thus tend to work to block borrowing decisions to install equipment. Hence, there has been some tendency for firms to procrastinate and to defer new capital installation. The failure of plants to modernize their technological outfit has undoubtedly had a serious impact on labor productivity, thereby enhancing inflation in a feedback effect which is adverse to the climb in real income on which our economic well-being depends. On balance, therefore, our dismal results in productivity growth over the last decade are not wholly unconnected to our weird inflation performance.

This is particularly true if expectations are rife that the inflation will soon abate, an assumption that, unwisely, has usually prevailed. For if interest rates are expected to decline, there is good reason to delay long-term borrowing decisions, for otherwise a plant erected today will have to compete with other firms borrowing at more favorable terms after the interest rate descent. The extra uncertainty engendered by the inflation course thus is inimical to modernization decisions as compared to a stable price climate.

4. Inflation has impeded the functioning of capital markets. The combination of inflation, the monetary policies adopted to thwart it, and the attempt by lenders to compensate for the price details, have led to a paralysis in the stock market from 1968 to 1980, at least. Over this long interval prices on the New York Stock Exchange glided virtually sidewise, despite many ephemeral and tempestuous lunges up or down. Of all sectors of the economy, equity prices alone have been cheap. Despite the growth of earnings the average multiple of stock market prices to earnings has tumbled from about 12 to 1 to about 5 to 1.

Implications here are profound. At the high ratio the firm must earn $1 to have its stock sell at $12 and at the lower ratio, $1 of earnings commands $5, implying a pledge, if it floats a new stock issue, to have new equipment yield 20 percent. Obviously, the implicit high commitment has been a roadblock to new equity financing; relatively limited amounts of venture equity capital has been raised over our long interval of high inflation-high interest-low stock market prices.

With the knocked-down and relatively depressed stock market, a rash of mergers has hit the brokerage business, with many established firms disappearing, and with most of the survivors looking upon the brokerage business as a diversionary sideline that might ultimately recover; they have embarked on a host of vaguely related activities, namely, Merrill Lynch entering real estate brokerage, bidding to purchase the Chicago White Sox, and Bache absorbing and being absorbed by an insurance Chicago White Sox, and Bache absorbing insurance business.

Wall Street, in the narrow sense of the stock market, thus almost ceased to function in its normal participation in financing the enterprise system or as an instrument for encouraging venture capital by its price signals; over our inflationary era these have mainly spelled out distress. Corporate takeovers from abroad have been commonplace, at bargain equity prices made more transparent by the foreign exchange slump of the dollar, which itself has been another casualty of our inflation.

Capital-market financing came through bond issues. These, too, as noted, are restricted and by 1980 had virtually dried up as a result of the abnormal interest rates and the plunge in bond prices. There has been a special aversion to long-term bond issues. Inescapably, inflation has impaired the functioning of capital markets and has effectually rocked the capitalist system at its financial market foundations where, presumably, the venturesome souls with enterprise know-how command savings and resources from the more timorous but parsimonious members of the economy. The frenetic inflation has made Wall Street an inefficient vehicle for fulfilling its select historic task.

5. Great financial institutions have operated under a suspicious cloud during the inflationary era. For example, life insurance policies have become something of a hoax. A $100,000 policy bought in 1968 is worth, in terms of 1968 purchasing power, about $40,000 in 1980. Simultaneously, as the portfolios of insurance companies contain a huge assortment of bonds, which decline in capital value as interest rates surge, at various times during the mid-1970s these powerful institutions were in the embarrassing position of balance sheet insolvency when their bond assets were valued at market prices. To circumvent the awkward facts there was the resort to the legal fiction, in violation of standard accounting practices, that the assets be valued at original cost prices, on the pretext that the bonds would be held to maturity.

The inflation trauma has thus fostered some chicanery to evade financial accountability; but no mode of compensation to reimburse the policyholder has as yet been devised; life insurance continues to be sold despite its vanishing value for the policyholder as inflation runs rampant.

6. Internationally, inflation has meant interminable foreign exchange perturbations and a debacle for the dollar. For example, the German mark had risen by late 1980 by 108 percent in exchange value since 1968, and the climb in the Swiss franc has been 150 percent. The Japanese yen moved up by 69 percent. Result: imports have become so much more expensive; Volkswagens and Opels now come in dribbles from Germany, while Japanese cars have virtually doubled in price. Only the ineffable Nixon, after engineering the dollar depreciation in late 1971, could go before the TV cameras, and, in a Checkers rerun, hail the dollar ignominy as a sort of domestic victory, attesting to our economic strength!

The plunge of the dollar has sky-rocketed the price of all imports, and has even lent plausibility to OPEC's poor-mouthing its *need* to raise oil prices which are stipulated in dollars. Likewise, the amenities of foreign travel have been made more secure for German and Japanese travelers, to the detriment of American voyagers condemned to postpone trips, or to hunt out the least expensive and less exotic fare. Universally, as the American tourist is lampooned for his poverty, the first-hand foreign observation of our colossal economic blundering has undermined respect for our leadership. Our exemplary world standing has been subverted in many small ways. Coincidentally, where once the world feared Yankee imperialism and the American colossus, the shoe is now on the other foot. Takeovers of American business by foreign enterprise abound, whether German, English, Japanese, or Middle Eastern in origin. Now Zurich, Frankfurt, and Tokyo are financial centers to be reckoned with, toppling our earlier dominance.

The international story is one of a sapping of our once predominant financial and economic strength. Inevitably, our voice in world councils carries less influence. And this weakness, exemplified in dozens of ways, is wholly a product of our monstrous inflation. What power we do wield rests mainly on our awesome military might and our stockpile of nuclear weapons rather than on any obvious mastery of economic policy. While we are still far from second-rate economically, our slips are showing as we travel the British path to nonglory, not via socialism or nationalization episodes, but by an inept capitalistic engine driven jerkily because of our unbraked inflation.

7. *Inflation imposes insuperable obstacles for long-range government planning.* As if the future did not hold enough hazards, the erratic course of inflation erects more barriers. Aside from the anxieties of householders, or the doubts that afflict firms in investment decisions for plant and equipment, government long-range budget planning becomes abject beyond even bureaucratic norms. Our social security system has become deranged because of inflation indexation of disbursements while the more rigid payroll collections are increased ratchet-wise, to place it on a pseudo-sustaining basis. Local budgets become disjointed, with the frequent tight money forays which raise borrowing costs and enlarge welfare outlays, even as they dismember tax collections as unemployment strikes under intermittent recession. Anti-government surliness develops as older property holders, living on fixed incomes, resist with cause the attempt to raise more revenue via property taxes to cover the inflated operating charges of government.

At the federal level, there is the tax escalation as individuals with inflated incomes enter progressively higher tax brackets.

Given the various budgetary imbalances, no mode of resolution appears rational or equitable in view of the assorted lags between the individual income movements and the price trend. All efforts to cope with the aberrations run into a sea of complications. Undoubtedly, our public policies would provoke fewer antagonisms, and show fewer fits and starts, in a more stable price climate.

A FAIRLY COMPLETE MALIGNANCY

From all sides inflation classes as a malignancy which is best averted. Unreality, inequity, chicanery, and organized deception in ordinary economic dealings impair the market system. Mugging is practiced on a colossal scale. Longer-range decisions are reduced to a gamble with excessive interest rates and price-level hazards. Many irrational decisions are fostered, in a vain hope to escape the price vagaries. Despite the complacency of too many economists, inflation is a very dispensable phenomenon.

UNEMPLOYMENT: THE IATROGENIC EFFECT

Because inflation is perceived as innately dishonest, and insidious in manifold ways, action to stop it becomes an automatic knee-jerk reflex.

Central bankers have a congenital dread of inflation, apparently chosen for their posts by this trait. By their monetary policies, they are perennially engaged in a war on inflation using the money supply arsenal in their possession. Unfortunately, their weaponry is as archaic as a stone pile in a nuclear war. Yet the central bank myopia is so ingrained that they actually boast of the sure-kill in their armory. They have a sublime faith: the consistent failure of their actions breeds only confidence of future success by divine revelation of a fresh operating formula. For artillery they elect sling-shots.

Their unremitting stone age war on inflation is not surprising for our Federal Reserve system, and indeed all central banks have the mandate to control the money supply based on the *theory* that in controlling the quantity of money they can subjugate the price level. The doctrine itself, with all its acquired subtleties, bears the Quantity Theory label. We shall have occasion later to debunk the ideas, and to charge that the monetary tools generate the double stagflation scourge or worse, of steering the economy into the slumpflation pit.

In the analogy of the prize ring, the Fed aims at its opponent and hits the referee. By its actions "our cup runneth over," and we are afflicted with the twin ailment of stagflation, or the triple dread of slumpflation. Recessions and unemployment are not made in heaven; they originate at the Federal Reserve as it bashes about in its ceaseless and futile war against inflation. The 7-member Fed Board is as feeble as the 7 maids with 7 brooms sweeping back the 7 seas. They mean well, but they do egregious harm. Their fight against inflation ends in conspicuous failure while dumping the economy in the unemployment ditch.

Unemployment is the sure outcome of the monetary therapy prescribed for inflation; unemployment, with or without recession, is the *iatrogenic* side effect of the medicine which fails to cure the disease for which it is prescribed.* It can be likened to a pain-killer which inflicts more pain.

FINANCIAL MARKET DESTABILIZATION

More will be said to buttress this strong indictment of the Federal Reserve as the "strategic center for maintaining unemployment." For its monetary policy is potent. But it hits jobs and not the price level.

We might also note that the Fed's efforts to stabilize the economy entail *destabilizing the financial sector. For as it invokes tight money,* interest rates rise and, because it is the interest rate inverse, bond prices automatically fall. Those who bought various series of that perfectly "sound and safe" investment, namely, United States government bonds,

*Cf. Hyman Minsky, "Symposium on the Carter Economic Policies," *Journal of Post Keynesian Economics* (Fall 1978).

are aware of this anomaly, for they have seen the prices of their bonds tumble from $1,000 to about $700 or less. This precipitous 30 percent tear—and "swindle"—is a product of the Fed's anti-inflation follies, even while it immodestly pronounces its own valor and vigilance, never advertising the conspicuous debacle. (The impact on insurance company and other financial institution portfolios has already been noted.)

In the same sequence the stock market has been rendered virtually impotent as an instrument for capital-market financing over the past 12 years while the Fed was flailing and wailing in its debauch with inflation. This major capitalistic appendage was severely undercut. Quixotically, rather than protest tight money and the drying up of their business, inspired by the articulate rationalizations of the commercial banks which write most of the ideological parodies advocating the measures, Wall Street has worshiped tight money. Surprise! The rise of interest rates from the 6 percent range to prime interest rates of 20 percent benefits banks enormously. They simply adore tight money. Remarkably, they have lifted a superb apology from economics; when farm prices go up, when industrial prices go up, they deplore the ascent as "inflationary." When their own price goes up, namely, the price of loan funds, they "explain" how this "fights" inflation! And academic economic theorists write learned papers which nourish and inculcate the twaddle on unwary students—who imbibe and preserve it.

Financial markets have been badly deranged in the course of our ongoing inflation. The absurdities have stemmed, in mixed dosage, from the price upheavals themselves and from the sadistic Fed measures to staunch the price tide, which perpetrate unemployment generally and financial sector instability in particular.

Financial markets will continue to reveal marked gyrations so long as monetary policy is pursued with a vengeance to "fight" inflation. Predictably, it will be ineffective on the price front. Invariably, it will generate capital-market instability.

UNEMPLOYMENT: THE UNKINDEST CUT OF ALL

The unkindest cut of all from the Fed's monetary flailing to fight inflation is the unemployment it engenders.

Fed stalwarts will think this recession indictment of their pet is a mite unfair. But their defense misses the point, for there can *always* be jobs and production if loan funds are available to business firms for legitimate business purposes. The clogging of credit lines do the damage to jobs and to output advances. To be sure, it is conceivable that some production will be misdirected. But it is never the function, or within the aegis of the Fed, to control the *direction* in which credit is used. This is mainly the function of the individual lending bank. The Fed's scope, in contrast, extends to the *quantity* of loan funds available, and not to its qualitative mix.

Table 2.2 indicates the unemployment and estimated GNP losses from the legion of jobless over the past decade. While inflation afflicts all of us, and is discernible whenever we go to the shops, unemployment burdens are borne by those affected directly, although some may be unemployed for a short duration, say, a month, and thereafter have their place in the statistics occupied by another person made jobless for a similar duration. The flat number thus conceals a churning magnitude. And, indirectly, through unemployment and welfare payments, through government tax losses because of reduced revenues, most of us are affected on the roundabout via government budgets, and in various social (street crime, for example) and political ramifications of the aberrant job climate. In addition, as the unemployment tabulation concentrates on only those who have previously held a job, and only those who were "actively" seeking a job, the unemployment data undoubtedly understates idleness. Many unemployed are not counted, for, they will reason, why look for a job when the only factory in town is *known* to be closed down?*

On these provisos Table 2.2 provides some evidence of our unemployment and output catastrophe during our decade of inflation distress. The gross national product (GNP) shortfall on high or low estimates, is just staggering either way.

The rock-bottom minimum unemployment has been taken, arbitrarily, to be 4 percent, although in 1968 it touched down at a 3.8 figure. Others may want to set the number at 5 percent because of the greater labor force participation by women. Minimum GNP losses are computed on a strict proportionality of jobs and production. The maximum totals reflect *"Okun's Law," where the late Brookings economist** calculated that* each percentage point increase in jobs lifted GNP by about 3.2 percent. Current dollars reflect prices of the particular year, while constant dollars denote 1972 prices. In the one case the volume of lost output ranged from about $0.4 to $1.4 trillion and, in constant dollars, the sums were $0.3 to $1.04 trillion. In 1982 prices a near $2 trillion top estimate would not be out of line.

*Definitional quirks are inescapable; any definition will fail to cover all the possible instances; the best we can do is to expect the concepts to be applied consistently. But the limitation must be kept in mind in evaluating the figures.

**Dr. Arthur M. Okun, recently deceased. See his *The Political Economy of Prosperity* (New York: Norton, 1970), p. 137.

TABLE 2.2

GNP Loss from Unemployment, 1970-1980 (in billions of dollars)

YEAR	ACTUAL UNEMPLOYMENT RATE MINUS 4 PERCENT NORM	CURRENT DOLLARS		CONSTANT 1972 DOLLARS	
		MINIMUM	MAXIMUM	MINIMUM	MAXIMUM
1970	0.9	$ 8.8	$ 28.2	$ 9.8	$ 31.4
1971	1.9	20.5	65.6	21.3	68.2
1972	1.6	19.0	60.7	19.0	60.7
1973	0.9	11.9	38.1	11.3	36.1
1974	1.6	22.9	73.3	20.0	64.0
1975	4.5	69.7	223.0	55.5	177.6
1976	3.7	63.6	203.5	48.1	154.0
1977	3.0	57.5	183.0	41.2	131.6
1978	2.0	43.1	137.9	28.7	91.9
1979	1.8	43.5	139.2	26.7	85.4
1980*	3.1	81.4	244.2	45.9	146.9

*Preliminary.

SOURCE: *Economic Report* (1981).

34

Visualizing these numbers in more concrete terms, say of $1 million projects, we have lost over 1 million school buildings, factories, bridges, museums, roads, hospitals, etc. In terms of $50,000 housing units, some 20 million structures could have been put into place, equal to 10 to 12 years normal construction. This is the size of the staggering disaster that has befallen us, mainly through the archaic and ineffective monetary bludgeon that the Federal reserve has wielded to "fight" inflation. The 7 maids with 7 brooms succeeded better in pursuing their impossible appointed task!

The conclusion can be succinct: The losses through the application of monetary policy to correct the inflation have been appalling. To add insult to the frightful injury, the Fed has *not* stopped the price upheaval. Its methods comprise a cruel exercise of mass sadism and, when supported by our political establishment, amount to brutal masochism lacking only in violent bedlam. We have revelled in a national folly on a massive scale that taunts our claim to a mature civilized bearing.

THE ROAD TO FULL EMPLOYMENT

Soothsayers exist in abundance, often honored with awards for pontificating that unemployment is a necessary and "natural" situation in an enterprise economy. This ranks high on the list of dubious propositions.

From February 1961, beginning early in the first Kennedy year, to November 1968, we had 94 consecutive months in which jobs and production rose steadily. For another 11 months thereafter, output continued to climb, though unemployment rates started to edge up under the Nixon monetary therapy to fight the incipient inflation burst. By 1970 both inflation and unemployment, to form the stagflation clot, began to appear.

The major point at this telling is that we *know* the road to full employment: abundant jobs *can* be created. There is much work to be done, as the most casual glance at our cities and suburbs will reveal, and as any list of national needs is cited. If the Fed would release the money brakes, which it could do under a viable alternative method to combat inflation, our economy could escape the recession or unemployment doldrums. Recourse to tight money keeps us mired in our sorry job plight where those who want to work, and those who need to work at tasks that our country must accomplish, could find jobs. It also deserves to be observed that in the Kennedy-Johnson years of steady climbs in jobs and output, the price level inched ahead in the 1.5 percent range, or practically a stable performance when measured by the subsequent dismal record. Those were the days, to be sure, of the Kennedy Guideposts when average pay increments were held to the 3.4 percent range, rather than the approximately 10 percent annual binge of the 1970 decade.

There are always nonanalytic souls, who excel in misreading history, who will allege that the 1960 growth miracle-decade must be assigned to the Vietnam war. Businessmen who utter the calumny thereby join Marxist critics who profess the doctrine that capitalism provides plentiful jobs only in wartime.

War did disfigure the 1960 era, on an inglorious scale during President Johnson's tenure. But it is not war that turns the job trick: it is the fact of massive market outlays. Expenditures make the market carousel go round; expected sales lead to production and job decisions. There is no valid reason why similar outlays, perhaps induced by cuts in business taxes, in personal income taxes, and lower interest rates to encourage business investment and home building, could not perform the same spectacular feat in a nonwar economy. There is no reason why massive civilian spending, mostly in the private sector, could not create the same type of growth environment as is commonly performed for military ends.

One of the weakest intellectual appraisals uttered in commenting on economic affairs is that "we can't spend our way into prosperity." Actually, there is no other way to thrive. The market economy lives on expenditures. What firm will produce goods for which there is no expectation of ample expenditures? The sales tune is the same, in peace or war. The only difference is in the nature of goods produced.

Full employment can be realized. But first the Federal Reserve must be disabused of its passion for self-inflicted wounds; another mode must be devised to inhibit inflation. This is our supreme institutional lack.

Later pages will detail the mechanics of an approach that has the merit of being compatible with our democratic ways and the market system. It will require mild modification in our institutional ways, but without yielding any significant features of the market system. It would be a concession of failure, and it would consign us to perpetual stagflation, to endure the tyranny of the monetary blight. That way lies a pack of troubles that will lead too many too often to cry for radical economic surgery.

Each year population grows. So each year should be the *best* on record on the job front. Each year, in the longer past, saw employee productivity grow. So each year should mean more output per capita and rising living scales. Each year should see a climb on the stairs to a better life for more people. But to attain what is within our grasp, we will have to revise our macroeconomic strategy. The moral of Ataturk and the fez should not be lost on us.

PART II

THE COMMON CAUSES OF INFLATION

Numerous causes of inflation are cited in the professional economic literature and by editorial writers, politicians, and in popular controversy. The next set of chapters dissects the catalogue and fastens on one dominant cause, with the other factors either incidental phenomena, complicating agents, or mainly emotional irrelevancies. Until we confront our basic hang-up, the control options chosen will not relieve us of our stagflation malaise. Many of the purported remedies compound our miseries by heaping unemployment on top of the price blitz.

We shall find much to condemn in the conventional wisdom which holds that the Federal Reserve can stop inflation, or that the government budget is the inflation culprit. It is possible to oppose many government programs, but cutting them to the bone can salve our ideological soul without stopping the price escalator. The budget folklore constitutes the monumental Reagan confusion.

The inflation position to be developed is devoid of either a liberal or conservative taint. It devolves from common sense based on a perspective of the economy in operation and an understanding of the magnitudes involved.

3

INFLATION: THE MAD ARITHMETIC

It is well to sketch the basic framework for grasping the inflation balloon. As a backdrop against which to appraise the incessant babble about the price index, we will develop the "law of the price level." This is an all encompassing *general* explanation which embraces all other diagnoses as partial or mystic elucidations.

What we seek is an explanation of *all* prices, whether foodstuffs, appliances, clothing, shelter, transportation, energy, recreational outlets, literally across the board. It is the *general* price explosion, and not any one specific price, that comprises our ordeal.

Also the preoccupation is with a market economy where goods are produced, bought, and reproduced, generally in growing abundance over time. Furthermore, and it should be axiomatic, to capture the flavor of the market economy, the focus must be on the largest payment flow in the economy, namely, on the money-wage and salary payments made for the productive services that translate into the valuable outputs.

It is a mild but conventional misnomer to designate our economy as a price system. Of course it is. But the characterization does not penetrate deep enough, for an economy in which goods rained down from heaven, as an act of God, and then traded for money, would also be classified as a price economy. The more telling feature of our economy is that it is a system in which labor is hired in *anticipation* of output to be sold in the market. Labor is paid a money wage, and the payments made comprise the major part of the cost side of the pricing equation. The same money wages constitute the major demand bloc in consumer markets. It is the money-wage aspect that conditions the cost-demand-price development in our market economy.

THE NATURE OF THE MARKET SYSTEM

Because labor earns a *money* wage, it is not surprising that money prices attach to the goods that enter the marketplace. If labor were paid in pairs of shoes, we would have prices stipulated in shoes; if workers were paid in TV sets, we would have TV exchange ratios as prices.

Money wages and salaries comprise roughly 75 percent of the national income total, and employee compensation covers over 52 percent of business costs. With depreciation, wage costs tally about 85 percent of corporate business costs. In consumer markets the wage-salary sums are responsible for about the same 85 percent of consumption purchases.

Chart 3.1 makes graphic the magnitude of wage-salary costs in non-financial corporate accounts; also when combined with the depreciation magnitudes, the chart reveals the magnitudes as portions of the total nonfinancial corporate output.

As the point is deceptively simple, its significance may be lost. What is claimed is that in stark outline our economy is one in which: (1) Goods are produced for market with the activities undertaken *in expectation of sales*. (2) Labor is thus hired in *advance* of sales, and *paid a money wage*. (3) Labor costs thus set up the foundation for *the cost side of the market price equation*. Finally, (4) the very same wages substantially shape the flow of purchasing power in consumption markets. The latter outlays tend to close the consumer-market loop in the circular-flow process. The wage costs to the producer are incomes to the wage earners, and constitute the demand side of the consumer-market price equation.

As these four synoptic propositions reveal, the process is circular and interdependent. Costs to the firms are incomes to the recipients which provide the underpinning for demand in the markets. "Cost-push" and "demand-pull" forces emanate from the same labor-hire phenomena.

This four-faceted conception is fundamental for comprehending the mechanics of our economy. It is not that individuals come to market with pockets flushed with money, and ready to buy regardless of the work process. Instead, our approximately 100 million gainfully employed acquire money *as income* in the labor hire act. Very few of us would be able to sustain our daily purchases without the regular receipt of income from our jobs.

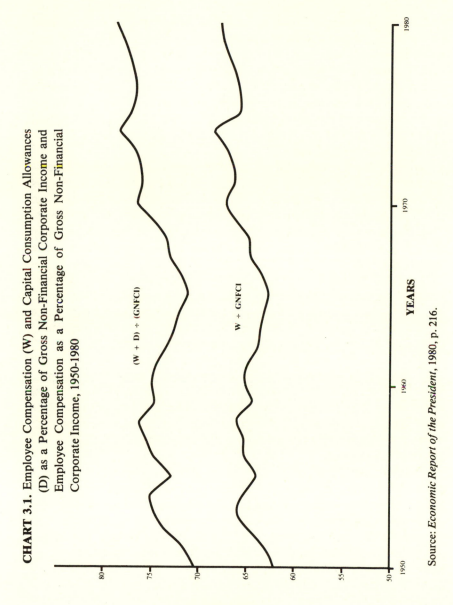

CHART 3.1. Employee Compensation (W) and Capital Consumption Allowances (D) as a Percentage of Gross Non-Financial Corporate Income and Employee Compensation as a Percentage of Gross Non-Financial Corporate Income, 1950-1980

(W + D) ÷ (GNFCI)

W ÷ GNFCI

PERCENTAGES

YEARS

1950   1960   1970   1980

50 55 60 65 70 75 80

Source: *Economic Report of the President*, 1980, p. 216.

41

A PURE EXCHANGE AND A CUSTOM-ORDER ECONOMY

The money-wage economy which revolves about an output sector which mainly replicates itself in reproducibles must be distinguished from: (1) a pure exchange *non*production economy or (2) a custom-order economy.

In a custom-order economy, a restaurant would presumably not prepare a sandwich until a customer came in. If a patron asked for a ham and cheese on toast, the restaurant would have to say: "Wait a minute; we'll rush out and buy some bread, ham, cheese." Even then, it would presume that the baker, and grocer, act on *market* principles and stock the items in *advance* of sales!

Similarly, we may often say that we are getting a "custom-tailored" suit of clothes. At a minimum this also presupposes woolens and threads are on hand ahead of purchase, or that the looms for making them are in existence. Moreover, for our custom-made home we may say that we are "building a house, with the architect drawing up the plans." Certainly this envisages existing tools and materials produced expressly for a *market* process.

The point is that in a strict custom-order economy the initiatives originate at the time the order is placed. In a market economy, the output operations build on *expectations*, and the latter are fulfilled by the same market income processes engendered by them, not excluding the banks' facilitating actions in financing the animated expectations.

Older economies, even of the 19th century and earlier, were primarily agricultural. They were economies of largely "fixed" amounts of output, year-to-year varied by stochastic vicissitudes in weather. In that past era when the metallic money supply changed—and it was gold and silver which for many countries came in from "outer space," or overseas—the inevitable impact of "more money on the same amount of goods" was invariably inflationary.

What has been hard for modern theorists to apprehend is that this is *not* a proper image of our contemporary economy; *it does not disclose how our economy works, nor does it offer a constructive account of how the money supply changes in the modern economy.*

Later, we deal with the always intriguing description of how our money supply grows. At this stage the significant fact is that the origins of inflation today differ from the operating causes in our country 200 years ago, or perhaps in Tahiti or some less developed country today. Explanations must be designed to fit the time and circumstances. So many of the conventional inflation exposés apply to past situations and are tangential to the contemporary scene. They retain their fascination only for people whose minds are rooted firmly in the past even though our economy has bounded vigorously ahead.

WAGES AND SALARIES: A DIFFERENCE WITHOUT A DISTINCTION?

Henceforth, the term "wages" will be used to include salaries. Spelled differently the words are synonyms, despite specious efforts to delineate a distinction. Long ago, wages were paid weekly, or daily, and in coin placed in a packet; salaries were usually biger and the province of white collar employees, paid by check, perhaps bimonthly. But the stereotype no longer prevails, and, if it did, the distinction would by no means be vital. Only a sentimentalist would protest if all salaries were hereafter labeled as wages.

INCOME AND OUTPUT STREAMS

Suppose all of us try, and succeed, in getting more money income per week while physical production runs at a steady pace. The end result *must* be inflation. This is the essential proposition that we must absorb no matter how uncongenial it is to our ordinary ingrained image.

The economy can be visualized as generating two economic streams over a period of time, such as a week or a year, namely, (1) a money income and (2) an output stream, with the price level serving as the balance weight between the two, giving a money dimension to output. Thus if $3 trillion is attributed as the productive factor costs paid to input participants for assisting in output, then $3 trillion is the amount of gross wage, interest, rent, and profit income, plus depreciation and business operating taxes incurred on the output. This is the *income* stream, broadly conceived.

But with these as the earnings—or *costs*—on output, the total *value* of output must comprise the self-same sum. Output value is the multiple derived from the *average* price per unit of output times the number of units produced. Thus the relation:

$$\text{(Average Price per Unit of Output)} \times \text{(Number of Units)}$$
$$= \text{Gross Income}$$

To illustrate, with 10,000,000 units of output, and consisting only of autos, and with each car carrying a market price tag of $7,000, then the gross income earned in the producing sector must be $70 billion, which would also include earnings by suppliers making sales to the auto sector.

Obviously our output consists of a heterogeneous mass. Nonetheless, if we conceive it as a physical amalgam of ounces, tons, gallons, pounds, and so forth, and as income on its production consists of money sums, any rise in money income *must* mean a rise in the average price at which a unit is sold. If the physical output amounted to 1 billion units, and money income was set at $3 trillion, the average price would be ($3 trillion ÷ 1 billion) = $3,000. If money income lurched up to $6 trillion and physical output held firm at 1 billion units, the average price level per unit would be $6,000.

Money incomes outpacing physical output compel a price rise; the arithmetic is inescapable. It is a truism remarkable only in the dimness with which it is perceived by economists, business leaders, and politicians. Every dollar of money income earned this year is a claim on physical output simultaneously produced. If money income goes up, and the physical output stays the same, each income dollar must unequivocally claim less output. This is merely a circumlocution for saying that prices are higher.

Schematically, the truism is:

$$\text{Prices} = (\text{Money Incomes}) \div (\text{Units of Physical Output})$$
$$\text{Example: } \$3,000 = (\$3 \text{ trillion}) \div (1 \text{ billion physical units})$$

Inflation is usually expressed in terms of a percentage price upcreep per annum. The equation yields the same essential price result.

$$(\% \text{ Price Change}) = (\% \text{Money Income Change}) - (\% \text{ Change in Output})$$

Thus if the aggregate money income growth is 10 percent per annum, and the output growth is nil, prices will escalate by 10 percent. With the same income growth, and with output 3 percent higher, prices will climb by 7 percent. And so it goes; the arithmetic is elementary and unassailable.

THE INFLATION SAGA

Inflation thus registers an old tale of a society attempting "to get rich quick" in money incomes, and unmindful that its well-being depends on "real incomes," meaning the growth in physical production where the latter consists of tangible goods or the intangible services which all of us buy from the doctor, lawyer, dentist, tennis coach, music instructor, or airplane, electric power company, teacher, and so on. When the goods and service flow inches ahead, while money incomes leap ahead, inflation is ordained by noncontrovertible logic.

AN OPTIMAL MONEY INCOME STATE

We cannot reshape history; we are where we are in time, and our economy is the evolutionary product of the whole interplay of humans acting with their beliefs upon physical resources. Suppose, however, we play the parlor game, just to grasp the inherent principles, of how, if we could wave a magic wand, we would want the economy to behave in the future.

On the presumption that a stable price level is most equitable, and that it best facilitates rational decisions, we would in our magic role try to foretell the annual production increase. Envisaging this at 3 percent, then we could decree that all money incomes, or all money incomes *on the average*, be lifted by 3 percent, for this could hold the price level steady. We would *know* that "real" income could not surpass this figure. So, to hold unit costs and prices in balance, we would establish a 3 percent norm as the *average* bound for money incomes. (Note that an "average" connotes some being above and some staying below the figure.)

This would yield an optimal price result. Abandoning the fiction of a planning chief with a magic wand, the same percentage rule is also an indispensable prerequisite for a stable market economy. Without the income-output discipline there will be *some* inflationary chaos, and more havoc as the breach between incomes and productivity widens.

GROSS BUSINESS INCOME AND THE MONEY-WAGE BILL

Incontrovertibly, the far largest segment of the money income aggregate consists of money wages, termed officially in national income data as *Employee Compensation*. This includes all payments for labor hire, in money, in kind as food or lodgings, or in fringe benefits; it also encompasses earnings at the minimum pay scales up through the munificent rewards of corporate presidents. Including proprietors' income, which is mostly the pay equivalent of farmers and owners of small enterprises, the totals come to over 80 percent of national income. (See Chart 3.2.)

THE WAGE SHARE IN GROSS BUSINESS PRODUCT

In Gross *Business* Product (GBP), about 53 percent of the current total consists of employee compensation. This ratio has tended to stay remarkably constant during the present century, especially on a year-to-year basis where a 1 percent annual shift is rather abnormal. Since about 1950 the portion going to labor has tended to climb by 5 or 6 percentage points, or about 10 or 12 percent above the earliest years of this century. This is a slow and small drift over the time span involved.

The relation between the gross business money income and the wage bill can be usefully written as:

Gross Business Income = A Multiple of the Wage Bill

CHART 3.2. Employee Compensation as a Percentage of National Income, 1950-1980

W ÷ NI

Source: *Economic Report of the President*, 1981

The wage bill is, of course, the average money wage times the number employed. Thus if the average money wage is $15,000, and the number of employees is 100 million—nearly the 1980 facts—the total wage bill is $1.5 trillion. If this total is ¾ of the *National* Income, then the latter would be $2.0 trillion.*

The implications of these ratios are profound: they compel recognition of the fact that to control the path of the price level it will be incumbent to check, in a way compatible with our democratic institutions, the explosive potential of the enormous money-wage and salary bill. Otherwise, there is certain inflation in our future. Tinkering with the money supply or toying with the budget will not stop the money-wage tide.

Consider this salient fact. The GNP employee compensation (1980) aggregate amounts to $1.6 trillion. Merely a 1 percent rise in the average pay rate amounts to $16 billion. Yet President Carter, in his solemn March 14, 1980, anti-inflation address, made a stern fuss over cutting budget expenditures by $13 billion to work the miracle. As pay increases have been gushing ahead by about 10 percent, the $160 billion *annual* rise in employee compensation, cumulated over four years, will *exceed* the total of *all* government expenditures!

It is an ancient political pastime to flay the small and disregard the large, to swat gnats and ignore elephants. Even as President Carter spoke so gravely about cutting outlays by less than 1 percent of the annual pay creep, he was easing restrictions, relaxing pay scales by 1.5 percent. This would translate into $24 billion and outweigh the budget "slash." The anti-inflation theatrics would end in succoring the price farce. Of course, the inflation itself would obliterate even the small but grave budget-cutting gesture: the Carter expenditures came in over $45 billion in excess of the March charade.

THE WAGE-COST PRICE-LEVEL EQUATION

Two key propositions have been elicited, constituting a verbal transmittal of the equations: (1) The price level *must* rip whenever money

---

*The gross business product is narrower in scope than the Gross National Product; it omits government (but not government enterprises such as TVA), religious, charitable, and educational institutions. It refers to the *market* or capitalistic sector of the economy which we usually have in mind in discussions of price making.

National income consists of all GNP income minus depreciation and business sales, excises, and property taxes. Thus wages of *all* GNP sectors is about ¾ of the total. This explains the discrepancy between the ¾ figure and 53 percent for wages in GBP.

incomes outpace physical output. (2) Far and away the lion's share of money incomes consists of wages and salaries—even though most of us bemoan *our* meager portion.

Real output, or Gross Business Product in constant dollars since 1950, and Gross Business Product in current (or changing) dollars, appears in Chart 3.3. The separate curves make a vivid contrast.

THE LAW OF THE PRICE LEVEL

In an alternative form, but with enormous ramifications for public policy, the law of the price level may be stated thus:

$$(\text{Average Price}) = (\text{Unit Labor Cost}) \times (\text{Average Markup})$$

To illustrate, if unit labor costs are $1, and the average markup is 2, or twice unit wage costs, then the average price = $2. If unit labor costs rise to $2.50, and the average markup is unchanged, prices will (on average) jump to $5. If labor costs go up by 1 penny and the markup remains at 2, prices will go up by 2 cents.

The interpretive significance of this relationship is formidable. If the markup is 2, and unit labor costs are $1, thereby making price $2, then out of the extra $1 of nonwage income business firms pay interest, rents, profits, corporate income taxes, dividends, and allocate depreciation allowances, and so on. If labor costs rise by 1 penny, and the prices jump by 2 cents, the extra penny contains the margin to cover all other costs.

This empirical law of the strong fastness of the markup is the key to the near perfect linkup of unit labor costs and the price level, or of money wage hikes and inflation. They go together, "like love and marriage"—and with even fewer qualifications in the modern era.

UNIT LABOR COSTS

Unit labor costs (ULC) are computed as the ratio of average annual wages to average labor productivity, or the ratio of average hourly wages to average hourly production. To illustrate:

$$\text{ULC} = \frac{\text{Average wage}}{\text{Average Output Per Employee}} = \frac{\$15,000}{1,000} = \$15.$$

In the illustration, if average productivity rose from 1,000 to 2,000 units, the ULC would drop from $15 to $7.50. On the other hand, if the wage rose from $15,000 to $30,000, with productivity still at 1,000, the

CHART 3.3. Gross Business Product in Current and Constant (1972) Dollars, 1950-1980

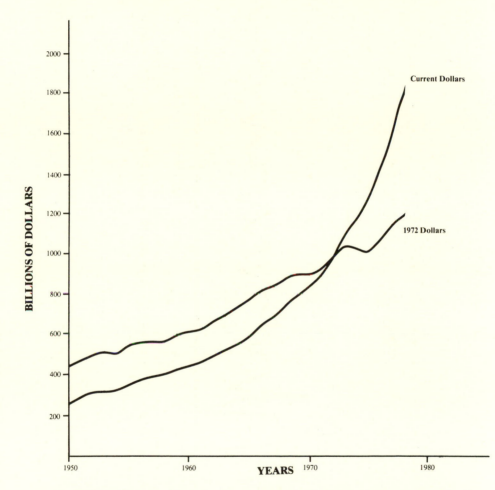

Source: National Income and Product Accounts of the United States, 1929-1974; *Survey of Current Business*, July 1979.

CHART 3.4. Annual Percentage Change in Average Markup, 1900-1978

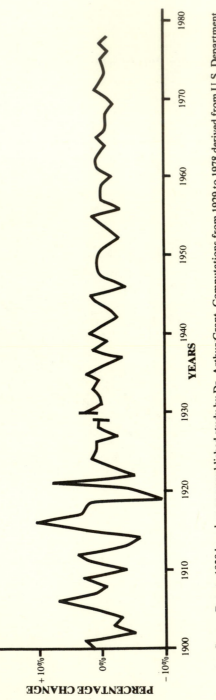

PERCENTAGE CHANGE

+ 10%

0%

- 10%

1900   1910   1920   1930   1940   1950   1960   1970   1980

YEARS

Source: Data to 1929 based on an unpublished study by Dr. Arthur Grant. Computations from 1929 to 1978 derived from U.S. Department of Commerce data.

50

ULC would explode to $30. If the average markup was 2, and with the ULC at $15 originally, prices would first be $30. Should the ULC mount to $30, prices would leap to $60. Conversely, with a ULC at $7.50, prices would tumble to $15.

The law reveals how the price level behaves. Deplore it or praise it, we nevertheless must resign ourselves to a price level which reacts fairly immutably to alterations in LUC. While the illustration is artificial and contrived, the facts affirm its harsh discipline.

Note the two ULC elements, namely, (1) the average wage and (2) average productivity. If one zooms ahead and the other tags well behind, the shock in ULC translates into price-level disorder.

THE REMARKABLE CONSTANCY IN THE MARKUP

Unmentioned so far is the affirmation that the average markup is equivalently the *reciprocal* of the wage share.* Thus if the markup is 2, the wage share is ½. If the wage share is ⅔, the markup is 1.5.

The most amazing economic fact with which we must contend is that the *average* markup of prices over unit labor costs has remained so remarkably constant over our modern industrial economic history. Since about 1900 when the first meaningful statistics were compiled, or since about 1929 when the first U.S. Department of Commerce compilations appear, the markup stability has been pronounced.

The constancy over time in the average markup is the most substantive empirical law in economics. Compared to other ratios often used in economics, whether it be the ratio of capital-to-output, which wavers up and down, or of capital-to-labor, which trends progressively upward, or the ratio of income saved, which often fluctuates in the 8 and 12 percent range—implying a fall of ⅓ or a growth of ½—the markup just plods along a sidewise course veering downward ever slightly. The velocity of circulation of money jumps about, with a historic tendency to fall, at least until recent years of tight money and peak interest rates. Money velocity vacillations contrast to the crablike motion of the markup.

Chart 3.4 depicts the markup on a ratio scale since 1900. Clearly, even more impressive than its strong historical stability, the year-to-year fluctuations are trifling: it is a rare year when there are 1 percent gyrations either up or down.

The markup, as the reciprocal of the wage share, has amounted in gross business product to a bit under 2, at approximately 1.9, meaning that of every $1 of business sales proceeds labor recoups about 53 cents.

---

*Obviously, this follows inasmuch as the markup is the multiple by which total income exceeds the wage share.

Explanation of this remarkable constancy in labor's share remains the unexplored mystery in economics. It is one of the best documented facts in economics, yet economists have been remiss in not attending to it, derelict in either unraveling the rather undeviating "law," or in applying it in their policy predilections. Considering its high stability, the main perplexity is less with its constancy than with why the markup originally got stuck at the particular figure of approximately 2—or ½ for the wage share—and not up to maybe 4 or 7 or some other high number. It cannot settle at or near 1 for then labor would get *all* income with scarcely any allowance even for depreciation.

In countries such as Canada or the United Kingdom, analogous phenomena exist, though in Canada the number seems closer to 2.2 and in the United Kingdom, a figure near 1.5 is a better estimate. Canada's economy is more agricultural, England's more industrial. The intimation is that the industrial economy yields a larger wage share—which is not surprising if the income of small farmers is lumped as a "proprietor's income" akin to profits.

THE CONFLICTING MONEY-WAGE AND PRODUCTIVITY TUGS

From these relations the law of the price level appears as:

(% Price Level Change) = (% Markup Change) + (% Wage Change) − (% Change in Average Labor Productivity)

Eliminating the percentage change in markups as about nil, we end with:

(% Price Level Change) = (% Wage Change) − (% Change in Average Labor Productivity).

The latter version expresses the *law of the price level*: The price level responds, percentagewise, to the tug-of-war being played out between gains in money wages and productivity events. If productivity growth is *negative*, we have the mutual price disintegration: both the money-wage bulge and the productivity decline pull in the same direction, accentuating the price-level surge.

DECLINING MARKUPS

Recent decades reveal some downward probe in markups. Since 1950, for example, the markup descent has come close to 12 percent. On this score, the 1980 price level should have been about 12 percent *lower*, if money-wage boosts merely matched the gradual productivity lift. Thus the actual price-level explosion attests to the gigantic takeoff of money wages over the period. Allegations that our inflationary debauch has been a result of business enhancing its profit share through exploiting mark-up opportunities betray a gross innocence of the available evidence. Ostensibly, markups in a few sectors have been unconscionable, with oil and the energy sphere being conspicuous offenders. Overall, in the full business spectrum, markups have dipped, serving to augment labor's income share.

IF LABOR GOT ALL THE INCOME: A MARKUP OF UNITY

Some will interpret this emphasis on money wages as an indictment of labor and a bias toward management, or censuring unions as the root of inflation and exonerating business as being a mere bystander to the event.

This is a distorted perspective. Nothing that has been said is intended to picture businessmen as meek victims, or to daub labor as carriers of the inflation bug. The issue is inflation, and not one of identifying good guys and villains. The incontrovertible point is that as most of the money income consists of wages and salaries—¾ in our economy—it is not possible to damp the money income tide without containing the ¾ share. Further, the importance of the descent in k (the markup factor) is to affirm that if ¾ of the income total is reasonably mastered, the other ¼ will pull in tandem, and not rush pellmell to garner more than the ¼ share. In fact, the several nonwage categories have persistently tended to recede, in inflationary season or out, with the recent exception of interest payments, even when the price level stood exceptionally calm and only barely advancing as in the 1960s.

The position can be put more strongly. Imagine that we dwelt in an idyllic socialist paradise—not of this world—where labor amassed *all* income, the full 100 percent, with none destined for capital, or management, or interest or rent, what then? The value of k would then be unity, of k = 1. Is there any doubt as to the outcome? Obviously in this situation prices would move in a *rigid* lockstep with unit labor costs: every rise in the average money wage would spell an exact proportionate price jump unless offset by enhanced labor productivity.

In this imaginary case where labor received *all* income we could *completely* neglect k as being utterly irrelevant price-wise. As matters stand, although k exceeds 1, it is neglected only because its perturbations are too small to make a difference. But when wages constitute all of income, k is *precluded* from changing by virtue of the very nature of the income arrangements.

Thus in that starry "ideal" world—where an exclusion of nonwage incomes is visualized as a dreamy ideal—the price level would *only* respond, and inflation could *only* occur, by outsized hikes in pay scales. The market economy operates in practically the same way, at least in its price-level dimension.

Not surprisingly then, in collectivist economies which have enjoyed a better price-level record over the last 12 years than the market economies, the average pay scales are set from the center. (This has, for example, touched off the Polish crisis.)* To emulate their insulation from price chaos we shall have to learn to do something akin to their pay principles, but by methods compatible with our democratic institutions, and through practices that conform to our own incentive modes for resource allocation.

But to talk of $k = 1$, and with only wage incomes covered by price, is to conjure a mythical inoperative world. There is the serious question of how the system would run if all other incomes dried up. Further, once labor absorbed all output, surely its share could not be increased further. There could be no demagoguery for an encore, for there would be no other incomes to be deflected to labor. Wage hikes above productivity gains would immediately usher in inflation and be perceived as a cynical hoax on labor.

In a world of $k = 1$ and only money wage income—to indulge the fantasy—*all* taxes would fall on labor. Granted a need for taxes, and a consensus in support of collecting them from the corporation because of administrative ease, then k would necessarily *exceed* 1. To demolish the mirage further, every business firm, whether private or state-run, must cover depreciation costs. On the rational attitude that product consumers are responsible for the costs entailed in using up equipment, to recoup depreciation k would have to surpass 1. One way or another, and to the consternation of those automatically protesting markups as always exorbitant, it is doubtful that they would disappear under "socialism." It would be absurd to pay out all *gross* income where depreciation is present, and where government taxes must be levied to finance the costs of nonmarket activities, such as police, fire, schools, roads, and defense.

The upshot of this digression into collectivist pricing is that so long as the market markup facts stay constant, or fall, they are *not* a live force in the inflation sequel. Only in rhetoric can one allege that they have been the catalyst in our price distress. There are always instances where they may be extravagent. By and large, they have at least been well behaved in the sense of no upward bump over the last decade of our dreadful inflation orgy.

---

*Ultimately, the Polish strikes have been over real wages, or the buying power of the money wages. The conflict thus also entails the productivity facts.

Where markups have jumped out of line they should be examined by the Federal Trade Commission and the Justice Department for potential antitrust violations.

MONOPOLY?

If money wages kept to the pace of productivity developments, and if prices still escalated, the outcome would connote a mark-up explosion. The surmise then would be that monopoly practices were afoot. We would then know that excess profit taxes and antitrust action provide the route to eliminate the competitive strangle.

As it is, when labor gets, say, a 10 percent pay hike, the industry involved tends immediately to raise prices; sometimes its price maneuvers precede the settlement date, anticipating events on the bargaining front. Invariably, labor protests that the price boost transcends the pay hike and business acts aggrieved, retorting that its boost barely covers the pay burden. Contending studies kick up dust to confuse unwary observers.

Better behavior in wages would put us in a far better position to decide business culpability. Also, if the size of k becomes inflated through the economy, signifying markup rather than wage inflation, it would be easy to cope with because, through the tax law, the gains could quickly be made unprofitable by forcing after-tax corporate income below the level attainable through a lower markup.

MONEY-WAGE MYOPIA

Labor is rightly concerned about its *real* wage, which is the buying power of its money wage. It can achieve improvement through: (1) a rise in its average productivity with its relative share of the total staying firm, meaning k being constant, or (2) extracting a rise in its share by somehow cutting down k. There are *no* other ways. There is scant popular perception of the inescapable logic of these succinct propositions.

When k is constant, labor merely maintains its share of the economic pie, so that real enhancement can come only through productivity lifts, economy-wide. This has been the traditional source of the remarkable growth in the real wage; some further but slight augmentation has also occurred through a fall in k.

With k holding firm, any single group of workers can aspire to higher real income by either: (1) the productivity gains of *all* labor or (2) inroads at the expense of another labor group, so as to lift their relative position in the pay pack. This latter proposition deserves elaboration.

RELATIVE PAY GAINS

Currently, each union bargains for its own membership; at the negotiating table it acts for its constituency. This can evoke some myopia when income shares are finally arbitrated in the price process.

Suppose that blue-collar steel workers are earning $15,000 and that the steel union bargains long and arduously for a 10 percent boost, and wins. The negotiators leave the conference room elated, and their members now, on average, end up with $16,500. In the flush of victory the leadership proclaims its triumph.

The ramifications, however, are more complex. Clerical and managerial employees, sooner rather than later, also eke out 10 percent more, perhaps with the management layer going up from a $30,000 average to $33,000, a $3,000 gain or double the $1,500 award of the production line people. At top echelons, the "underpaid" $100,000-and-over executives moan over their struggle in trying to survive on their pitiful pay. New numbers may come to $10,000 more for the $100,000 person, and $50,000 more for the $500,000 steel gold brick executive.

As the same ritual soon unfolds in other firms, the heralded union pay gains evaporate in the inflation smoke. Relatively speaking, the steel workers are back where they started or even fall behind as executive pay scales break the average percentage barrier that the union punctured initially. It is no surprise that the miraculous pay gains of unions that provoked glee at settlement time have proved so illusory. By attending only to its own pay orbit, and disregarding the chain of events in other divisions of the firm or industry, the union has effectively clouded its own vision.

The income struggle is basically a conflict over *relative* pay positions. Perversely, union bargaining procedures have focused only on income absolutes. While a union may pride itself in getting a good slice of the bankroll, other groups may grab off a larger part of the pelf. It is a continuing source of amazement that income shares, under the much vaunted and feared union thrust, have made only a slight dent in k which is the ultimate arbiter of wage and nonwage income *shares*. With k holding firm, it is a zero-sum-like poker game where one labor group can only benefit at the expense of another; all can gain only through a general lift in productivity. Union leadership has not been cognizant of the important facts of life in the hullabaloo over confrontation tactics.

PROFIT MARGINS

Not only are present bargaining practices myopic, and guaranteed to obstruct organized labor from progressing on the relative income scale, but there is another dimension to the short-sightedness in the union's practiced disregard of price-making forces.

Winning what it perceives as a favorable contract, unions have given scant heed to the pricing policies of the firms with which they bargain; they have not only condoned but they have often even welcomed price increases within their employer firms to meet the labor costs of the contract. Implicit is the wage-price spiral. Rampant illustrations occur monotonously in urban mass transit disputes.

But when the phenomenon happens within all firms, the effect must be either to hold labor's share constant so that real wages are immobilized, or, when k pokes up, for labor's share actually to fall. If labor did a better job of monitoring industrial markups, it might be able to whittle away at some extravagant profit margins and enhance labor's well-being beyond the normal per annum productivity increment.

In these inflationary years of low productivity advance, it is a rueful commentary on the superficial penetration of fundamentals that there has been no serious concern with these industrial market aspects which are, nevertheless, fundamental to labor's economic well-being.

A NEW "IRON LAW" OF MONEY-WAGE INFLATION?

Over a century ago the socialist Ferdinand Lassalle christened the real wage aspects of Thomas Robert Malthus's population doctrine as the "brazen" or "iron law of wages." Recall, this held as *real* wages rose, and living standards improved, more children would be born ultimately driving real wages back. Of course, this was long ago when sex was one of the few amenities, besides beer and carousing, open to the working class. There were not the other distractions of TV, movies, and spectator sports.

By the age of about 8 or 10 children were ready for work of the most irksome sort, doing menial tasks in a coal mine or factory: Karl Marx in his diatribe on capitalism gained much mileage and human sympathy—and disciples—by documenting the brutal and inhumane facts of child and female labor in those early harsh days of capitalist organization. Thus a large accretion to the working force could be generated fairly quickly when pay scales allowed more consumption fare than minimal necessities. Population placed a lid on real wages.

AN IRON LAW OF INFLATION

Economists today reject the "iron law of wages" for the Western world. The economic system has shown its ability, through technology, to drive production on to outpace the labor force augmentation, and to raise *real* incomes. Indeed, the gains from productivity have negated Marx's pessimistic prognosis that real wages would inexorably fall and that labor would be so "immiserated" that it would naturally revolt. Because of real wage gains his doomsday knell tolling the demise of the capitalistic system by a grim proletariat has gone awry.

Nonetheless, the "iron law of the price level" does prevail. It stipulates that barring small dips in markups, any increase in labor's *money* wage beyond the minor bulges in average labor productivity will dissolve in inflation smoke. The price escalation is inescapable. And from inflation, under our usual monetary policies, unemployment, high interest rates, and a concatenated chain of events spell assorted havoc to sap our political, social, and economic well-being.

Real wages rise with productivity improvements. These have been the benign increments which have suspended the "brazen" law of wages. But the price level remains victimized by the vigorous striving to obtain more *real* income under existing productivity conditions and the prevailing mark-up forces which are entrenched in the *modus operandi* of the market economy.

4

Money Supplies: Relinquishing Some Myths

Some will recoil at our feat of isolating the inflation virus without mention of the money supply, or without attaching any credence to money volume in the inflation script. The inadvertence has been deliberate. For in the modern inflation drama money comes on as a bit player. Nonetheless, the potency of money is not to be underestimated: it is crucial in determining production and jobs. It can under*write*, or under*mine*, the magnitude of real GNP at the price level established by the money-wage and productivity nexus.

"Too much money chasing too few goods" is the venerable monetary dictum on inflation. In today's stagflation world of business below capacity operations this is a muddled explanation of price-level events. Its shortcomings extend to market economies most like ours, for example, the United Kingdom, Canada, Australia, Germany, Japan, France, Italy, and Scandinavia. Those who plead that inflation comes from money excesses have the causation reversed. Essentially, it is a case of higher market prices *requiring* more money to facilitate the transactions flow.

"STOP PRINTING MONEY"

When asked about inflation and how he would stop it, as the Republican presidential candidate, the now President Ronald Reagan was prone to hold up a dollar bill and quip, "Stop printing these." Other equally misinformed public figures say something equally absurd. By and large, the declaration brands the pundit as a carrier of the monetarist economic doctrines which have visited the stagflation tragedy on our nation. Too many in high places are the captives of deluded ideas imbibed long ago and now expounded as verities. The reiterated myths contribute to mass confusion.

Does President Reagan want the Mafia to print dollar bills? Counterfeiters? Does the president want us to use blank paper? Or carry around the trees from which the paper is derived and on which the money is printed? In back of his mind is the absurd notion that the government has been printing currency in various denominations to pay its bills. This purveys the falsehood that we are financing our federal deficits by printing money.

This is a mischievous and misguided description of events, wrong from start to finish; if any secretary of the treasury has been guilty of the practice in either the Nixon, Ford, or Carter administrations, he should be jailed for a criminal offense.

Ultimately, the casual rhetoric constitutes opposition to an unbalanced government budget, and the borrowing undertaken to close the gap between tax collections and outlays. If this is what the president has in mind, it can be said simply instead of reiterating the naive intellectual crudity urging that "we stop printing dollar bills."

HOW MONEY GETS INTO CIRCULATION

How do coin and currency get into circulation? In the immortal comic-strip words of Pogo, "We have met the enemy and he is us." We, the public, share complicity for the money in circulation. Paper money survives because each of us finds it convenient to hold currency to make some payments, instead of drawing checks on our bank deposits.

Think of a simple illustration. Suppose I have a checking account amounting to $5,000. Simultaneously, suppose I carry no cash, no nickels, dimes, quarters, dollar bills. Of course, if I want to make a purchase I can usually, with proper identification, draw a check for the exact amount, say $70 for a pair of shoes, or $20 for a meal. Most of us find that for the everyday small purchases such as a newspaper, bus fare, coffee, it is easier to use cash. Most of us thus go to our bank and write a check to withdraw, say, $200 in coins and currency. In doing so, surely the *total* money supply is not altered: my total money holdings are still $5,000. All that has hapened is that the *form* or *composition* of the total has changed, from $5,000 in a bank account to $4,800 in the bank account and $200 in currency.

This is the typical process. Why are coin and currency in circulation? Answer: Because *we* the people want them there. Because we find it comfortable to hold a good fraction of our weekly money income in cash form.

If we preferred not to hold coin and currency, we would merely drive to our neighborhood bank and deposit the sums there, swelling our bank accounts. Would this *decrease* the money supply? Surely not, for it would only mean a concentration of our total money holdings in checking accounts.

Perhaps this outcome would please President Reagan, but it would hardly appeal to most of us. Maybe, with less currency outstanding President Reagan might conclude that our inflation crisis was solved! Most of us would see this as a hallucination. The altered money-supply composition would not abort our inflation mess.

VARIATIONS IN THE OUTSTANDING CURRENCY TOTAL

Normally, as July 4 or Labor Day approaches, and we know that banks will be closed, and especially if we contemplate travel, we are apt to draw down our checking accounts to hold more coin and currency. Over these dates there is usually a *seasonal* increase in currency outstanding. Likewise, the seasonal phenomenon is pronounced during the Christmas gift season, or over the Thanksgiving and Memorial Day weekends. The Federal Reserve allows for recurring seasonal regularity in its operating decisions. Seasonal movements hold few surprises by virtue of the perennial experience.

Despite confused political partisans who blunder egregiously on these matters, the mechanics of a net increase in currency (and coins) outstanding are elementary. Normally, in their daily operations, banks will find one group of people depositing currency and another set making withdrawals. Where there is a good matchup, an operating harmony prevails: bank tellers collect deposits from the one person and pay out to the withdrawing party.

When, on balance, the bank is faced with net withdrawals, say $25,000 or more, it will phone the Federal Reserve Bank of its area and request funds, thereby drawing down on its own deposit which it holds at the Fed. The transaction is completely routine. (If the bank is a local branch of a larger chain, it will call on the head office. If the bank is a non-member of the Federal Reserve, it will draw on its account usually held with a Fed member.)

EVENTS AT THE FEDERAL RESERVE

When local banks are making net demands on it for currency, the Fed will ship out the notes and deduct the withdrawals from the member bank's deposit accounts. Finally, if the Federal Reserve itself must replenish its own stock of currency, it will deposit various forms of collateral—in the gold standard days, substantially gold certificates, and now mainly government bonds—with the Government Bureau of Printing and Engraving. The latter is administered not by the secretary of the treasury but the treasurer of the United States (customarily a woman, since the days of President Franklin D. Roosevelt). In exchange for the hypothecated collateral the Fed will receive the requisite supply of currency and coin and comply with the needs of the local banks who are, in turn, responding to the requests of its customers—you and me.

THE PUBLIC DECIDES ON THE CURRENCY IN CIRCULATION

Thus you and I, we the public, govern the *amount* of money in circulation. It is not the case that the government is "forcing" us to hold the coin and currency; the holdings follow from our conscious decisions based on our income, wealth, and spending proclivities for "small" purchases. If we decided to hold less pocket money, the totals of money in circulation would fall dramatically.

Conforming to the Reagan strictures to "stop printing them," we would end up with a maladroit money system. When we went to our bank and asked for nickels, or dollar bills, the tellers would say, "So sorry, President Reagan stopped printing dollar bills and producing coins to 'sell' to the Federal Reserve." But, they could add, "Draw checks against your deposit. Creditors will have their deposits increased, and you, as a debtor, will have yours decreased." The result? Whenever we buy a newspaper or a cup or coffee, we would draw a check!

Obviously, this would be "conservative"—and awkward—in the extreme. But it would logically follow from the Reagan recipe. Obviously, the candidate was bamboozled by his "experts," and foisted a snow job on his audiences.

It would be a crude money system if our checking accounts kept increasing but, by the president's peculiar sophistries, we could not have our moneys in denominations which we preferred. President Reagan would be on stronger ground if he argued that the full money *supply*, and not just currency, be brought under better control. Thus if the money total stopped growing we would be limited in the sum of bank balances *and* coin and currency. If our full holdings grew more slowly, then our outstanding coin and currency aggregate would be capped.

Table 4.1 lists the various bank deposits and the coin and currency outstanding on December 31, 1980. We forego the appellations M1-A, M1-B, M2 . . . usually assigned to the various aggregates although mastering these conventional definitions is often enough to vault one to eminence in the inner sanctums of Wall Street.

TABLE 4.1

Seasonally Adjusted Money Supply and Its Composition, December 1980
(in billions of dollars)

Currency	$ 116.5
Demand Deposits	268.9
Savings Deposits	395.5
Time Deposits	1,011.1

SOURCE: *Economic Report* (1981), p. 302.

HOW MONEY IS BORN

The money stock is what it is, a proposition quite true but trite. The perplexing aspect is: how does it change? Thereafter the more complex subject concerns the effect of the money supply changes, which is tantamount to the profound teaser on the type of monetary policy we should pursue for optimal economic performance.

It would be possible to wade through our checkered past in a historical exegesis on how the existing near $400 billion of checking accounts, and coin and currency, originated. But for contemporary comprehension the foray would be equivalent to exhuming Egyptian mummies; for a description of modern man the ancient facts are mostly irrelevant for purposes of future policy and control.

With minor qualifications hardly worth mentioning, our money supply changes whenever commercial banks—meaning banks which hold our checking accounts—grant loans or purchase bonds (generally they are precluded by law from stock purchases, with few exceptions). This is it: this is the sum and substance which can make everybody an expert on how our money supply trundles out into time and space.

Banks, to repeat, lend to their customers, or they buy commercial paper—which consists of promissory notes of the larger corporations—or they buy government, public utility, corporate, or mortgage bonds. It is on the interest from loans and bonds that banks earn their living, doing quite handsomely over the last decade as interest charges surged skyward.

Consider the trivial details of the money-augmenting process. Suppose the reader enters the bank to request a loan of $5,000 to purchase a car and agrees to repay in installments. When the bank finally grants the loan, with adequate collateral as a safeguard, the bank will notify the borrower that "as of that day your deposit account will be increased by $5,000." (Usually, under the discount process, if the term ran for one year and the interest rate was 10 percent, the deposit account would be increased by $4,500, with repayment totaling $5,000.)

Obviously, the net effect is to increase the total of *demand* deposits by $4,500. As the loan sum is withdrawn by personal check to the automobile dealer, the latter's deposit account is increased, while the purchaser's account dwindles by the same sum. But the purchase transaction does not alter the total money supply any further: it has been augmented by $4,500 through the bank loan. As the dealer pays his help who make purchases, and so forth, the money total remains swollen by the $4,500 loan amount, though the volume of currency in circulation will almost certainly change under the different preferences of individuals who comprise the payments stream.

Alternately, suppose your commercial bank grants a mortgage loan on the new home you are purchasing, or suppose you want to sell your bank some government bonds that you have inherited. The process, in either case, is quite parallel: you turn over the $25,000 mortgage bond, or government bonds, to the bank, and the bank *credits* your deposit account with $25,000. Thereupon, you are free to write checks for this sum, or to make withdrawals, perhaps to demand $25,000 in pennies, if the fancy seizes you. Either way, the money supply is *increased* to the extent of the bank's purchases of the securities.

This *is* the way in which our money supply changes. The mechanism is practically the same in most of the Western-world market economies. Without the banking system we would have to invent another means of altering the money supply in order to facilitate our payment needs as money incomes, output, and labor force grow over time.

Note, *no* judgment is being cast on the money-creating process; the above serves merely as a description. We forego questions on whether our money-creating method is a ''good'' or ''bad'' means of altering the money supply. Suffice to say, it *is* our method. It can obviously operate for good or ill but, to return to the major quest of this work, the money-creation process is only dimly related to our inflation rot. An exposition of how money affects the economy, and its potency, is reserved for ensuing chapters.

To anticipate some queries of those who wish to pursue the process further, when savings banks grant loans or buy mortgage bonds, it is mainly a matter of transferring ownership of your deposited check to a new owner, with the savings bank as intermediary and getting some interest cut on the deal. For the most part, the various savings institutions also maintain deposit accounts with commercial banks. Thus as we deposit checks with them, they deposit the same checks in a commercial bank. At the moment, our banking system is in a transition phase with checking accounts, or equivalents, being available at savings banks.

Nonetheless, barring the future metamorphosis of the commercial banking system, the process recounted above describes the money-creation process in our country, or in Canada, United Kingdom, Australia, Japan. A future scribe may have to drop the distinction between "commercial" and "savings" banks.

GOVERNMENT DEFICIT FINANCE

How does the government fit into this picture? Later, we examine the operational control by the Federal Reserve which occupies an uneasy status as an *independent* government agency, with its policy-making officials appointed by the president but responsible, in a reporting way, to Congress. Owing its legislative life to Congress, the Federal Reserve always treads a narrow line. In practice its independence is reminiscent of Mr. Dooley's sage remarks on the Supreme Court's ear to the election returns.

To finance its deficits the federal government must issue its own promissory notes, either in the form of Treasury bills or longer maturing government bonds. Inasmuch as it sells them in the open market to willing buyers, it is inevitable that some part of the offering is bought by commercial banks. During the 1930s, for example, with other borrowers absent from loan markets, banks acquired a sizable portion of the government bonds issued to sustain the deficit finance of the Depression days. After all, government bonds are the nearest thing to a "certain" investment, with *no* prospect of default in payment of interest on due dates, or repayment of principal when the bond matures. (Of course we have doomsday prophets who contend otherwise—or predict the impending end of the world.)

It follows logically that when commercial banks buy government bonds the money supply expands, just as in the case of bank acquisition of bonds from nongovernment borrowers. In working out the details, the bond-buying bank increases the Treasury's deposit account with it as payment and, when the Treasury wants to spend the proceeds, it withdraws the funds, deposits them with the Federal Reserve, and invariably draws its checks on the Federal Reserve. As the checks are acquired by individuals and firms receiving money from the government, the checks find their way back to the banking system, enlarging the checking deposits of private citizens or corporations. One way or the other, the total money supply is expanded. Every time, therefore, that the government sells bonds, and when commercial banks purchase them, the effect on the money supply is exactly the same as when bonds are acquired from private nongovernment issuers.

Insofar as the government sells bonds to finance its deficits it is competing for part of the pool of funds with private borrowers. This has been called the "crowding out" effect, suggesting that money-market access is made more onerous for private borrowers. Generally, the argument is confused, for it assumes that Federal Reserve policy would be the same *without* the government deficit; it conveys the impression that Fed policy would be immutable despite a different economic climate. Conceivably, the Fed policy could be more lax—or stricter. One can never be certain of the chain of events under different circumstances.

Between December 1960 and November 1980 the commercial banks' loans and bond holdings increased by $1,024 billion. Their acquisition of government bonds amounted to $49.4 billion. Despite all the fuss, the latter sum hardly contributed to any massive augmentation of money supplies or "printing press money," as President Reagan and others allege. Tales of "crowding out" effects also come more from Aesop's *Fables* than reverence for the facts.

President Reagan would nonetheless be on far more solid ground if he abjured the showy rhetoric of "stop printing money," and objected to deficit finance, or to banks buying government bonds—though the latter are decisions reached by banks in the light of interest rate portfolio alternatives, rather than being mandated by government. Better still for Reagan to object to the money supply increase, namely, in checking accounts, coin, and currency. Concentrating on "printing paper money" conveys a dim understanding of the United States monetary system.

THE FEDERAL RESERVE POWER NICHE

Emphasis has been placed on the loan and bond-buying proclivities of the commercial banking system in determining our money supply. We might glimpse the part played by the Federal Reserve governors and their power niche in the grandiose scheme.

As noted, the commercial bank system members must keep a deposit with the Federal Reserve Bank of their region. It happens that the preponderant banking strength of our country, measured in terms of either total loans and investments, or total deposits, are Fed members. Under law, the larger member banks must keep an amount equal to 16¼ percent of their own demand deposit liabilities as a deposit—or reserve balance—at the Federal Reserve. They receive no interest on these sums (though there is pressure to alter this, for in these inflation days of high interest rates it means a substantial income sacrifice by member banks). Unless the member carries an ample reserve deposit the bank is in violation of the law.

Here then is the lever to control the checking accounts of the public which arise through bank loans and security purchases. As banks try to keep "loaned up" to augment their earnings, the Fed operates to control the reserve balances that the banks hold with the Fed. For as they possess more reserve balances, the banks are free to make more loans which, we have noted, augment the public's deposit money. Thus when the Fed engages in maneuvers to curtail the bank's reserve balances, the banks must exert restraint in granting new loans; they may be compelled to actually contract loans or cut their bond portfolio, by refraining from new loans or by selling some of their inventory of bonds.

Open-market operations arise in this setting. As the Federal Reserve also owns government bonds, acquired not from the Treasury in financing deficits but in purchases in the money markets in the execution of its money supply policy mission, the Fed can decide to sell off some of its bond holdings. If it decides to sell $1 billion of bonds to willing buyers, and as the checks in payment to the Fed are drawn on the various local banks, in short order the member bank reserve balances will diminish by $1 billion as the Fed confronts the banks with the checks for collection; the banks redeem their debt obligation to the Fed (for the checks) by drawing down their reserve balances. The commercial banks, losing $1 billion in reserve balances, and with a reserve requirement of 16¼ percent, must perforce contract their loan and bond portfolios (and thus their deposits) by approximately $6 billion (or about six times in view of the fractional 16¼ percent requirement).

This is a broad-brush description of the Federal Reserve "open-market operations," always portrayed as intricate and arcane machinations by financial writers. There is very little mystery about them. When the Federal Reserve, in its discretion, decides to sell government bonds it mops up reserve balances and places a lid on banks' loan expansion. The money supply is thus placed under restraint.

Conversely, when the Fed wants to encourage bank lending, it will *buy* government bonds in the open market. The upshot is for the Federal Reserve to issue checks for $1 billion and, as these are sent by the various bond *sellers* back to the Federal Reserve for collection, payment is made at the Fed by *increasing* the reserve balances of the member banks submitting the checks. As the latter now acquire extra reserve balances, in amounts in excess of legal requirements, they can grant loans to augment their earnings as they expand the money supply.

THE FED: KEEPER OF THE MONEY SUPPLY

The Federal Reserve is thus the ultimate custodian of the money stock; effective practical control of the money supply lies within its grasp. In

December 1981 it held a total of $117.6 billion of government bonds. Reserve balances of member banks were $44.9 billion. Indulging in a fantasy, if the Fed sold off $45 billion of its holdings, and on the fractional 16¼ percent reserve requirement prevailing for large banks, the total of demand deposits in the commercial banks would have to be slashed to zero. Of course, it would usher in a massive money deflation, and we would have to invent a new money system!

Thus if President Reagan really feels that the money supply is too large, and that its total should be dammed, then his quarrel is with the Federal Reserve. Its governors *are* in a commanding position to decrease the total. It is a red herring to aver that we have "too much money," alleged to come from the printing-press process. The latter reference is extravagently misinformed—on a generous assessment.

INTERNATIONAL MONEY FLOWS

Inflows or outflows of funds from abroad hardly trim the main outlines of the money process. If some Swiss citizens want to buy dollars, they will go to a bank willing to sell dollars for Swiss francs. Ultimately, as the foreign currency—dollars owned by Swiss banks—becomes scarcer, either the value of the dollar in foreign exchange markets will rise, or the Federal Reserve (or some foreign holders of dollars who want to acquire Swiss francs) will make them available. The effect: the Fed ends up with more foreign currencies, and member bank reserve balances, and the money supply in the United States will rise. (It is as if an open-market operation by the Fed, to acquire Swiss francs, takes place.)

Likewise, for an outflow of dollars. The dollar holder will have to sell dollars to amass Swiss francs, or German marks, or Japanese yen. Someone must buy the dollars. If it is a foreign central bank anxious to control the exchange value of its currency, the foreign central bank becomes the dollar custodian. As these funds are not held for domestic United States expenditure, if the Federal Reserve wanted to neutralize the departure of dollar balances it could buy government bonds in the open market and thereby restore the basis for the active domestic money supply.

In sum, the Fed is the ultimate monarch ruling the money supply by controlling member bank reserve balances through its open-market operations. These are under its tight grip, at least over a period, though, for several reasons, there can be some modest intermittent slippage. If our complaint is that the money supply is steaming ahead too fast, or moving at too lumbering a pace, we are engaging in the ever-popular all-season sport of Fed-faulting. Criticism sent to any other address is misdirected.

The serious censure of the Fed, elaborated below, is not that it cannot control the money supply amply but that it claims too much in professing its ability to prevent inflation. In its misguided inflation obsession, considering its sparse, clumsy tools, it has contributed mightily to our stagflation distress.

THE GOLD STANDARD NOSTALGIA

We might digress to note here a revival of a gold standard bug among some Reagan economic advisers during the presidential campaign. Others, of another generation, undoubtedly yearn for the restoration; they have long mourned gold's dethronement.

To explain our abandonment of gold in 1933 would take a tome in itself. But we were the last, not the first, of the major countries to take our leave of the ancient order, literally forced to do so. There are these factors to note: (1) The gold standard is an expensive standard. It means a heavy cost for countries without gold mines to give up goods to acquire gold. (2) The gold standard was a mechanism for fixing international exchange rates. This could not occur unless other countries restored the system. There seems little interest and less urgency on the part of Western nations to do so. Amusingly, some of the original advocates of "floating" exchange rates now advocate the gold fixity. (3) The gold standard was a "fair weather" standard. Our country, and other countries, always suspended gold payments when there was a run on the gold held by the treasury. Thus it worked in placid times. In emergencies it let us down. (4) There is the vital issue of the price of gold. Those who advocate it are silent on the issue but its main feature was that the price of gold was fixed, at $20.67 an ounce until 1933, in 1934 and thereafter at $35, and since 1973 officially at $42.22. Thus those who advocate the standard to *control* the money supply would usher in a spectacular money binge if gold was monetized, say, at $500 an ounce which has been near its recent market price. The present Federal Reserve holdings would scoot up in value from approximately $11 billion to about $130 billion by the stroke of the official pen. It could, unless neutralized (as it would have to be) touch off an immense augmentation of the monetary base—all in the name, for the Reagan monetarist campaign advisers, of "fighting inflation." Consistency does not rank high as a commendable virtue among economists.

Gold restoration seems to be an archaic method of providing, or controlling, our money supply. The gold standard concept is frequently drummed for its promise in "backing" or "regulating" the money supply. We know where a linebacker is in professional football, say 5 or 8 yards behind the line. How far back does gold stay? When help is needed, the gold standard is abandoned any time too many clamor for gold. Thus the standard resembles an ace quarterback who is so valuable that the coach fears to see him injured—so he holds him out of every game!

The gold nostalgia omits the past instability under the gold standard, the many banking panics, the runs on gold, and the fact that the departure from gold occurred during the Great Depression which it scarcely helped avert. In fact, the more usual analytic threads suggest that the standard was a major contributing factor to the depression severity, if not the major causal strand.

Vague hints on the revival of gold foreshadow the prospect of another whale of a red herring being injected into our national economic dialogue, diverting us from the stagflation issue. Without alluding to the price of gold to crown the restoration, the gold bugs are toying with an idea as sound as making an automobile sing by reversing the tires.

5

MONEY POLICY:
THE BULLDOZER IN A FLOWER POT

Money incomes, especially money wages and salaries relative to average productivity, have been indicted as the inflation maker. How do money supplies fit in? After all, excess money supplies have long been held to be the root of all inflation. This is the subtle poser to challenge us in this chapter, following our description of how money supplies emanate from commercial bank loans and bond purchases.

Money supply mythology has it that an increase in the money supply speedily elevates prices, qualified only by provisos on a slower velocity of money circulaton or bursts in the volume of physical output. This was the essence of the Quantity Theory of Money, which is the most significant relic of past thinking. Prior to pointing just where the theory went wrong, we first etch in how money supplies enter the picture on our conception of the price level evolving from the lopsided battle between nominal wages and productivity.

SOME FUNDAMENTAL PROPOSITIONS

Our economic system is often described as a capitalist system, or a market system, and it is always viewed as a price system. Fundamentally, on a prior concept it is a *money-income* system. For the ubiquitous product price phenomena result from the fact that incomes, with wage-salary pay being the dominant type, are dispensed in money. Because of money wages our workers make money purchases at the shops, paying out money prices for the goods. Food prices, clothing, gasoline, appliances, and rents, are all stipulated in money terms to confront the employees with money-income sums to disburse. If employees were paid in shoes, or food, or gasoline, or any other commodity, we would have relative prices expressed in those items rather than in terms of money. Prices reflect the pervasiveness of money incomes, in a causal image. While the system may have originated as a price system, it is best comprehended now as a money-income system. This revised conceptualization best illuminates the economic process. Fogginess is dispelled compared to versions which stipulate consumers coming to market fortified with spending money, without any reference to the income source of the spendable money.

The organization and operation of our economic system can be posed as an amalgam of the following interrelated propositions: (1) Entrepreneurs hire labor at an agreed money wage in order to produce goods, in the expectation of later market sales. Thus General Electric hires labor to manufacture light bulbs, in anticipation that market sales will eventuate some months hence. Likewise, clothing manufacturers will produce shirts, blouses, coats, suits, well in advance but on the expectation of retail disposal.

(2) The hire of labor in the production chain will largely set up the cost side of the pricing equation, and control the amount of output that will become available. The wage-salary bill for nonfinancial corporations amounted to 67.6 percent of their gross product (in 1980) and, if depreciation is included, to 78.4 percent of total production charges.*

(3) The same cost sums, paid out in money wages and salaries, act as bread thrown on the waters: wages and salaries become the purchasing power of the mass of the household-consuming public. These incomes utterly dominate the consumer side of the price equation. Wage and salary recipients absorb about 85 percent, and about 90 percent in the longer past (before the welfare state), of consumer intake. The rest of consumer demand emanates from welfare, professional school students, social security, and unemployment insurance recipients, supplemented by retirees eroding their past savings. Only a small portion of the consumption intake emanates from capitalist "coupon clippers" living on dividends, rents, or interest.

Thus it is not a handful of rich persons such as the Rockefellers, the Gettys, Hunts, Kennedys, or other prominent scions of wealth, who consume most in our economy. Instead, it is the wage and salary employees who consume the most; they crowd the supermarkets, clog the highways, browse through the appliance shops, brush against one another in dis-

*Economic Report of the President, (1981), p. 246.

count and department stores, occupy the beaches, and engage the garage mechanics and auto dealers.

This is the nature of the circular economic process and its three distinct and elemental phases. At desks, work benches, or job sites, money incomes are tendered, to tote up to the costs of doing business and the purchasing power for consumer demand. It is a gigantic circle, with the originating point set at the business firms who hire employees for production in advance of their sales processes. And it is the same business firms who bask in the ebb tide of sales from their cost outpayments: the outgoings ultimately make their cash registers ring in sales. The more they pay out, the more they recoup at their sales counters. And the merry-go-round goes on and on, with the only serious flutters stemming from either a break in (1) the aggregate employment number or (2) the *average* pay scale.

The concept of the circular process can be made more complicated, and more exact, by recording details on other incomes such as dividends, depreciation reserves, or interest payments. But the immersion in details would blur the bold image with faint inconsequential strokes.

THE CAPITAL-GOODS SECTOR

In the capital-goods sector the circular flow is apt to be disjointed so as to disrupt the image. Capital goods are produced only in part for the anonymous market, for they are to a large extent "custom-tailored," as in a construction contract for a factory, apartment house, office building, or for machinery ordered to comply with buyer specifications, and negotiated prior to the production startup.

This capital goods aspect can make a difference. Whereas in the consumption sector the purchases by households are made almost wholly out of income, in the capital-goods sector there are bank loans to capital-goods purchasers. Alternately, borrowers flock to a pool of *past* savings accumulations which become finally deflected to the capital-goods sector. This dependence on *finance* for expenditures, and the more eminent part played by bank lending, destroys any easy "circular" symmetry and forms an amoebic pattern compared to the direct incomes flow to consumer markets.

Note the accent on bank loans to underwrite the new capital-goods formation. We return to this aspect shortly.

MONEY WAGES, MONEY SUPPLIES, AND JOBS

Denying the direct potency of money supplies upon the price level surely is not even remotely to be construed as averring that the money magnitudes are economically impotent. On the contrary, the influence of money-supplies or monetary policy is awesome and potent. But the immediate and major money clout is on *jobs* and on their production analogue. More bank reserves provided through the monarchial (but not divine) aegis of the Federal Reserve, and filtering out through the banking system to business firms, provide jobs and incomes in the firm's orbit. The pressures can release salubrious winds or impose shattering recession storms on the economy.

BORROWING OPERATIONS

Business firms borrow to finance current production activity from their existing production facilities, and to acquire temporary finance for building new plants, or to accumulate inventories, or to acquire fresh equipment. Contractors need temporary finance while constructing new office buildings or apartment houses or private homes. Money loaned— or borrowed—spells jobs, less unemployment, more production.

An example can lend concreteness to the sequel. Suppose a construction firm is in the habit of borrowing *at the existing wage and price level*, where both are denoted by an index of 100, a sum of $10 million. Suppose, too, that this line of credit is open through some consortium of banks, or available to the firm by issuing commercial paper for sale to banks intervening in the money markets. With the funds available the firm proceeds with its construction schedule, creating jobs and income in the process. After the building is in place and sold, or rented, the contractor or the new buyer can issue bonds for the long term finance of the project and, on receipt of $10 million in bond proceeds, it can redeem the outstanding short-term loans.

Imagine that in the subsequent year the firm is confronted by money-wage agreements which raise its wage bill by 10 percent. To keep the illustration simple, suppose that the prices of all the materials it buys escalate by 10 percent. If the firm contemplates the *same* volume of activity as before, it will have to borrow not $10 million but $11 million. It must borrow *more* money *because* of the higher money wage and material costs merely to maintain its previous production volume.

If banks (because of Fed adamancy) are not in a position to lend $11 million, confessing that despite the firm's creditworthiness the bank does not have ample reserve balances to finance the higher lending position, the firm will be compelled to curtail its productive activities, roughly by 10 percent due to the unavailability of funds.

The sequence will *not* entail any fall in prices—by stipulation they are 10 percent higher because of the higher wage and cost bill. But there will be a drop in production. The lack of funds will claim an activity downturn and jobs as victims. Prices, however, will sit higher. The failure of money supplies to match the price pace inevitably exerts its toll on jobs and output.

Consider a university which waits each year for its tuition receipts in September or October. Suppose it requires $5 million to tide it over the summer months and ordinarily borrows this sum over the short period. To inject a fanciful assumption, if the average university salary *doubles*, beginning July 1 and with a tuition rise of 100 percent slated for the new school year, unless the school can temporarily borrow $10 million over the summer period receipts-gap, it will have to lay-off some normal staff —or ask them to defer pay until October.

The situation differs only in details for an industrial firm which relies on its internal sales finance instead of borrowing. As the prices of the things it buys mount, and as depreciation accumulations erode under the pressure of rising prices, the firm must have greater recourse to loan markets. Not finding the money available in banking circles will compel it to cut back on its production activities. It will buy less material and dismiss some help because of money stringency. One way or another, unemployment will spread.

In the case of building construction, of homes, offices, or factories, financing is indispensable between the commencement of operations and completion and sale of the project. Where building materials and construction labor costs go up, the contractor will have to borrow more on short term. Without the extra sums there will be a curtailment of activity onsite and in the various back-up sectors selling construction supplies. Fewer new houses will mean lower appliance and furniture sales, touching off a domino effect through the broken multiplier chain.

Inventories, too, require financing. At higher prices the same inventory volume ties up more cash. A lack of ample credit will foster liquidation and dampened activity in industries which produce the goods which comprise the "normal-sized" inventories.

Money is the oxygen to keep the exchange process alive. With the higher prices resulting from higher wage costs, more money is required, generally almost in exact proportion to the average money-wage increase, and the tandem general price jump. Without ample funds, production and jobs will slacken.

THE MATTER OF MONEY VELOCITY

Our description has assigned ample weight to the domineering importance of money supplies. The money punch, however, is directed to jobs and production rather than prices. In fact, a ubiquitous point has been that higher prices *require* more money. But more money is *not* culpable for the price rise.

In older accounts of the Quantity Theory of Money it was surmised that the number of times each piece of money was used per annum—the average money velocity—remained constant over time. That is to say, if individuals are paid on average $100 weekly, earning $5,000 per annum, then each piece of money is used 50 times per annum. If they are paid just once a year, to take a far-fetched illustration to cinch the point, then each piece of money is used *twice*, and individuals will ordinarily hold about $2,500 daily in their possession. The point is that the less frequent the pay period the less the money velocity. A fixed money velocity thus rests on: (1) an unchanged pay cycle and (2) unaltered spending habits. In the circumstances, money literally wanders about, spending itself. In addition, higher incomes, in the given conditions, require for the same number of jobs or income recipients that more money be made available.

According to the modern monetarist theorists, the constancy does not extend to velocity in the sense of the *absolute* money turnover but to the *relative* change in money velocity: presumably, a 1 percent increase in the money supply leads to approximately a 1 percent *increase* in money velocity. The rate of change is deemed constant.

Implied in this recent velocity version is the proposition that if prices escalate by 10 percent then about a 5 percent increase in the money supply must be generated merely to *sustain* the *previous* level of production at the *new* price level. A lesser money increment will dismember production and employment.

It is possible to be underwhelmed by the alleged monetarist finding of a constant percentage link between velocity and aberrations in money supplies. Surely, as interest rates trend higher, banks will compete more keenly for the available money supplies, and individuals will direct their money holdings to loan markets of highest return; various economies, such as through money market funds, can be practiced in managing checking accounts. The velocity of money will reflect these altered behavior patterns.

Within elastic limits, therefore, higher prices make higher money aggregates imperative to perform the same *volume* of money work, thus to finance the prevailing level of employment. A reasonable rule-of-thumb seems to be that for approximately every 2 percent hike in the price level, a 1 percent increase in the money supply is incumbent to guard the economy from sinking into an unemployment abyss.

IMPLICATIONS FOR MONETARY POLICY

Vast implications abound from this analysis. Once prices rise because of an immoderate hike in money wages, more money must be provided by the Fed just to *sustain* the previous output and employment level. Consider the upheaval of 1970-1980, when the average money wage more than doubled as the GNP price level reacted by about 90 percent. If we maintained the same money supply as in 1970, we would be pinched in jobs and production because of a short supply of money. According to the statistics, we observe the validity of these broad patterns. With the money-wage and price ascent, in order to avoid massive unemployment far beyond our decade experience, the M1-B money supply series, consisting of coin, currency, and checking accounts, went up by 91 percent between year-end 1970 and 1980. Obviously, the statistics lend themselves to refinement, but the broad pattern is clear. Prices rose, money supplies rose less rapidly, interest rates escalated significantly, and economies in the use of money were practiced so that the money velocity jumped markedly.

To grasp the main principle at work, recall the fundamental synoptic proposition underscored previously. If a firm is going to hire labor at $100 per week, and contemplates hiring 1,000 individuals at the pay scale, then it will normally have to have $100,000 in hand each week to "meet its payroll." Manifestly, if the average pay advances to $300, then it will need to have access to a weekly money reserve of $300,000. And in our monetary system, to reiterate, the only way in which the money supply can be augmented to maintain the *same* activity volume at the *higher* money wage and price level is through bank loans *and* bond purchases.

Money is still the "life-blood of trade" for us, as it was for the ancients. But insofar as the average pay scale escalates, more money is needed as extra plasma to finance the higher money incomes. When we also contemplate the growth in the labor force, and the intent to absorb the unemployed, the demand pressure on money supplies becomes excruciating in the price and growth sequence. Unless the Fed is accommodating on the money-supply side we can be victimized to witness the replay of a Great Depression.

STAGFLATION: THE DOUBLE TROUBLE

Stagflation refers to the double trouble, the sorry juxtaposition and simultaneous twin plague of too much inflation and too much unemployment. Implicit in the foregoing remarks are the ingredients which cook up the twin evil. The Federal Reserve swings at inflation and misses the mark badly; at the same time it deflects the economy into the unemployment swamp.

MONEY RESTRAINT AMID RISING PRICES

Once prices rise *because* the money-wage advance has surpassed gains in labor productivity, the economy requires more money merely to finance the dynamics of the already prevailing job situation and output flow. In addition, a rising labor force commends a money augmentation to support the ensuing potential. It is not surprising, say, that on just this score our 225 million population requires *at least* a 70-fold money expansion compared to that in George Washington's time. Year-to-year the money stock *must* grow.

As an illustration, *if* prices rise by 10 percent, and on the assumption that a 1 percent increase in the money supply leads to about a 1 percent increase in velocity (so that the accretion supports a 2 percent increase in money payments) *then* a 5 percent increase in moneys is prerequisite just to *sustain* a production standstill. At the same time, if jobs are to pick up by 4 percent through absorbing the unemployed and labor force growth, there will have to be a 2 percent extra money increase to underwrite the rising job trend at the new higher prices. The annual money-supply increment will have to approach 7 percent to avoid unemployment distress.

If the Federal Reserve fails to build an ample bank reserve base to assist bank lending, the upshot will be output recession and mounting unemployment. Herein, in the incomplete and begrudging money support by the Fed, is the genesis of stagflation. The "tight money bit" fails to compress prices, but it reins in jobs and production, and fosters higher unemployment rolls. In "fighting inflation" the Fed has displayed the deftness of a bulldozer churning up earth in a flower pot.

Thus in recent years, as money wages and salaries have zoomed, the Federal Reserve has sought to "fight" inflation by tightening the money tap. The sad sequel: prices have irresistibly followed a skyward course of 116 percent between 1970 and 1980 in consumer prices while the money brakes have compounded our economic miseries by inviting unemployment of 7.5 million in absolute numbers on average in 1980 and in a 7.1 percent unemployment rate. Stagflation has been our dismal lot. Our economic report card registers our squalid status.

To change the metaphor, the Federal Reserve zeroes in at the inflation target, and because it is unable to deflect the surge of money wages it is wide of the bull's eye for prices, but is only too effective, unwittingly or not, on maiming the "next of kin," namely, jobs and production.

Unless the Federal Reserve can halt the rate of money wage increase, it will *never* succeed in inhibiting inflation despite its self-serving professions of its valor; the Fed has been too eager to parade its heroism on how it stands at the ramparts in protecting the nation's economy. While the Fed boasts of its valiant stance and brave defense, even its unpopular and heroic antics, it monotonously releases the lugubrious monthly statistics tolling our inglorious retreat in the inflation battle. It is all so reminiscent of the Austrian army communiqué of World War I declaring "an advance in a retrogressive direction."

The Fed's incredible exercise in futility is no accident. The Fed does not have the tools, or instruments, or the weapons to implement its anti-inflation forays. The fact that the price level is about 5 times higher than it was in 1914, when the Federal Reserve began its melodramatic struggle, attests either to its faulty generalship, or to the lack of ample weapons in its monetary arsenal to get the job done. After listening for 67 years to its bewildering *promises* of stability, we can dismiss its solemn self-serving pronouncements as the babble of a general who constantly sees "light at the end of the tunnel." Its optimistic assurances that it can succeed if unimpeded, and ominous tones of hostility if it is impeded have long been devoid of substance.

Of course, the press and the TV media, backward a generation or more in their thinking, continue to transmit, file, and inscribe the banal statements of Fed officialdom. All Fed chairmen are treated as oracles; we exonerate their public misdeeds, while failing to examine the track record of the "star performers" who persistently fail abysmally to establish their prescribed price stabilization goals. Never have the Fed people wavered in their faith in the efficacy of monetary policy despite their dismal record of disaster and economic disarray. This is the supreme irony and the saddest hoax of all, that the Fed's posturing to deny an output lubricant always commands applause as it masquerades as an inflation policy.

PHILLIPS CURVE DEPRESSION THINKING

Why is the Federal Reserve, and its 7-member board of Governors, as effective as the 7 maids with the 7 brooms sweeping back the 7 seas in its interminable and vain struggle against inflation, when it always promises victory tomorrow after releasing the sorry price data on defeat today? Obviously, the economy has changed, but the Fed's thinking has remained frozen except in a search for a new money-supply formula.

There are several reasons for the Fed's abysmal ineffectiveness in applying the band-aid money antidotes, as compared, for example, to the pre-World War I tight money panics before the Federal Reserve was born. (1) There was the long wave of immigration in the late 1800s which provided a stream of workers eager to take jobs *below* the prevailing pay standards. Wages could thus *decline* under growing employment. (2) Unions played little or no role. Big unions came of age only after the New Deal in the 1930s. (3) Unemployment compensation played scant part in alleviating the misery of joblessness; hence money wages fell in a business slump, regardless of the incipient—usually a money clamp —cause of the downturn.

Even now, if the Federal Reserve made money scarce enough to induce an utter collapse in production to rival the 1930s Great Depression, money wages *might* drift down amply to *lower the price level*. More likely, under today's union resistance, they would stay flat or edge ahead only slowly. This unmitigated disaster could thus free us of the inflation blight at the cost of massive job and output distress. This would be the "trade-off" that economists offer in their textbook fancies. In medicine its analogue would be the infliction of one malignant disease, as a fatal kidney impairment, for a menacing coronary arrest. This unsavory medicine would treat half the problem, in striving for surcease on the price front by substituting irreparable damage on the job and production frontier. Medicine would not claim pride in a half "cure" that leads to an irretrievable death. In economics we have enshrined this as a "trade-off" principle; we dispense with no regret the sacrifice inherent in this apocalyptic "remedy."

To reiterate, money policy is a laser that operates *directly* on jobs and production. Focused long enough, and pursued with a vengeance, money therapies can create enough unemployment at frightful costs to retard the money wage tide, and indirectly thereby to mitigate the price advance. Technically, among economists such recourse to the bitter "trade-off" pill is identified as the *Phillips curve relation*, where unemployment is purveyed as an alternative to money-wage increases. Sometimes it is espoused by Keynesians—though the stress involves a hoax that mocks Keynes's work, which aimed at *curing the full patient*, the full economy in both its job and price dimensions.

The true "cure" must banish inflation *and* unemployment, and erase the stagflation malaise. Half-a-loaf solutions, or the substitution of more of one disease for less of the other, does not resolve the peril, and the tactic betrays a faulty diagnosis of the system's infirmities. Too often in our inglorious recent past our inflation blitz has been only partially, imperfectly, and weakly dispelled by injecting an unemployment virus to revive the job boom-bust cycle. Today, when only a deep depression through monetary measures will "stop" inflation, new strategies to insulate us against the inflation madness should be invoked. Otherwise, the stagnation ravages will endure.

MONEY SUPPLIES CHOKING OFF INVESTMENT

Tight money depresses economic activity when banks, strained by a lack of reserves, are forced to deny loan credits even to their most credit-worthy borrowers.* Interest rates are perforce driven up; in 1980 and

---

*A $1,000 loan, discounted in advance at 20 percent yields $800 cash to the borrower. Normally the latter is expected to hold about a $200 "compensating balance" as standard practice. The exact interest toll then comes to $200 on $600 of available funds.

1981, with prime interest rates at 20 and 21 percent, the actual charge often worked out to over 30 percent for many smaller borrowers who could rightly mutter about "usury made legal."

The price of money is an obvious deterrent to borrowing and economic activity. Firms contemplating new plant and equipment at 7 to 10 percent will shy from a prospective obligation of 14 or 16 percent. Operations are set aside, stillborn, when long-term interest rates hit the stratosphere. Why build at 16 percent when, by patience, the project may be financed next year at 10 percent, after a recession deepens and interest rates tumble? The discrepancy between 14 and 10 implies an interest cost surcharge of over 28 percent.

HOW TIGHT MONEY *RAISES* PRICES

Those who cling to the dictum that the Federal Reserve money hampers will exorcise inflation overlook the perverse potential of tight money fostering a *higher* price course. There are several possible slips between the Fed cup and the price lip.

1. Almost invariably, as the money spigot slows, interest rates edge up. Just as little boys on sleds come out after the snowfall, the higher interest rates spur public utilities to petition their regulatory commissions for rate hikes, for telephone services, railroad rates, electric power, or gas. Thus when yields on government bonds are 8 percent, for example, A.T. & T. may plead for the right to earn 10 percent, as a "fair" return. As bond rates advance utilities will also aim for a higher rung on the earnings ladder. As the petitions are routinely approved, despite some showboat political wrangling, tight money passes the higher price pill to consumers, not because of higher operating costs (except for fresh borrowing) but because of the legal doctrine of "a fair rate on reasonable investment value," the historical doctrinal pillar in rate cases. All is clear in this legal mandate except the words "fair" and "reasonable." Invariably, tight money spells higher utility prices.

2. Tight money invariably slams construction and the housing industry. Growing population and relative scarcity in new homes lift the price of this vital component of the consumer budget.

3. When interest rates are in the 4 to 7 percent range, as they were for so long, the amount of interest charges was a fairly nominal part of business costs. At the recent "usury-made-legal" rates, they bite more than twice as hard, and this is reflected in prices. Carrying costs for inventory become onerous, as auto dealers can attest. Prices must carry a higher tag.

4. Installment purchases exemplify the price burden. Borrowing $5,000 to finance the buying of a car, the purchaser pays an extra $750 at a 15 percent rate if the term is one year. At 20 percent, another $250 is tacked on, making cars that much more expensive.

In buying a $75,000 home, and assuming a $50,000 mortgage, at 8 percent the interest cost the first year is $4,000. At 16 percent it is double, of course. There is no doubt of the inroads of interest payments on home purchases on consumer budgets, offset in part by the generous government tax treatment unknown in other countries. Rental properties reflect the higher interest charges in the staircase climb in rents, with renters denied any tax alleviation.

5. In carrying our 1980 national debt of about $1 trillion at 8 percent, an $80 billion sum of tax revenues must be allotted to the task. At 10 percent the servicing charge scoots to $100 billion. At 15 percent, $150 billion. Either more taxes must be levied—inviting wage earners to seek higher wages, or firms to squirm for higher prices—or more Treasury borrowing must hit loan markets, feeding back on interest rates in a dog-chasing-its-tail syndrome.

6. Higher interest rates, as noted, cause firms to defer plant modernization thereby deterring a productivity advance. Deferral is undoubtedly an inflationary factor. It is probably no accident that the 1970s, which saw historic highs in interest rates, was the decade of our startling productivity shortfall.

7. Insurance firms, and other financial institutions, hold enormous amounts of marketable bonds. Every rise in bond yields compels an ineluctable fall in bond prices, as a matter of arithmetic. Many financial institutions, as noted earlier, were in the 1970s in serious financial jeopardy on capital account, with assets dropping below liabilities, engendered by their pursuing a normally prudent investment policy of acquiring gilt-edged bonds. Beside window-dressing their balance sheets to evade the dour solvency aspects, insurance premiums and policy values (because of inflation) have been driven higher as a salvage measure. Consumers shoulder the burden.

BANKS AND THEIR RATIONALIZATION OF TIGHT MONEY

Thus it is a myth to aver that tight money fights inflation. Through the channels enumerated, and doubtlessly others, the money clamps feed inflation. Nonetheless, with plaintive innocence and unflagging adamancy, the Fed, with unanimous commercial bank support, is congenitally prone to defend the money vise as an undiluted inflation breaker.

This self-serving attitude of the banking community must be taken with a whole carload of salt. In their grave monthly bulletins viewing inflation with alarm, and applauding each Fed turn of the monetary screw, they are hardly the objective doctor rendering a diagnostic judgment on an inflamed appendix, without a stake in the decision. The banks' analysts always express dismay at the perceived trend when industrial prices march the upward trail, but shuddering ceases and turns to glee when the price of money turns up. Interest rates, which sustain their livelihood, "fight" inflation!

Banks, and their apologists, thus have a wonderful rationalization in professing virtue every time interest rates spurt up. Manifestly, they are the primary, maybe the only, beneficiary of the Fed's whacking of the economy. They unhesitantly inject a patriotic note of national purpose which miraculously coincides with their undiluted self-interest. Borrowers and buyers in sectors affected adversely by higher interest rates are unlikely to concur. Persons drafted into the "army of unemployed" would also quiz the identification with national interest as spurious after their squeeze on a tight money rack.

6

How Tight Money Is Supposed To Work: Some Mindless Wall Street Support

Tight money has been censured for *de*stabilizing jobs and output while misfiring at the price level. The burden of the argument is that it is an overachiever in setting up a mine field under the employment and production fronts. The indictment becomes more far-reaching, however, for the Fed's manipulations decapitate values in the financial sector. Not only have the gilt-edge markets for high grade bonds been deranged but a pall has been cast over the stock market. All capital markets have been subject to the whiplash.

Monetarist apostles, in expounding their conception of the cause and remedy for inflation, sketch a scene in which the money stock (or volume) is suspended as a Damocles sword over the volume (or quantity) of goods on hand. In the mechanistic model, after an increase in the money total, presto, the sword will smite, and prices will bounce up as a reflex action. Of course, in the refined, less mechanistic, versions of the price-level reverberation, an allowance is always made for a variation in the available goods and for disturbances in the velocity of money over the considered time span.

These few statements contain the essence of the venerable Quantity Theory of Money doctrine that reigned supreme, with only intermittent challenge, for over two or three centuries (depending on the assignment of priorities). Its cardinal features are unaltered, despite the copious writings of the modern monetarists whose minor embellishments incorporate revised institutional operating practices. Policy precepts remain frozen: to subjugate prices, press firmly on the money lever. In former epochs, where a paper money was involved (rather than today's checkbook money), the injunction in the devastating inflation in England during the Napoleonic wars or during World War I, was an admonition "to burn the paper pound."

As remarked, there were qualifications for output variations, with the growth in money supply to be choked a notch below the output push in order to drop the price level. Presumably, if the match-up in goods growth and money bulges balanced, the price level would edge sidewise over time. While conceding that money velocity could show flux in an evolutionary development of the economy, any major revisions were largely—not wholly—brushed aside in the applied doctrine because of the presumption that the "structure of payments" was not susceptible to rapid vacillation. In John Stuart Mill and Alfred Marshall, "waves of confidence" could provoke cyclical oscillations in spending but these were pathological aberrations, minimized in projecting the secular trend.

FROM CONSTANT VELOCITY TO CONSTANT RATE OF CHANGE

In dropping the older conception of a nil change in money velocity over time, modern monetarists have averred that as individuals (and society) became more "affluent" there would be a greater demand for money as individuals sought to enlarge their holdings. But this was statistically estimated to induce a mere modification in the concept of "constant velocity." Formerly it was interpreted as a nil change, and thus a nil percentage change; now the proposition was transformed to read as a "constant percentage change," as in an emendation from "no percentage change per annum to 1 percent change per annum." In application, either form of "constancy" would entitle us largely to neglect the phenomenon.

These provisos are injected here mainly for some reasonable completeness in expounding the monetarist creed. Nonetheless, press a monetarist or Quantity Theory disciple, new or old, for a recipe to stop inflation and the reply will echo President Reagan: stop printing money, either in currency or bank accounts.

The legend is hardy, unswerving, timeless—and wrong.

DAVID HUME AND MILTON FRIEDMAN: A TECHNOLOGICAL GAP

Vivid fables have been concocted to color the tale of how money supplies succor inflation. Two of the more famous fictions are recounted here.

David Hume, in writing his essay "Of Interest" (*Political Discourses*, 1752), propounded for his readers this parable:

> For suppose, that, by miracle, every man in Great Britain should have five pounds slipt into his pocket in one night; this would more than double the whole money that is at present in the kingdom; yet . . . this money, however abundant . . . would only serve to encrease the prices of everything, without any further consequences.

Likewise, in his essay "Of the Balance of Trade":

> Suppose four-fifths of all the money in Great Britain to be annihilated in one night, and the nation reduced to the same condition, with regard to specie, as in the reigns of the Harrys and Edwards, what would be the consequence? Must not the price of all labour and commodities sink in proportion, and everything be sold as cheap as they were in those ages?

This was Hume's excursion in imagery. Women today might demur at the "male chauvinist" tinge; others might quiz his nationalistic sentiment; but this can be only mild criticism, in concession to the tenor of the times. But there is no gainsaying the Damocles sword conception of "money suspended against goods," with the cutting stroke yielding the price level.

For the economy of Hume's day his model was valid enough. He saw merchant trading ships and pirate vessels carrying specie to England; a historian might even demur at distinguishing between the buccaneer plunder and trading ventures. Effectually, in the agricultural English economy, production was "fixed," subject only to the vagaries of the weather and hence, the image of "money versus goods" was not an inaccurate portrayal.

Milton Friedman, in influential writings over 2 centuries later, entertains us with the fantasy of a helicopter dumping money on a community, and invites us to ponder the price-level impact. Shades of Hume, with concession to the technological gap! To nobody's surprise Friedman emerges, triumphant he thinks, with the Humean price-level proclivities. Only the details of the "miracle" are revised, though there may be an eccentric somewhere who "experimented" with the "theory" over a small domain on a magnitude as forgettable as small potatoes.

VOIDING THE FABLE

Granted either the Hume or Friedman tale of money bombardments from outer space—which would be a queer way for Martians to punish us—the Quantity Theory conclusion seems sturdy enough. The only thing to fault is its reality.

The fantasies have absolutely nothing to do with our economy. Both parables *assume* that the amount of output is already, and magically, in existence and that thereafter money is dumped into the economy.

Legerdemain in creation, or in annihilation, is the Hume-Friedman trademark. Money, apparently, plays only a subordinate part in *funding* production; the output is somehow available to be gobbled up by buyers whose money holdings are divorced from the production sequence. Perhaps in no other place in all of economic theory or policy, and surely not on any concept of such primordial importance, has so much credence been given to a model so palpably false. Fascination with it has been incredible, despite its tenuous connection to reality.

Rather than adventitiously poking up on the scene, production occurs in response to price anticipations gauged against unit cost calculations. To finance the material purchases and labor hire, firms have to use their internal funds and rely on their banks to fund their production activity. As explained earlier, hiring and paying labor sets up the cost side of the market equation and the same cost sums, as income to their recipients, are returned in purchasing power in consumer markets. Behind the entire process, to start production and to provide income and underwrite market demand, are money aggregates. That part of the money total provided by banks—often technically called "inside" money—comes into existence in the production act and would vanish into thin air if production dried up.

Money does not appear as a magician's rabbit regardless of production, as in the Hume-Friedman conception, but the money supplies are instead intimately dependent on the labor hire, production volume, and average money wage. If output shoots up, with the money wage unchanged, more money through bank notes will be born simultaneously. Correspondingly, if production holds rigid but average money wages go up, more money will be demanded and created in response to the demand; if it is not provided, higher interest rates and job losses will be the outcome.

The Friedman-Hume conception of money on one side and goods on the other, as antagonists, is thus a misconception of events. The two phenomena interact; money and production emerge from the same house rather than from separate abodes; the money volume is strongly conditioned by (1) the production volume, (2) the average money wage, and by (3) the assorted fears and the dose of theology and the small dash of wisdom that pervades Fed policy deliberations.

To illustrate, at a money wage of $1 an hour, a firm contemplating the production of 100 million gadgets may have to borrow $10 million to finance the enterprise. At a money wage of $10 an hour, the firm will have to plead, hat in hand, for the bank to lend $100 million. In stark contrast to the Hume conception, costs and prices determine the amount of money that business firms implore banks to clone as a lusty offspring in our institutionalized money creation process. If the Fed is a reluctant parent, once removed, then it will not be prices that will be aborted—as Hume and Friedman contend—but production and employment. Stagflation is the name of the game when the Fed refuses to bless—immediately, but it comes around after an interval—the emerging price process inherent in the settled money wage amplitude.

Money supplies thus facilitate *output*; money wages (and labor productivity) govern the price level. Restraining money supplies, despite Hume and Friedman, will not cause the price level to bend or break; instead, it will spell the stagflation malaise. Depending on the size of the catastrophe that the Fed is willing to underwrite, the money tap will hold the key to the gravity of the job malaise. While the Fed is politically insulated to jolt the economy by its zealous commitment to Hume-Friedman, and thereby draft people for what Karl Marx called the "army of the unemployed," it is not entirely immune to political facts as to foster a really big depression. It can bash jobs under the illusion that it is our saviour from inflation, and testify gravely to Congress about its tenacity and courage even as it chronically reports rising prices and persistent defeat. Its bulldozer tactics bow to political and economic realities as Congress, through tax cuts and expenditure boondoggles, runs to a rescue mission for the unemployed.

Central bankers, as unreconstructed Hume-Friedman kin fatuously interpret their posturing as a fight for the price level; in reality their huffing and puffing is invariably in a bout with jobs, of maintaining enough economic slack and in plying an ample "army of unemployed," to damp money wages and thus the price level. It is an ill-conceived and roundabout ploy and, worst of all, it has been ineffective on the price front. "Victories" have consisted of demolishing jobs and income.

To reiterate, contra Hume-Friedman, by lending money banks lubricate the *production* process. Individuals receive money income in the workplace, and not from a helicopter bombardment or overnight miracle; either of these conceptions belongs in a children's fable, and not to an analysis of the economy. By its capacity to apply the money brakes, the Fed can determine the job and output speed of the economy, but not its price altitude.

The Fed rules the job roost. But it has too often adopted Humpty Dumpty antics, knocking the economy down in order to revive it. Usually, the restoration stretches longer than the destruction. There would be a point in its games, play acting, and pretensions if the fuss and flurry inhibited the price-level escalator. Unfortunately, its tally sheet shows only zeroes in the many games it has played.

MINDING OUR PS AND QS

Symbolically, if the letter Y is written to denote our gross national product (the GNP captioned by the media), then $Y = PQ$, where the P represents the price level (or average price) and Q encompasses the total mass of output.

As our monetary guardian, handed a mission to stabilize P, which it ardently wants to do, the Fed through its monetary maneuvers takes careful aim at the P-targets. Despite its accumulated 67 years' experience (since 1914), its dedication, its ample staff, and "expert" advisers making intricate studies, the Fed's expertise has only scored hits on the Qs—while shooting for the Ps! The P-target survives intact, and out of danger, for it is immune to the Fed's monetary blast. Only if the Qs are fatally demolished, as in a Great Depression, can their wound spill over to some minor P-bleeding as the jobless, victimized by the toppling of Q, consent to a money wage slowup.

The Fed, even outside a strong recession or depression sinking spell, is foolhardy enough to extol its competence to contain the Ps. The more often it reports failure on this front, the more often it insists that it has discovered a foolproof operating recipe. And Congress, the country, and too many economists stay awed by its somber dignitaries, candidates for statues, that the Fed trots out to sing its song for "Just One More Chance." Given the gravamen of the glee club, it is a bit wearing after 67 years, though each generation treats the Fed's utterances as an infusion of wisdom or a new revelation.

The Fed, in claiming "light at the end of the tunnel" after 67 years of communiqués reporting defeat, mimics the prize fighter, floored 15 times and unconscious for 15 minutes, who moans, "Let me at him; I can lick the bum."

We need a sure and accurate rifle to hit the Ps whenever they threaten to get out of line and spurt on an upward course. The Fed's weaponry cannot, except by a costly unemployment probe, accomplish the task. The Fed, however, can do violence to the Qs. It should be confined to the mission of *facilitating* the Qs so that they flourish at a near maximum pace. But we will have to adopt nonmonetary tactics to cap the Ps and to prevent the Fed from ushering in a national job misfortune.

Yet the nature of conventional wisdom is so opaque that each time the Fed fails in its assault on the price salient, a cheering legion assures the bewildered public that it can still capture the height. Yes, even a punch-drunk fighter has a loyal cheering band, sustained not by reason but by faith.

THE TEDIOUS DESTROY-TO-REVIVE FANTASY

To dispel any confusion about it, these pages have not denied the potency of money supplies. Quite the contrary; their wallop has been highlighted at every turn, in practically every phrase. But the punch has been sited on jobs and production, and either tenuously at one remove, or generally not at all, on the price level or inflation domain. MONEY MATTERS, the monetarists never weary of repeating. Their error is in confounding its clout on jobs with its ineffectual stab at the price level; monetarists are confused on *how* and *where* money matters.

The one exception, it has been reiterated, is through the indirect (Phillips curve) route where the Fed creates an outrageous volume of unemployment to stifle the ascent of money wages; a hammerblow of a Great Depression might be entailed; a mini-recession is unlikely to offer any price-level abatement. Either way, the tactic is costly in national (and personal) income and output, and mostly ineffective. The overwhelming evidence must finally lead us to conclude that the Federal Reserve is vastly overrated as an inflation fighter.

The Fed surely is not an inflation *killer* entitled to a proud place in the Hall of Fame by virtue of its economic stabilization achievements. (In this sentiment, for other reasons, there would be agreement by monetarists who prefer an automatic monetary formula to the discretionary Fed antics.) The Fed, indubitably, is a supreme *under*achiever, with its record showing scant connection between its claims and its accomplishments. Over time, under the aegis of the Fed, our price-level record has deteriorated. Its bite on prices has been that of a toothless squirrel with each occupant of the publicized post of chairman strutting in the limelight of publicity, while destined to inflict human misery by augmenting the jobless army.

We have been exposed to a tedious revival of a destroy-to-revive fantasy. It is an ongoing travesty, freshened up by journalistic inattention or short memory. Whenever we are on the high road to full employment, the Fed slams on the brakes to "fight inflation." The economy is knocked down, with production kicked down and workers expelled to the unemployed ranks. Yet the price swath is hardly interrupted. After wreaking its havoc, some political sanity surfaces and either through congressional tax or expenditure action, or by the Fed's own awareness of its political vulnerability, the Fed then sets about to restore the situation. To a great extent the "restoration" occurs with the worst disasters averted through the Fed's withdrawals of its pet thought-relieving formulas on augmenting the money supply.

Destroy-to-revive seems to be a silly though not an innocuous game. But it is the one the Fed plays best, as inflation goes more or less unmolested. The Fed can rightly be condemned for the Humpty Dumpty wavelength to which its strategy is confined. There is its pompous deception that some extraordinary virtuosity is involved, and that there are truly profound subtleties involving delicate maneuvers, when all that is afoot is a Humpty Dumpty lawn game: let's knock down the economy "to fight inflation" and then we'll collect the pieces to put it together again. It is doleful entertainment on a lavish scale. Worst of all, it parodies the Fed's serious mission, namely, to fund production and jobs.

A LESSER QUALIFICATION

A very minor qualification and one entered for some completeness is that the tightening of credit may do a little something to curb daily speculation in commodity prices, as on wheat, cotton, corn, copper, gold, and so forth, in commodity markets. For these operations are financed by credit. But if, as we are told, these markets "foretell" future prices, their incessant flurries will have little effect on the general price level which reflects the unit labor cost and markup phenomena. Forestalling bank loans to the speculative markets, and best of all, a non-Fed direct attack on the price level, would dissipate most of these Fed concerns. Commodity markets erupt in speculative behavior only in an inflationary market environment caused by nonmonetary factors.

WALL STREET'S MINDLESS AFFAIR WITH TIGHT MONEY

Tight money not only has devastated income and jobs but it has also decapitated the bond market and checked the stock market over the 12-year period 1968-1980 despite the often wild gyrations, now up and now down, making a secular sidewise path. it has driven many old stock brokerage firms into merger or exit, and literally prevented the new-issue capital markets from functioning. Yet such is Wall Street's sublime faith in tight money, led by articulate self-serving commercial bank special pleading, that it has cheered on the Fed which has prepared its noose. It is a scenario not unlike the contemptuous (but apocryphal) remark attributed to Lenin: "When we are ready to hang the capitalists they'll outbid one another to sell us the rope."

Consider the sequence. In Old Quantity Theory reasoning, slowing up the money spigot would thrash only Ps, and not at all the Qs. In the modern Phillips curve's versions not uncommonly embraced by monetarists, the money choke lowers the Qs (and jobs) and indirectly transmits its fatal blow to the Ps. My own view agrees *partly* with this version, alleging that the Qs are suppressed but that the Ps remain free to run rampant on their inflationary track, according to modern experience with rising money wages and salaries.

Both views concede that money tightening subdues Qs, one arguing it is a necessary sacrifice to curb Ps, while the other position avers that the act of self-immolation does *not* propitiate the inflation gods. It merely promotes needless anguish. Either way, on either interpretation, the Fed's actions *de*stabilize job markets and the production evolution.

Most directly, however, the Fed affects interest rates as it sets its control levers on member bank reserve balances. In the Fed's open market operations it buys Treasury bills to ease reserve positions, refrains from renewing its portfolio holdings on maturity (in lieu of selling bills) to tighten reserve positions. Or it buys or sells long-dated government bonds. When the Fed sells government bonds (the easiest illustration of the open market sequence), member banks, after the Fed collects on the checks at the clearing-house settlement, inevitably lose reserve balances.

But the Fed's very act of selling the bonds also serves to depress their price. Furthermore, as the banks have fewer reserves their loan position is hampered so that short-term interest rates tend to climb. The higher short-term interest rates are transmitted to the long-term spectrum, namely, to the so that short-term interest rates tend to climb. The higher short-term term rates are transmitted to the long-term spectrum, namely, to the yields on bonds. As bond yields mount, inasmuch as bond prices automatically move inversely to bond yields, the prices of bonds tumble.

This precipitous decline of bond prices was alluded to earlier in commenting on the balance sheet erosion of various financial institutions under the tight money, described more vividly as a "credit crunch," during the 1970s. Tight money invoked by the Fed has been a guillotine, decapitating bond values of all owners who bought gilt-edge bonds, such as Treasury bonds, in the expectation that their price would be generally stable. Instead, they have helplessly watched the bond values plunge. Government bonds bought by trust funds, to protect "widows and orphans" by trust departments of banks, for which they paid $1,000 each a decade ago, were selling for $700 or less in 1980. For estates needing immediate cash, or estates being liquidated, it meant a capital loss of 25 percent or more on each bond; this happened alongside the purchasing power drop through inflation of about 60 percent. "Widows and orphans," in these special instances, received about $375 or less in 1967 purchasing power, in 1980, say, for each $1,000 "prudently" invested for their protection and benefit. (Bank trustees, of course, charged customary "management" fees for this exemplary service!)

The financial havoc does not end with the mighty impact of tight money in slashing bond prices. For as bond yields are higher, the dispersion between stock earnings and dividends, and bond prices, tends to fan out. If bond yields are 7 percent, and stock dividends are 4 percent on current stock prices, the stock market may appear attractive on growth considerations and higher future dividends. When bond yields go to 11 percent, say, stock prices are less magnetic as individuals contemplate the bond yields. Over most of the 1970s, the stock market recoiled in some horror, falling each time the Fed turned the money screws another notch in its vainglorious heroics to throttle inflation. Bondholders suffered, and stockholders were a gloomy lot as Wall Street endured the tight money shakes.

In 1968, the Dow Jones average of stock prices stood at 906. In 1978 it was at 820 and at 844 for 1979. In September 1980 it started to move slightly above the 1968 mark. It is as if this generation of stock market analysts, in our tight money bouts, has been brought up on the experience that the stock market never rises, it just drifts sidewise over time. "Smart" money thus fled the financial markets for the sanctuary of real estate in the stagflation seventies.

If the effects were confined merely to financial markets, this might be a matter of limited concern. But the ramifications are more profound. For low stock market prices are a signal to firms of heavy financial costs if they propose to expand by means of a stock issue. It is a trifle mad to finance plant expansion in a low and falling stock market.

The functioning of our capital markets has been impeded. Equity financing, in the jargon, has dried up. High bond yields have made the bond market a legatee mainly of state, local, and federal government issues, rather than of industrial borrowers although utilities, able to persuade regulatory commissions of the higher cost of capital and thereby to elicit rate hikes, have been active in selling their obligations.

With a "Great Depression" in the stock market, brokerage firms, as remarked earlier, have disappeared, by merger or other route. Merrill Lynch sought to buy the Chicago White Sox. Baseball is a queer outlet for a firm that boasts that it is "bullish on America."

Yet despite the self-inflicted devastation wrought by tight money, Wall Street remains supportive, even elated by each Fed tightening act: It is the loudest cheerleader at its own funeral. Its devotion and attachment are astonishing. Its fealty is touching—and mindless. Insurance companies, brokers, bond dealers, and the varied assortment of Wall Street firms have interests which do *not* coincide with those of commercial banks that benefit from tight money; nevertheless they all approve of the Fed dropping the napalm, capable at any time of raising interest rates, destroying jobs, income, and output.

Financial instability is thus another bent cutting edge to the tight money saw. As the Fed tries to compress the Ps, and with a lackluster report, not only does it destabilize the output Qs and the employment Ns, but it swells the interest rate Rs. And in the process it compromises our entire financial network. With "friends such as the Fed, capitalism will not want for foes.

7

GOVERNMENT PROFLIGACY:
A SCOTCH VERDICT ON INFLATION

In conversation and in despair, in editorials, TV chitchat, on the election stump, and among businessmen and economists, the conventional myth lambastes government spending for our inflation woes. Cut governmental spending, the line goes, and all will be well. We implore the government to be "business-like," and conveniently forget that we ask it to do the things that business cannot do.

Unfortunately, there is a smidgen of truth smothered in a ton of illogic; it cannot withstand scrutiny despite the ease with which it is muttered by ideologues who flick prejudices for thought. It is politically inspired dogma to appease receptive audiences wanting to see government excoriated as an unremitting foe, and ready to protest taxes when the discussion revolves about expenditures, in a whimsical progression of thought. Jimmy Carter, before Ronald Reagan, in the manner of a string of predecessors stretching back to colonial times, denounced the "bloated" bureaucracy as the inflation goat in his 1976 election campaign. He reverted to the spending themes in his episodic "new, new" war on inflation on March 14, 1980. He proposed cutting government outlay and, with the stern mien that politicians can impart to non sequiturs, argued that pruning government outlays by $13 billion—about 0.5 percent of the GNP or 2 percent of federal expenditures—would deter the 20 percent inflation then (early 1980) in progress.

Dissent on this point is capable of arousing feverish passions, attesting more to a refusal to think than to economic insight. Surely, it is rational to oppose wasteful government expenditures at all times, in inflation season and out. Even when the price level remains stable or even when it falls, everybody can stand foursquare for nonwasteful expenditure. President Reagan is not unique. Ideally, we yearn for honest and efficient government services in return for our tax dollars. Wasteful spending precludes better programs, or impedes tax cuts and more prudent deployment of taxpayer money.

Therefore, a conclusion that government expenditures are no more than a tiny part of our recent inflation misery should not be construed as a plea for government profligacy, or for a bigger Leviathan, or an ideological protest in opposition to the drive for tax cuts. The author is a congenital, though not strident, subscriber to the petition that government act as a less exacting partner in sharing his income.

TYPES OF GOVERNMENT EXPENDITURE

The inflation that torments us is a *market* phenomenon, exemplified in the price of bread, meats, or foodstuffs generally, or in clothing, housing, medical care, autos, and other consumer durables.

Consider, then, the types of government outlays before trying to apprehend their capacity to affect these everyday prices. For not all government outlays will have a market clout.

CIVIL SERVICE

Obviously government spends on the hire of civil servants, the bureaucrats that we flay in our captious moments. The cast can be stretched to include consultants hired on an interim basis, and the appointments in the higher administrative echelons, plus elected officials, and the entire military establishment.

Clearly, government pay constitutes wages and salaries to the recipients. The latter also pay taxes, and descend on the shops for the purchase of the usual assortment of consumer goods, and thereby supplement the consumer demand pressures on prices.

In order to show that our recent inflation stems from the "bloated bureaucracy," and that the number of civil servants (broadly conceived) has urged on price jumps year-after-year, we would have to show: (1) that pay scales in the government sector have risen faster than in the private sector and (2) that their numbers have grown inordinately relative to the private sector.

Chart 7.1 is instructive in this respect. It shows most strikingly the relative growth of state and local employees. But apart from the bulge during the Korean and Vietnam periods, the federal establishment has *not* been growing disproportionately. On the contrary, it is contracting relatively to the other sectors. In regard to average pay scales (Chart 7.2), government employees have largely conformed to the general trends in the pay scramble of recent years. Much of the castigation has thus been misdirected, and the bureaucracy maligned. The numbers at the federal level do not confirm the fingerpointing demagoguery of blustery misinformed prophets.

To repeat, this is not a defense of government operations. It is a denial of the attribution of the decade's runaway inflation to bloated bureaucratic miscreants!

GOODS

Government buys a vast and diverse heap of goods, from the paper, pencils, typewriters, chairs, and desks for bureaucrats to occupy—and mostly to do vital public work—to the airplanes, missiles, tanks, and submarines for cavorting by the military. Only a telephone book could list this infinite catalogue.

Chart 7.3 graphs GNP, federal defense and nondefense purchases of GNP output, and state and local purchases, since 1929. Obviously, it is emotional sputtering to allege that the government intake has swelled disproportionately. Over the last decade the totals have tipped down a bit, relatively, and this happened during our period of chaotic inflation.

The important fact is that when government outlays buy milk and bread for school lunches, or desks and autos, or typewriters, paper and computers, the market punch is exactly parallel to these goods being bought by individuals or business firms: the expenditures generate market demand. The sums impel jobs in the *private* sector, and not in the government sector. And if we maintain that the expenditures are "inflationary," then we are decrying *all* expenditure, all purchases from whatever source—of autos by households, or the buying of bread or milk, and not decrying government expenditures alone. As federal expenditures in 1979 amounted to about 7 percent of the GNP total, the diatribe flails the far smaller component of the aggregate, in mainly venting our ire, while evading the remaining 93 percent of the total. Including state and local outlays the combined intake comes to just over 20 percent.

If we are serious in thinking that expenditures must be slashed to stop inflation then it must be *all* expenditures that warrant the vitriolic abuse ordinarily reserved for government. (The Reagan tax cuts must, on this score be labelled inconsistent.) Of course, if we think government expenditures comprise only frivolous items, they deserve the venom. On the other hand, a nation overindulgent in casinos, electric toothbrushes, stereos, electronic toys, or autos, might on reflection assess these as the grosser superfluities.

CHART 7.1. Wage and Salary Employees in Non-Agricultural Establishments, 1950-1980

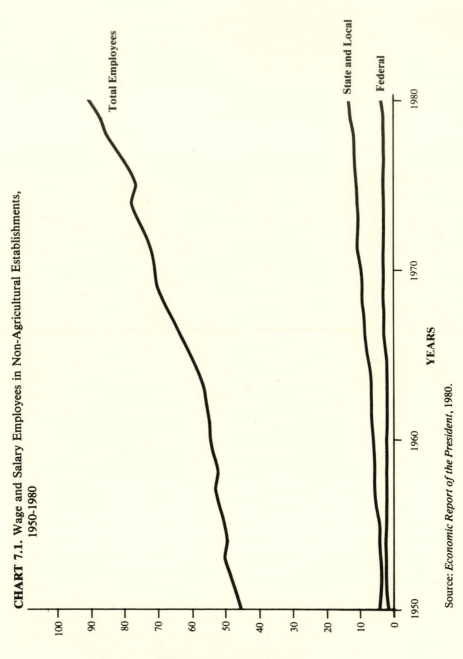

Source: *Economic Report of the President*, 1980.

CHART 7.2. Average Annual Employee Compensation, 1950-1980

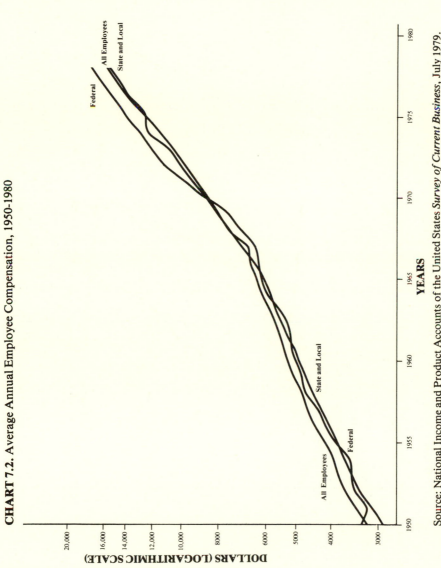

Source: National Income and Product Accounts of the United States *Survey of Current Business*, July 1979.

99

CHART 7.3. GNP, Federal Defense, Federal Non-Defense, and State and Local GNP Purchases, 1929-1979

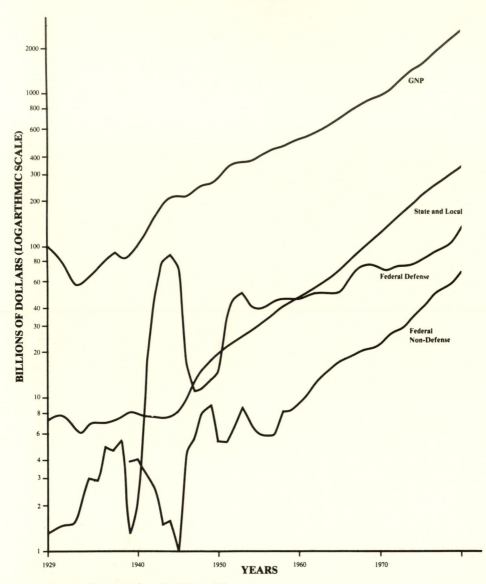

BILLIONS OF DOLLARS (LOGARITHMIC SCALE)

GNP

State and Local

Federal Defense

Federal
Non-Defense

YEARS

Source: *Economic Report*, 1980, p. 203.

To reiterate, this is *not* a plea for government expenditures but for more luminous thinking. Government expenditures mould demand, just like other expenditures; obviously, they generate jobs and production. They *may* affect the inflation rate by absorbing workers and lowering the jobless pool, so *indirectly* enhancing money wages. But exactly the same consequences ensue from private outlays; there is nothing special in this respect about public outlays.

Considering the government outlay trends relative to the GNP, there is nothing spectacular in them over the last decade to support the allegation of culpability for the inflation ordeal. For those who insist that government outlays are too high, the assertion is at bottom an expression of ideological aversion to the nature of government operations, with which many of us may agree. But to denounce the outlays as the special cause in our price madness is a bias not grounded in the facts. If we think the road to a better price record lies in slicing demand, then we should advocate universal expenditure restraint, and not curtailment in government alone.

Confusion also enters by the practice of classifying all government outlays as operating costs, although many outlays would appear as *capital* investments in the accounts of private firms. For example, the government may contract for a bridge to be built by a construction firm in the private sector; the bridge may last for 50 years. Yet, for government, the construction cost of the bridge, or dam, or submarine, or park land, or road, or office building, will be listed as "current outlays," in the same way as quickly "consumable" paper or pencils or school lunches. No private firm would think of using an accounting system which lumped capital items with *current* expenses as a drain on *current* income. By throwing capital expense outlays and operating costs in the same outlay pot in the federal budget, too many critics commit the shallow error of indicting the government deficit as equivalent to a "business loss" on current operations. This is a grotesque misinterpretation; the government ledger is not analogous to a business income statement, and it is a display of naive innocence to read it in the same way.

Private enterprise bookkeeping has not been adopted by government, for to do so would engender interminable legislative controversy over operating and capital accounts. So confusion is engendered in popular controversy accusing the federal government of "failure to balance its books," considering that income and capital account entries are not segregated.

TRANSFERS

The federal government also makes *transfers*, namely, payments unrelated to any civil service work currently, or for goods purchased in the marketplace. Thus there are social security disbursements, unemployment compensation, welfare, medicare, medicaid, as well as veterans' pensions, farm subsidies, and a host of other programs. Interest on the national debt is also listed under the transfer heading.

It is tempting to conclude immediately that these outlays are "inflationary," but this would be a hasty judgment. In the case of social security, the government makes outgos and amasses tax receipts from future social security recipients. It is thus largely a case of income sums pouring in on one side and shoveled out on the other. Over the years the social security system has been self-financing, with younger groups, continuously renewed, paying sums to retired persons who performed the identical mission in the past. Technically, it is an intergenerational transfer, undertaken on the sure knowledge that all of us will, before too long, get old. Chart 7.4 depicts some trends in the pension system. From its origins in 1938 till more recent years, inflows exceeded disbursements. This then turned around to near balance; with a big excess of outpayments threatening, the future will bring diverse modifications to the program, for it is subject to perennial review.

For inflation, the main point is that under the current program retirees largely spend more, and employees have less income for consumption outlay. The consumption expenditure switch, one group by the other, is substantial but with only a minor net drain, on balance, on GNP consumption.

As ordinary Treasury revenues are disbursed for agricultural subsidies or veteran benefits it is tempting to call them "inflationary." But the government expenditures themselves do *not* absorb goods and services for the government; they accrue to the transfer recipients. Likewise, the welfare beneficiary engages in the actual purchases of the consumables. In the absence of these sums there would have to be some fallback on charity, and others, perhaps relatives, would have to dip into small savings accumulations, while many current recipients undoubtedly would have to live as forlorn paupers. The total market expenditure drop in the economy would not be significant; the burden would shift from the Treasury, or the general run of taxpayers, to those must vulnerable to charity appeals, whether relatives, churches, the Salvation Army, and the like. The main issue relating to these government transfer outlays is thus not their inflation aspect, but their distributive burden.

The interest charges on the national debt are also a transfer paid out of tax revenues. The debt is a legacy of the past; the interest outgoings will somewhat affect the consumer demand of the interest recipients. Where the debt is owned by business or financial firms, as banks and insurance companies, the interest sums augment their operating revenues and are thereafter distributed as salaries, rents, dividends, and so on. Not directly,

CHART 7.4. Old-Age Survivors Insurance Trust Fund, 1938-1975

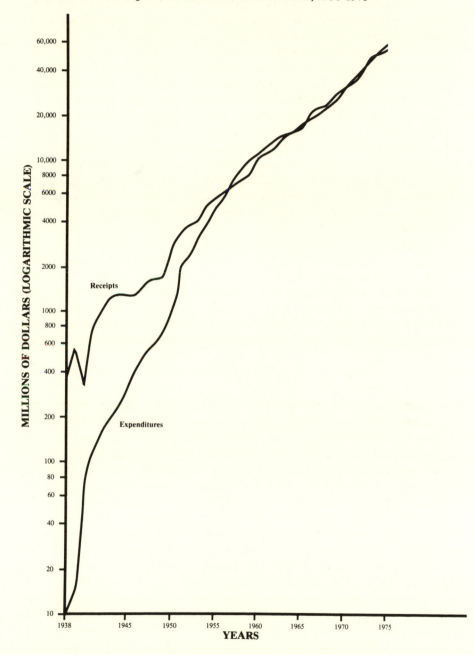

Source: Statistical Supplement to the *Social Security Bulletin*, 1975, p. 65.

but only at one remove, do they result in market expenditures. In addition, when the debt financing charges constitute direct net income to recipients, personal and corporate income taxes remain to be paid. So, GNP market purchases stemming from interest on the national debt are substantially less than the interest disbursement listed in the federal budget.

Likewise, the federal government allots grants to state and local government and as foreign aid. Without these funds state and local services would fall off, though many of them would come to be sustained out of local tax revenue sources at a lower level of funding. To a large degree, therefore, there is a shift in the financing burden from the local government unit to the federal treasury. If the transfers were discontinued, the result would mainly be a redirection in the burden, and thus in income distribution. Foreign aid is something else again; we make it as a humanitarian gesture and to our friends and allies, mostly to keep them out of the Soviet orbit.

The total amount of federal budget outlays since 1950 is depicted in Chart 7.5, along with the federal GNP purchases of goods and services. The difference between the two series provides a rough estimate of "transfers." Both series, though increasing, have not quite kept the GNP pace although transfers have mounted. Again, the reminder that a good part of the transfers consists of the redistributive operations of the social security system and interest payments on the national debt.

OUTLAYS FOR CAPITAL ASSETS

The government also makes outlays to acquire existing capital assets, such as land for a national park, or land and buildings for office space, or land for roadways, military bases, or other purposes.

These, too, are jumbled among current "operating expenses" though the outlays are not a drain on current production and have little—or nothing—to do with the market inflation in consumer goods. Some of the outlays, such as for highways, tend over time to reduce hauling costs, thereby to raise productivity and *lower* market prices. The government also sells offshore drilling leases, or drilling rights on public lands, or disposes of some property, or otherwise realizes capital revenues from asset disposal, as of wartime or military surplus. These constitute a revenue offset to its capital asset acquisitions.

The chief conclusion that emerges from this examination is that it muddles understanding merely to look at total federal outlays and put a perfunctory label on them as "inflationary" or "deflationary." A more careful disaggregation of the totals can be less alarming. President Reagan, on February 18, 1981, proposed to hold the 1981 budget down by $4.4 billion, and to slash the 1982 figures by $41.4 billion. These are big absolute sums; yet out of a GNP of over $3 trillion they are piddling sums. Their inflation impact will be practically nil despite the publicity and fanfare. Their displacement will consist of private expenditures out of ensuing tax cuts.

STATE AND LOCAL EXPENDITURES

Despite all the emotional railing at Washington, the obscured truth is that by far the larger part of expenditure is at the state and local precinct. Chart 7.3 portrays the facts on GNP purchase outlays since 1950 by the different government bodies. Chart 7.6 specifies the main types of the state and local expenditures. Obviously, the kinds of expenditures can also be classified, as at the federal level, between civil servants hired, goods purchased, transfers, and on capital assets.

The major state and local outlay categories consist of education, highway construction, maintenance and repair, public welfare, and public safety, including police and fire; these broad groupings absorb upwards of 80 percent of the total. It follows that any severe cut, or failure of the figures to grow parallel with inflation trends signifies a curtailment of public services. While waste undoubtedly abounds, this ailment seems to be a mainstay of the human condition, not unlike death element seems tobe a mainstay of the human condition, not unlike death or taxes. Taxpayer indignation, too, comes naturally. We can wish President Reagan every success. But muscle will be cut along with fat. We will still have to debate what we want of government.

REDUCING THE SIZE OF GOVERNMENT?

If we are really committed to scaling down the size of government, of "getting it off our back and out of our pocket," the big opportunities lie at the local, and not at the federal level. The media, in fixing their gaze at the national news and Washington events, regale us with the fascinating small stories—relatively—and neglect the larger profligacy in city halls and state capitals.

Government Expenditures: More Consequence Than Cause of Inflation?
The point that can be made unequivocally is that government outlays, by bolstering market demand, lead, directly or indirectly, to production of goods and services by individuals and firms. In the case of civil servant hire, this aspect is manifest in the flow of household-consumption purchases contingent upon the earnings of government employees. With respect to the physical goods bought by government, there is an equally certain creation of jobs in private sector firms whose output caters to public sector needs.

Grants, transfers, and capital asset transactions are more complex to categorize, but, overall, they do not deflect current productive resources to do duty for public purposes.

GOVERNMENT EXPENDITURE AS A CONSEQUENCE OF INFLATION

Going beyond the direct and indirect multiplier in the job and output creating aspects, a sharp rise in government expenditure is far more a *consequence*, or a *result*, of inflation than a *cause*. The only plausible qualification to this proposition would be in a situation where there is a *sharp* upward surge in the scope of government activities relative to the private sector. This has not happened during our historic wave of inflation in the 1970s. Rather, the federal spending role has diminished slightly.

The conclusion follows that so long as the federal government is not the dominant employer, and so long as Congress monitors pay scales so that government pay does not leapfrog the private sector, pay scales in the government sphere largely *follow* earnings in the business sector. Whenever the average business pay rises, the pay of government employees must before long thrust forward. It is the inflation in *private* pay scales that drives the civil service pay chariot; if the average private sector pay scale leaps by 30 percent in the next three years, we can surmise that civil service pay will progress by approximately the same percentage.

For the goods the government buys it should be transparent that government expenditure is an undisputed bystander of inflation: a result, not a cause. Just consider the military hardware which constitutes the sustenance of the armed forces. Every time the prices of tanks, missiles, planes, submarines, aircraft carriers, communications systems, and other materiel leap ahead, in order to maintain the same level of military preparedness, defense outlays *must* jump proportionately. When the prices of desks, typewriters, paper, are marked up, the outlays go up. When the cost of paving a road or building a bridge skyrockets, government outlay must also zoom.

In fiscal 1981 federal expenditures after President Carter's stern address were budgeted at about $615 billion. At the prices of 1960 they would have been about $235 billion! Why the steep jump in expenditures? *Because* of inflation the prices of everything the government buys have sky-rocketed; the budget sums are higher because prices are higher, and *not* the other way around.

When we consider social security or welfare payments, or medicare, this is obviously the case. As prices go up, in order to maintain the real payments scale, the government has inserted cost-of-living escalator

CHART 7.5. GNP, Federal GNP Purchases, and Federal Budget Outlays, 1950-1980

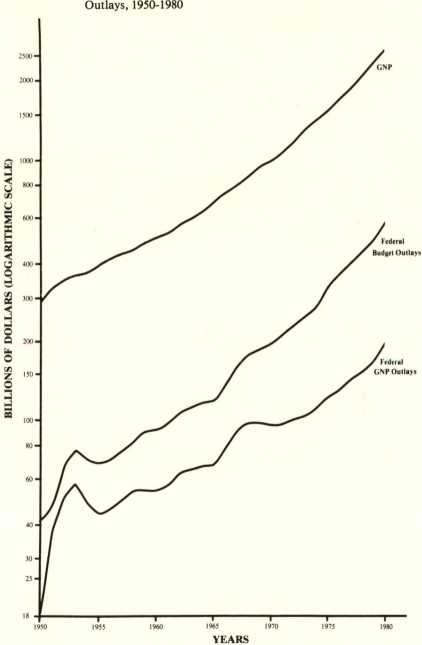

Source: *Economic Reports of the President*, 1980, pp. 203, 286; 1981, p. 315.

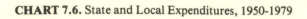

CHART 7.6. State and Local Expenditures, 1950-1979

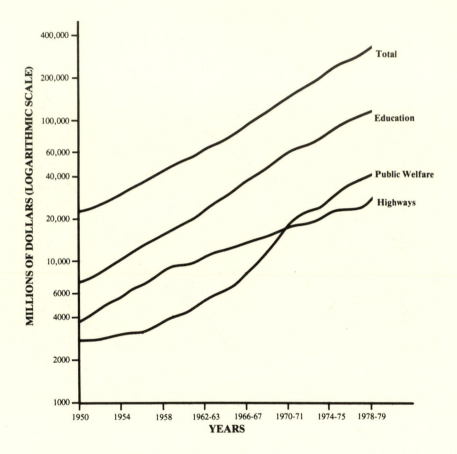

Source: *Economic Report of the President*, 1981.

clauses to keep pace with the inflationary times. Clearly, the flights into orbit of these transfers are ineluctable *consequences*, far more than causes, of inflation: they vault as prices leap.

TIGHT MONEY

Chart 7.7 depicts the total interest-bearing national debt and the annual interest carrying charges. Manifestly, the interest costs of carrying the national debt have shot up faster than the debt total. When we inquire why, we learn that interest rates are higher *because* of the inflationary phenomena and the tight money policies of the Federal Reserve adopted to fight inflation. Either way, the rampaging costs of servicing the debt are not an inflationary *cause*, but a *consequence*.

The conclusion is inescapable. If we do a better job in curbing inflation, we will do a far better job in containing government spending: the latter is a consequence of the former. Beyond a peradventure of doubt, if inflation runs at its high recent tempo, government outlays will also maintain their skyward momentum.

The inference is chronicled as a prediction of things to come. It does not signify approval nor approbation of unfolding events. After all, in predicting the winner of a horse race, the opinion expressed does not connote an unflagging love of the horse: it conveys no more than a judgment on the outcome.

THE MORAL: THE MISLEADING POLITICAL RHETORIC

Government outlays are mainly the prisoner of prices; despite political claims to cut waste, outlays are destined to balloon as prices surge. As an inflation maker, if we adopt a demand-outlay version of inflation—which I think utterly mistaken—and argue in terms of the relative size of outlays by consumers, business firms in investment, and government, the latter are dwarfed by the former two in the ratio of 4 to 1. In magnitude, government sums are more the tail than the body of the dog. Further, while we denounce the federal charade the larger farce happens locally. The political posse has gunned the wrong suspect as we have become beguiled by our prejudices.

On inflation government expenditures are not the inflation culprit, a small accomplice maybe. Even for those who weigh the evidence differently, if they do not subscribe to a judgment of full acquittal, they might opt for the Scotch verdict of "not proven" on the sheer score of trends and magnitudes of the GNP.

CHART 7.7. National Debt and Interest Charges 1950-1980

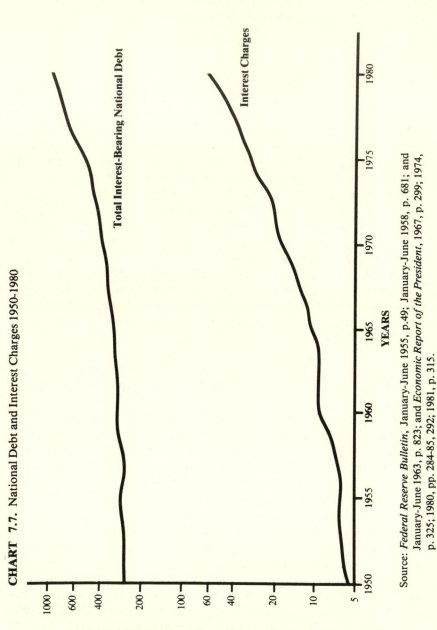

Total Interest-Bearing National Debt

Interest Charges

BILLIONS OF DOLLARS (LOGARITHMIC SCALE)

1000
600
400
200
100
60
40
20
10
5

1950   1955   1960   1965   1970   1975   1980

YEARS

Source: *Federal Reserve Bulletin*, January-June 1955, p.49; January-June 1958, p. 681; and January-June 1963, p. 823; and *Economic Report of the President*, 1967, p. 299; 1974, p. 325; 1980, pp. 284-85, 292; 1981, p. 315.

President Reagan, on February 18, 1981, proposed to cut outlays by $4.4 billion for 1981. This *is* a miniscule amount in a $657.8 billion aggregate. For 1982 there is a weightier slash, of $41.4 billion, from $729.7. The numbers are conjectural and contain an optimistic inflation surmise. Considering that GNP may be as high as $3.5 trillion, it is possible, in any demand inflation context, to be somewhat unimpressed by the $41.4 billion number, for it is under 1.2 percent of the prospective GNP.

Government comes to about 20 percent, or less in the future, of GNP. President Reagan proposes to whittle it down about 3 points. The big splash is over cutting the dog's tail without concern over the dog's size.

8

TAXES: AN INFLATION SIDESHOW

Until recently, economists would scoff at any proposal to cut taxes during inflation. The advice would have run the other way, to *increase* taxes to stop the price scourge. Today, given the magnitude of our price upheaval, and the recession, the idea is broached in serious quarters—if one regards the halls of Congress as a forum of responsible debate.

Taxes are considered in this chapter. The discussion fits naturally, for when expenditures, as the inflation vehicle, are debunked, political spouting will quickly seize on taxes as the inflation sources. Thereafter, the stream of illogic fastens on the deficit which, with the national debt, is fervently held, in all inconsistency, to be the inflation maker.

It is just not possible to cover everything simultaneously, in one breath or one sentence, although common demagogic puffery makes an arduous try. Our own analysis proceeds more slowly. Logic, too often, goes out the window in these shrill discussions, with a tax cut lumped alongside a denunciation of deficits with a simultaneous advocacy of more defense spending.

THE TAX PROTEST

Tax cuts are always popular: who wants to carry the existing tax load, much less to pay more taxes? Indeed, our country was founded on a tax protest, although modern demagogues, noting a fertile soil of public sentiment, have sold the idea as novel, and surely rich for political fishing. Too many in the beguiled, bewildered, and self-interested electorate have grabbed at the bait, as if there have been many—or any—political aspirants who ever ran for office on a pledge promising to *raise* taxes. The tax denunciation always seems good for one more—many more, really—election, however irrelevant the slogan, and the banalities, concord with the facts. The attitude has so often gulled the electorate in a cynical ploy inimical to the preservation of a viable democracy.

THE JARVIS PROPOSITION 13 AND KEMP-ROTH

Clamor for a tax cut, on property taxes, became a veritable crusade in California where the Jarvis Proposition 13 ballot referendum in June 1978 called on voters to mandate a ceiling on property taxes. Apparently, the Jarvis brainstorm was an "original" thought never before contemplated, to wit, that people will vote to cut their taxes! Hoopla and dumb solemnity presented it as a grand innovation and, with success in California, a broadside was fired nationally.

Compassion comes easily in sympathy with the plight of older (and younger) homeowners, many of them living on fairly fixed incomes and enduring higher property taxes in an era of inflation. Property owners can readily perceive that if *they* paid less in property taxes, they would be better off. In this respect the Jarvis tax revolt represents a self-serving reaction to inflation; *it does nothing to stop it*. Indeed, with property owners shelling out less tax income, they have more to dispense on other goods and so, on the demand theory that market expenditures *cause* inflation, lower property taxes add fuel to the consumer price pyre.

Moreover, if property taxes are constantly eroded, while state and local expenditures continue upbeat, then the lost property revenues will have to be recouped either by higher sales or excise taxes, or a variety of state and local income taxes. Thus a property tax slash can succeed, on balance over time, only if a lid is clamped on government expenditures to render higher taxes superfluous. The long term campaign, therefore, must be devoted to expenditures. In keeping with this imperative, the Jarvis movement also assails government spending, thinking to block it by tighter rein over the tax purse strings. This tether, even when we deplore cuts in library services or other communal projects, cannot be faulted in its logic. Condemnation of this aspect of Jarvisism is moral, or ideological, and pragmatic.

Blocking property taxes without curbing spending must shift the tax burden to other tax forms, as sales or income taxes. Ultimately, the issue becomes one of *who* is to be taxed and by *how much*. The Jarvis amendment thus emerges as a plan to alter the income distribution, to treat property owners better and other tax payers less favorably. It is thus a "redistributional" measure, to aid Paul and hurt Peter, and overlapping for many Peter Pauls. If we like Paul (the property owner) and don't care much for Peter (the sales tax payer) we can applaud the outcome. Unraveling the full effects can be complicated in a dynamic setting of changing Pauls and Peters.

A great pity of our existing world is that horses, trees, or birds, don't pay taxes; if they did we could tax them and forget the whole business. Unfortunately, people pay taxes; we can change only the types but somebody must shell out. The only way to honest succor is to check government expenditures to a level such that the tax imposts are acceptable.

Of course, we must strive for equity, but realism commends the conviction that all of the citizenry will be pleased only in some other blissful world. Most of us are persuaded that the only fair tax is a tax on somebody else. We favor "good" communal projects but we shy away from volunteering to be the taxpayer. We hum the piper's tune but prefer to have somebody else pay to keep him playing.

The Kemp-Roth bill, which entered the legislative hopper in 1979, was born of the same sense of tax protest. It, too, found a receptive audience, and the chant was picked up by President Reagan during his election campaign. Briefly, a version frequently discussed proposed cutting federal income taxes by $30 billion over a three-year period. Politicians smelled votes. Of course, the same people spoke of cutting government outlays while hiking military outlays. As the maverick presidential candidate John Anderson remarked, in the Iowa campaign "debate," it will be done "with mirrors"—the pithy derision did not faze his rivals who went glibly on, not bothering with the trifles of "how." Of course, they all opposed inflation!

SUPPLY SIDE ECONOMICS

The Kemp-Roth bill would not be worth singling out, for it is a manifest pitch for voters' favor, if it did not wave an anti-inflation banner through some exaggerated rhetoric, latched on as a rationalization, hailing a new and miraculous "supply side economics"!* Briefly, this underpinning held that a substantial tax cut would touch off a burst in productivity to assist the "war against inflation." The productivity

---

*The idea and term came into the literature in the presidential address of Nobel winner Lawrence Klein to the American Economic Association. (His scholarly address was not devoted to Kemp-Roth.) See the *American Economic Review*, March 1978. When Klein cited original sources of the idea, the references were to my 1955 and 1956 works.

miracles would follow from the politicians' recurrent dream of cutting taxes.

Seldom has so much nonsense been perpetrated on so lavish a scale to throw dust in our eyes to win support for a tax cut. The policy might—conceivably—help in trimming a percent or two of inflation, by cumulative effects through plant modernization, in the year 1990! The shallowness of it all did not deter the Democratic chairman of the Joint Economic Committee—Senator Bentsen—from inserting the specious argument in the committee report as a promising "solution."

Not unexpectedly, the congressional sponsors of "supply side economics" articulate only the pleasant half-truth. Obviously, a quantum leap in productivity would be a source of jubilation; only with higher productivity can all of us enjoy a rising standard of living. But an emphasis on productivity to retard inflation conveys only half of the equation. If we are to ward off inflation, the productivity rise must be matched exactly, and never outpaced, by *the advance in money incomes*. On the pay prerequisite, the Kemp-Roth proponents are notoriously silent.

No wonder. It could damage beyond repair their vapid anti-inflation claims, and the reined income aspect could be awkward to explain; it might offend their voting constituents. Yet without this adjunct on moderation in money incomes, inflation will wend its unmerry way, playing havoc with lives and forestalling our march to undisputed economic leadership. Inflation will not be stopped by the vacuous Kemp-Roth or Jarvis jingoism. President Reagan in his February 18 budget measure straddled the matter by adopting the undiluted Kemp-Roth proposal but, in deferring the starting date, he pruned the 10 percent annual figure to 5 percent the first year and delayed the cuts a bit thereafter.

TAXES AND INFLATION

We consider some of the tax magnitudes and their variety. Thereafter, there is some assessment of the connection of particular taxes and inflation.

TAX DATA

The recent mainstays of the federal revenue system appear in Chart 8.1. Manifestly, the personal income tax towers over all others, coming to dwarf even the corporate income tax which is dwindling in significance. Social security taxes, as remarked before, are collected as a prelude to disbursements.

Although trial balloons surface on a value-added tax (VAT), which amounts to a national sales tax, the federal government abstained from the levy of a sales tax though there are some fairly equivalent excises,

CHART 8.1. Federal Tax Revenues, by Source, 1960-1980

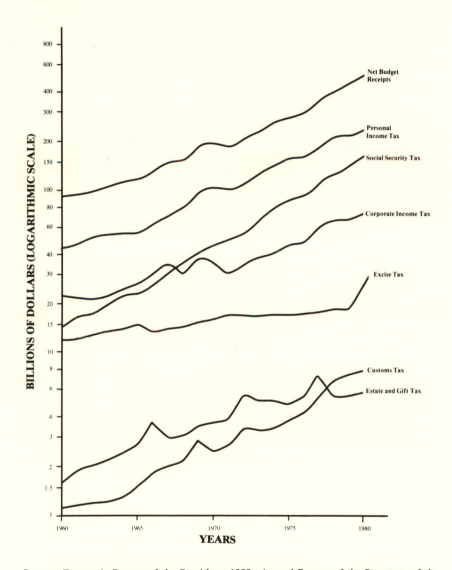

Source: *Economic Report of the President*, 1980; *Annual Report of the Secretary of the Treasury, Fiscal Year, 1978*.

such as those levied on the production of cigarettes, whiskey, gasoline, jewelry, leather goods, and so forth. Also, there are estate taxes and customs taxes on imports. Other revenues include fines, sale of offshore drilling rights, or of military surplus. We forego discussion of the latter as being fairly unimportant currently.

The income, sales, and property tax (hitherto) have been the backbone of the state and local system, with property taxes (more realty than personalty, such as stocks, and bonds) decreasing in significance in recent years, and probably destined to faster degeneration because of Jarvis-type amendments. Under the lashing to which property taxes have been exposed, new revenues are likely to come from state grants out of its revenue collections. The nonfederal tax complex appears in Chart 8.2.

THE PERSONAL INCOME TAX AND INFLATION

Consider what would happen if personal income tax rates were precipitately axed, as under Kemp-Roth. Would the proponents also advocate raising taxes in depression times, such as the 1930s? Surely, this latter would only make matters worse by stripping personal income recipients of purchasing power. Exposed to the logic of symmetry, Kemp-Roth is a travesty on reason.

A personal income tax cut in the 1980 inflationary recession climate would leave income recipients with more purchasing power, say $30 billion more, to go to the shops. As 1981 consumer purchases project to about $1.85 trillion, the figure could run up by nearly the entire tax cut. It would be utterly incompatible with the ongoing Federal Reserve monetary policy invoked to *depress* consumer purchases in the vain hope of wringing out some illusory demand inflation.

This would amount to a case of one arm of the government undermining another; fiscal and monetary policy are being primed for a head-on collision, each charging at one another. Kemp-Roth is a grotesque display, in the current inflationary environment, of congressional negation of monetary policy even as the sponsors *implore* the Fed to tighten its monetary stance to stifle inflation. Seldom has so brazen an effort been made to confuse the electorate by paying lipservice to the Fed's monetary maneuvers while simultaneously erecting impenetrable barriers to their success. Fiscal policy via the tax cut pulls directly counter to the Fed's recession antics in restraining job expansion.

A POSSIBLE INFLATION ASSIST?

As an anti-inflationary tool the Kemp-Roth bill is a monstrosity undeserving of serious contemplation. It could have a saving grace, however,

CHART 8.2. State and Local Tax Sources, 1960-1979

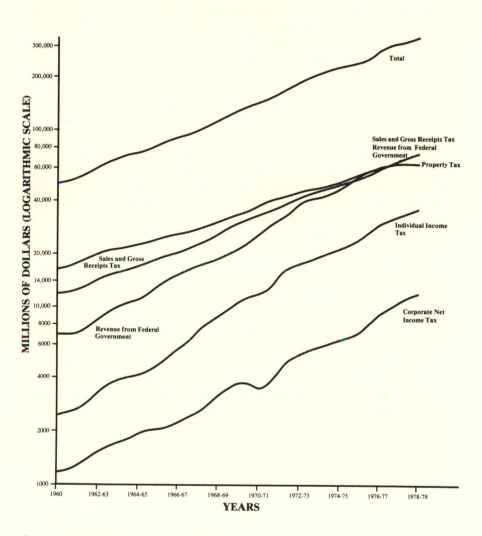

Source: *Economic Report of the President*, 1981.

in that higher take-home pay through a tax cut might slow up pressures for excessive pay grants. But Kemp-Roth, in its myopia, lacks a provision to link tax cuts to pay moderation. Later in this work, just such an amendment will be proposed.* This could be (1): anti-inflationary, (2) of major relief to taxpayers, and (3) an aid to foster smaller government outlay growth.

Would a cut in taxes slash government expenditures so as to make replacement revenues unnecessary? While specifications for outlay containment have been sparse, and are unlikely on any large scale, Senator Roth, to his credit, has sought to lead an antispending brigade in the Senate. But this is apt to be unsuccessful, at least on the scale contemplated by the Kemp-Roth tax cut; politicians are prone to give us the ice cream without the bitter dose of medicine. To his credit, whether we agree or not, President Reagan and Budget Director Stockman have acted in a way hitherto unknown to wield the expenditure axe.

Vague talk prevails, especially by Congressman Kemp (about the economist Arthur Laffer curve), depicting how a tax cut can engender so much more economic activity that the drop in tax rates fosters a more than commensurate GNP gain, to more than recoup the revenue lost.** The curve appears in chart 8.3. Note that so much depends on where we are in the graph; if *below* the "optimal rate," higher taxes will mean *more* tax revenues; above it, GNP and tax revenue will fall. If the figure traces a wide flat arc, higher or lower tax rates will scarcely affect revenues. If it is a sharp sidewise pyramid, slight tax changes will take a frightful revenue (and GNP) toll by acute economic sensitivity to minute tax perturbations. Empirically, we are in rather complete ignorance of the curve shape, but in the current environment it is possible to be skeptical of the pronounced optimism; a reduction in inflation, and in interest rates, might give us a solid upkick in real GNP even at *current* tax rates. This inference implies *shifts* in the curve over time, depending on the economic milieu.

The curve then is appealing—and obviously specious as an antidote for recession. We would have no difficulty with inducing an increase in real GNP—if we wanted to stimulate production we could simply reverse the restrictive Fed money policy. But without pay restraint this would be merely the familiar recipe for inflation! Thus an unadulterated Kemp-Roth is a queer strategy to advocate in 1981 when inflation is zipping ahead toward historic price heights. As observed earlier, Congressman

---

*See below, pp. 181, 200.

**For interesting and incisive analytic and econometric comment, see the letter of A. B. Atkinson and Nicholas Stern, *Lloyds Bank Review* (April 1980), pp. 43-46.

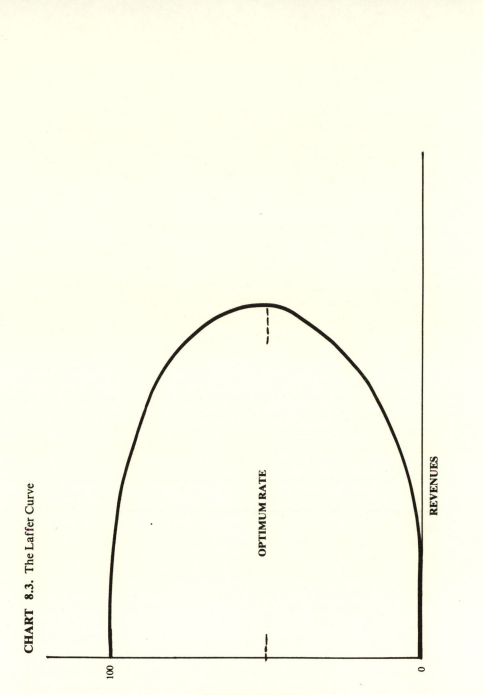

CHART 8.3. The Laffer Curve

Kemp plays only one string on the fiddle, picking out an investment and productivity tune while refusing to muffle the pay restraint theme. Kemp-Roth, with Laffer curves to boot, grabs headlines; Kemp's remarks pass for serious perception in the halls of Congress. Support of the old quarter-back dodge means that higher inflation rates lack congressional defensive foes.

THE CORPORATE INCOME TAX AND INFLATION

Kemp-Roth also projects a slash in the corporate income tax, on the apology that this will revive productivity through encouraging plant investment. Omitted entirely is the inflation climate and the Fed's invocation and tolerance of historic high long-term interest rates. As Kemp-Roth shuns this aspect we can surmise that the productivity claims represent a wishful yearning which will not be realized. In ignoring inflation and Fed policy Kemp-Roth envisages a world other than the one in which we happen to live.

On the corporate tax cut there is much ado over supply side economics. Lower personal income taxes, the proponents aver, will lead individuals to work harder for more "marginal income" so that less will redound to government; this may, or may not, be so depending on some esoteric economics; in practice it is probably so unimportant as to foreclose discussion, for most individuals are hired to work a standard workweek.*

For the corporation, the Kemp-Roth thesis maintains that firms will, because of the lower tax and higher profit opportunities, build new factories, and install new equipment to touch off a wave of technological modernization.

Some firms will be encouraged undoubtedly by the lower tax prospects to hasten new structures, others will not. To grant the Kemp-Roth theme the best argument, the issue is how much modernization will this accomplish? How much of a gain in labor productivity will be forthcoming?

It can be contended that so long as inflation prevails and the Federal Reserve fights it with tight money, as in tolerating the prime interest rate at 20 percent and over, most firms will remain very reluctant borrowers, or remain unwilling to venture internal funds, because of the rampant inflation and the altitudinous interest rates always threatening to provoke a recession collapse. Stopping inflation, and bringing down interest rates, would do far more to induce an era of capital formation. Kemp-Roth looks squarely at the problem—and evades it.

*Kemp and Roth seem to have some very, very mythical corporation executives in mind who are withholding their abilities because of taxes. Somehow this gets translated to production-line employees in an absurd hyperbole.

It is naive to assume that plant modernization merely awaits a tax break, which thereafter would herald a substantial productivity surge. This is a doubtful premise; it is a wild tax-cutting rationalization when it is also contended that it will combat inflation. Productivity over the long term, in our glory years, tended to progress by 2 to 3 percent per annum. In the 1970s the average productivity increase per employee inched forward by about 1 percent per annum. In 1974, and again in 1979, productivity actually *declined*, with the descent each time about 2 percent. Something beyond lower taxes is required to turn the trick.

To lift productivity by 1 percent, from 1 to 2 is not merely a 1 percent jump, but a 100 percent leap! From 2 to 3 percent involves a 50 percent vault. For confirmation of the enormity of "mere" 1 percent gains, compound interest tables can be consulted to show the path of money cumulating at the different rates. The miraculous supply side economics, to rationalize its tax ventures, skirts the hard questions by screeching "productivity"—a probable minor development—while squelching any debate on the pay boost aspect.

In track and field events, world records are shattered by fractions of a second or, in the high jump or pole vault, shaded by fractional inches. Can we realistically expect enormous strides in output? Unless some sensational inventions are on the drawing board we can be dubious of our politicians' productivity claims. For with energy prices boosted by OPEC, the better guess is that the current productivity shortfall is more than a passing phase, for the history of production progress has been one of human muscle being replaced by mechanical aids. This option was easier to embrace in past times of tumbling energy prices than it is now. New innovations will occur, but some will be stymied or retarded by the cost of energy.

Mostly, the Kemp-Roth bill begs the question in asserting the unknowable as immutable truth; for proof, they speak louder and profess faith. Productivity growth belongs to the future; it will come from technology still to be invented or, when known, still to be innovated in practical usage. The claim that a mere tax cut will accomplish the productivity miracle without assessing the energy shortfall or its pricing obstacle smacks of the spiels of the patent medicine pitchman. The promises are simply offered as a rationalization for a corporate tax cut; they are even more fantastic in claiming a capacity for stopping inflation. To suggest that Kemp-Roth can resolve our inflation impasse without income moderation is to mutter a wish unencumbered by any facts.

The Kemp-Roth bill is an undisguised corporate tax cut, with a play on words appealing for voter sanction. In some deception it omits the major factor responsible for our inflation, namely, the hasty money income acceleration.

SOME VALID ARGUMENTS FOR A CORPORATE TAX CUT

Despite our indictment of Kemp-Roth, a case can be made for latching a corporate tax cut on as an adjunct to pay restraint. Thus, if a tax cut were granted to firms that restrained their prices and pay, inflation would be under better control. The combination of lower taxes *and* lower interest rates could then usher in a massive era of plant modernization and updating. Too, in many instances such as in public utilities, lower corporate taxes could bring some prices down, as a "once-and-for-all" plunge. Corporate tax cuts thus have a future—when tied to pay moderation practices. Kemp-Roth merely omitted the star player from their supertax spectacular.

THE ALLEGATION OF DOUBLE TAXATION

Advocates of corporate tax reduction—or elimination—commonly allege that the corporate tax is a "double tax" in that the firm's earnings are taxed and that thereafter, the dividends are also taxed under the personal income tax code.

Double-taxation is a play on words. Undoubtedly, the burden on stockholders is higher than it would be if only dividends were taxed, and the corporation tax was eliminated. But then, for the same amount of revenue, other tax rates—probably the personal income tax—would have to go up, so the issue boils down to a choice of tax forms and a division of tax burdens. Second, despite all the self-serving protests seeking the abandonment of the tax, the very existence of corporations generates government costs, to provide police and fire protection, roads, schools for teaching necessary business skills—including the 3 Rs—to supervise sanitation and health standards, as under the Pure Food and Drug Act, to prevent pollution, and so on. The catalogue of supervisory tasks is long. But the argument is that if the production of goods generates communal costs, the business firms involved should contribute to the list of government protective activities incumbent in facilitating production.

It should be obvious that if only dividends were subject to taxation, in order to avoid corporations winding up as tax shelters, legislation to compel the disbursement of practically all corporate earnings would have to be enacted. Firms could no longer be permitted to retain as much of their earnings for internal financing of corporate growth; they would have to exercise more recourse to capital markets for venture capital. On this consideration, not all firms would regard the elimination of "double taxation" as an unmitigated blessing.

Finally, in the nature of the modern government colossus, the corporate income tax is relatively easy to administer, as compared to most other taxes. About 3,000 firms produce 90 percent of all business output. Collection and administration costs would be far higher with most tax replacements.

But these great issues extend far beyond the inflation tangle. To use them in the present inflation context is to ramble away from the great issue of the price blitz. Reform of insubstantial elements in our tax system can be contemplated more calmly and judiciously after the price level has been brought to book. Currently, the price-level consequences of tax modifications should be the chief ingredient in policy design. Whether to delete taxation of dividends or to retain the levy, is of no serious significance in this context.

SOCIAL SECURITY TAXES

Social security taxes, amounting to 13.3 percent on incomes up to $29,700 in 1981, raise another question. Clearly, if they declined, costs would be lower and employee take-home pay higher. But if the old-age survivor's disbursements are preserved, what other tax forms would replace the levies? Unfortunately, social security tax dissenters are often hesitant to provide details.

The vital point is that while lower labor costs could drop prices, the decline would be confined only to the year or thereabout in which the change was triggered. Thereafter, from the new tax and cost level, the same perplexing issue would emerge, namely, of stopping the price rise: no encore to assist could come from lower social security taxes once they are abolished.

This is another instance of a "once-and-for-all" side show. Inflation, on the contrary, comes from *persistent* influences and not just a one-time shot. Our inflation is insidious, for the trouble is ongoing. Of course, we could whittle social security taxes a bit each year, and each time report some slight price relief—with the accent on *slight*.

The conclusion follows that social security has not been our inflation bane except for the years in which its tax levies have been increased. The price-level lift imparted by the social security levies has played a fairly minuscule part in the price saga.

SALES AND EXCISE TAXES

State and local units rely heavily on sales taxes. Economics has long taught that sales taxes raise prices not quite proportionately, because of some technical niceties of supply and demand elasticities. For our purposes we can suppose that they raise prices in nearly the same amount as the tax collection. Abandonment thus would lower prices. Again, how would the revenue be replaced?

This reduction would also be a "once-and-for-all" slash. As sales and excise taxes have not been substantially raised during our unbroken period of inflationary travail, they can scarcely be blamed for the inexorable upward trend. Once they are built into the price mechanism they account for the *level* of prices, but not for the untrammeled climb that spells inflation.

PROPERTY AND MISCELLANEOUS TAXES

Levied on property, and calculated on the assessed value, property taxes are nevertheless paid out of income. It is generally fantastic to declare that they *raise* prices. They lower property prices, by and large, whenever they go up.

Consider what would happen if suddenly they were eliminated. Business-property owners would find their annual net rental income increased by the amount of the tax savings. Any prospective buyer would thus estimate higher income returns, and would be willing to pay a *higher* price for the property. For example, suppose net rents, after operating costs, on an apartment house were $100,000 before a bill for property taxes was entered, say, for $20,000. If these taxes did not have to be paid, income would be $100,000, and not $80,000. The extra $20,000 of income, capitalized at just a 10 percent rate of return, would tend to raise the value of the property in the marketplace from $800,000 to $1,000,000. At 20 percent the property would jump in value from $400,000 to $500,000.

Over enough time, presumably, new properties would be built and the extra supply might—in a decade or so—result in lower rentals. But this is a purely conjectural long-run conclusion. Immediately, the tax relief would offer no succor against inflation.

Miscellaneous other unmentioned taxes display the several features of the tax-types already considered. Thus there are school and sewer taxes, water taxes, franchise taxes, corporation taxes, and so on. The total intake is small, compared to the tax mainstays considered. They have a walk-on bit part in the inflation drama.

TAXES: MORE ANTI-INFLATIONARY THAN INFLATIONARY

Mostly, taxes play a more prominent role in suppressing demand-side inflation tendencies than in evoking price increases. In the few cases of positive correlation between higher tax rates and prices, it would have to be shown that tax rates increased substantially during our inflation epoch. The demonstration is lacking, for the event never happened. Moreover, a removal of the offending tax would amount to a one-time wonder: the price escalator would run as before. Inflation trends would only spurt up from a lower starting gate.

THE KEMP SPOOF

In a variety of explanations to puff his stagflation spoof, and in a manner that mimics John Kennedy, Congressman Kemp has not been above praising the JFK tax cut and hailing it for its miracle work. The Congressman claims the same wonder work for his pet.

On this, Kemp displays either fancy footwork in the fast-talk to which athletes are addicted or has a convenient memory in executing a quarterback dodge. He omits: 1) the Kennedy-Johnson *Guideposts* which gave us price-wage stability and a flat price record to 1968, and which permitted, 2) the Federal Reserve to tolerate interest rates in the 5 to 7 percent range, and 3) under Kennedy-Johnson, government money and real expenditures rose. Really, none of these facts prevail in the Reagan budget, and government outlays will be especially contained. Kemp has thus wheeled out a Swiss cheese containing only holes in his striving for popular support in making an analogy to the Kennedy years.

9

DEFICITS, DEBT, AND INFLATION: MOSTLY SOUND AND FURY?

Mostly noise parades as plausible contention in the fervor with which too many hold the view that the government deficit is at the bottom of our price-level disorder. Usually, the error comes from seeing the government as an extended family business. "What is prudence in the conduct of every private family," wrote Adam Smith in 1776, "can scarce be folly in that of a great kingdom." Alas, in this, the astute Scotsman was mistaken. To take a trivial example, one person can murmur, "there's room for one more on the bus," and act on the proposition. But 225 million people cannot step aboard the vehicle.

DEFICITS AND INFLATION

Deficits are the arithmetical excess of government outlays over tax revenues. Thus their impact should be elicited from summating the general effects on the economy from the outlay side minus (or plus in surplus years) the tax out-take. Deficits themselves should not exert any extra thrust.

This would be the generally correct inference, except for two aspects: (1) the financing of the deficit, and its influence on the money supply, and (2) the deficit cumulating into the national debt so that there are supplementary debt management issues. En route to some examination of these matters we shall look at some confused alarms, and some of the facts which too often are submerged despite their ready accessibility.

DEFICITS, DEBT, AND BANKRUPTCY

Most of the confusion over the deficit emanates from the Adam Smith dictum, in one guise or another. A debt-free individual is surely relieved of financial anxiety. But in the economy at large, a debt for one person is a credit for another: the plus and minus nets out to zero. Largely, except for foreign-held debt, something of a zero sum holds for the national debt.

The notion that an "individual" is more secure when out of debt is hardly tenable for an economy. Where would entrepreneurs, the big-wheel decision makers of our economy, get the wherewithal to operate without incurring debt? How would funds pass into productive hands if all of us obeyed Shakespeare's Polonius injunction? What would happen to banks, to home ownership, to corporations, if all loans dried up and all debts were paid off? Capitalism would disappear with banks the first to go, and the market economy would be unrecognizable without debt— including government debt.

This is not to opt for mountains of debt. But debt, and government debt, also have a place in our economic system.

BANKRUPTCY?

The ominous fears of debt generally come from viewing the government as "just" another individual or super-giant corporation. But government is "immortal," in a sense that transcends individual lives or even the longevity of a corporation. Above all, few future events are as certain as the ability of the United States government to fulfill its commitment to honor the annual interest charges and the principal, on maturity, of its domestic debt.

Too often, the strong in conviction but weak in perception inject the bogey of government "bankruptcy" as ensuing from extended borrowing. Obviously, individuals have a dread of bankruptcy, which compels handing over practically all assets to creditors who, under the law, acquire them as a lien to cover their claims.

Bankruptcy for the federal government? Bondholders seizing government "assets"? This is a fanciful concept indeed and exposes the shallowness of the use of the term. The world has witnessed many revolutions, of political and economic "outs" displacing the "ins." Bondholders occupying the White House and auctioning off Congress because of a United States Treasury debt default is one revolution that will never come to pass! Taxpayers may revolt at the election booths or in street marches. *Policies* may be bankrupt but not our country.

Bankruptcy is a *legal* state, with the inherent rights of creditors conferred by *law*. It can *never* apply to the federal government which is the abode of the *law*. Those who bandy the term in denouncing economic policies of which they disapprove are guilty of a play on words to exploit the gullible—including themselves—to fear impossible situations. If they merely mean that they adjudge the policies to be lame and weak, and the governing political party to be "bankrupt" in the sense of being devoid of ideas, the term is merely a pejorative figure of speech. To use the word to convey shudders and alarms over government debt mostly exhibits an impenetrability in economics and a superficiality in law inasmuch as the legalism is ripped out of its proper context.

DEFICITS INCREASE THE MONEY SUPPLY

Most sophisticated analysts claim that deficit finance involves government borrowing from the banks, thereby augmenting the money supply and thus spelling inflation.

At this point, scares about the deficit merge with the monetary theory of inflation, of "too much money chasing too few goods." This has been analyzed previously. Note, however, the criticism at this phase leaves the deficit domain and concentrates on the money supply increase. The inflation contingency devolves about the Quantity Theory of Money rather than around government profligacy and borrowing.

LIVING BEYOND OUR MEANS?

A final theory opines that the deficit reveals that "we are living beyond our means." Ordinarily, this judgment replicates the Adam Smith conception of the government as simply an extended family or corporation.

It is hard to disabuse ourselves of the notion that the government should conduct its affairs in a "business-like" way. Unfortunately, the government is not just a business. Is there any private firm that can provide national defense, spend billions in developing radar, missiles, or nuclear fission bombs without any prospect of return? Or undertake experimental and costly space probes and communication and weather satellites, provide low-cost housing, and so forth? If businesslike merely means *efficient*, then the thought is impeccable. But the government must do many things that we want done that businesses simply cannot or will not do. And government revenues do not ensue from sales to voluntary market purchasers but are rather coerced from taxes on involuntary subjects, for the most part.

As to "living beyond our means," we can either: (1) cut expenditures, (2) raise taxes, or (3) borrow.

Cutting expenditures depends on the will—and whims—of legislative bodies and pressures from constituents. President Reagan and his ardent supporters are of the opinion that the spenders have gone too far. Democrat rivals share contrary views. If the outlays were less, taxes might better cover outlays—unless legislators reduced them in concert with the lower expenditures. This is the current fashionable trend.

For analysis sake, take outlays at $550 billion and tax revenues at $500 billion, with borrowing needs at $50 billion. When the government taxes in amount $500 billion the Treasury disdains even the issuance of a receipt to the taxpayer marked "Paid." Individuals' spendable income is depleted by this amount, and the repercussions fall unevenly on consumption and savings, according to the tax progression and taxpayer expenditure-savings proclivities. Overall, about 90 percent of after-tax personal income goes into consumption spending.

Suppose government upped the tax bite to $550 billion. Again, there are ramifications on consumption and savings. However, when the government *borrows* the $50 billion, individuals do get "a tax receipt," mailed out in the form of a government *bond* which promises to pay a definite amount of interest, say, 12 percent, over the stipulated period of time. At the time the government borrows, and individuals lend, the transaction may tend *somewhat* toward cutting consumption but it is more likely to divert savings from other forms of personal portfolio acquisitions. (Or, if the moneys are borrowed from commercial banks, the money supply would increase.)

Should the government borrow? Should it tax more instead? Should it cut outlays? These are decisions made by duly elected legislators subject to pressures from constituents, ideology, awareness of political and economic interplay, and attitudes on national needs. Perhaps they are wrong in their judgments. But when we look at the facts it is hardly obvious that we have suddenly started "living beyond our means." For example, Chart 7.7 shows the amount of interest on the national debt since 1950 and the debt total.

Obviously, the absolute amounts of interest payments have soared. But all other numbers have also ballooned. As a percentage of government revenues the interest total has been fairly flat. As a percentage of the national income, likewise, it does not betray any sharp trend; quite the contrary, compared to the 1950s the importance of interest payments has declined dramatically.

To finance the charges on the national debt out of Treasury revenues, 11 percent of the full tax collections (in 1981) must be deflected to this purpose. Or looked at differently, we have to tax ourselves to the extent of 2.7 percent of the national income, in good years or bad, to pay the interest charge on the national debt.

Manifestly, the situation *is* manageable. Over time, *so long as national income grows faster than interest charges*, the interest burden will be lightened. Whatever the past reasons for incurring a debt of the $1 trillion magnitude, the moneys to pay interest can be found: the remedy for the debtor position is always at hand. To solve the "predicament" peremptorily, the drastic remedy would consist of paying off the national debt.

THE DIMINISHED BURDEN OF THE NATIONAL DEBT

Apparently, the annual interest charges on the national debt are tolerable and readily manageable. So far as the debt total itself goes, the total will not go up so long as we act to bring tax revenues *above* government outlays totals. Otherwise, the national debt must rise. This is the serious resolution of those who want a remedy rather than for those who deplore the situation with fervor.

Often, there is the bogus concern of whether the government will be able to sell its bonds. If we think about it, this is entirely a matter of the price, or of the rate of interest the Treasury pays on its bonds. Most of the ghastly, dread fears are unfounded; if the Treasury can't sell bonds to yield 10 percent, it offers 11, or 12 percent, and so on. Ordinarily, as one bond issue matures, and if the government has no tax surplus with which to redeem it, the Treasury issues new obligations, extending the maturity into the longer future; it happens that the subscribers to new refunding issues consist mainly of the former bondholders who substantially "roll-over" the old in exchange for the new, often in the amount of 90 percent of the new refunding.

THE DEBT-GNP RATIO

Chart 9.1 depicts the national debt as a percentage of the gross national product. Confounding the alarmists, the national debt bears a *lesser* proportion to the GNP today than in earlier years. Largely, this result signifies that the GNP, through real output growth and inflation, has shot up far faster than the national debt, and in the process has *alleviated* the debt burden. Manifestly, this is a remorseless byproduct of debtors being beneficiaries, and creditors being victimized, in a period of inflation. Under inflation, despite some contrary wild rhetoric, the debt burden has become lighter, not heavier. Bondholders, holding claims expressed in nominal dollar amounts, have been mulcted. They have a most legitimate right to protest inflation, and not to be bewildered by the specious reasoning of those who profess that their lending, or the debts

CHART 9.1. Net Public Debt as Percentage of GNP, 1929-1980

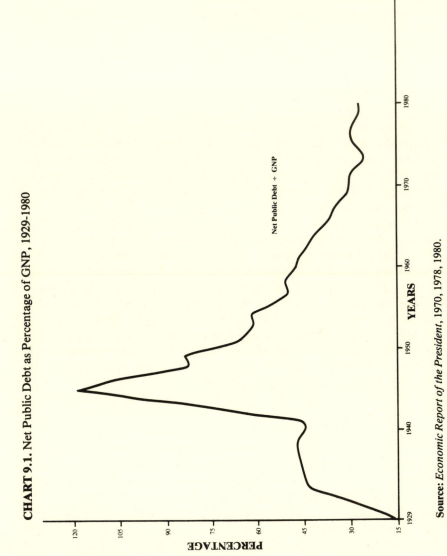

Source: *Economic Report of the President,* 1970, 1978, 1980.

134

themselves, *cause* inflation. The debt burden has lightened, and it has not become more burdensome. Inflation is the culprit, and not the debt load. The rhetoric misfires at the wrong targets in condemning the debt. Inflation merits the vitriolic abuse.

Even in a stable price climate the national debt burden, however we perceive the load, ineluctibly will be mitigated so long as the GNP outstrips the national debt increment. So long as we conduct our national affairs in a way conducive to real economic growth and to contain our government deficits, the debt burden will dwindle.

PAY OFF THE DEBT?

Sometimes a frenetic chorus cries, on private analogies, for the government to pay off the debt, and wipe the slate clean. This betrays a peculiar confusion. The out-turn would be that we would tax ourselves well beyond the bill for current government expenditures. Depending on the tax forms adopted, there would be ramifications on consumption and on investment, and thus the GNP income evolution. At the end of the analytic line, we would make checks payable to the Treasury, and the Treasury would turn about and make checks payable to bondholders to redeem the bonds outstanding.

After the swap, bondholders would hold the *same* amount of money —minus administrative charges—but without bonds! Would taxpayers feel richer in donating an extra $10,000 in taxes in order to enable the Treasury to erase their $10,000 of bonds? Private asset holdings would be decimated; taxpayers would be stripped of this wealth, tending to curtail consumption per annum, conducive generally to a more stagnant economy unless there was a perverse burst of capital goods investment by firms ardent to build factories for a public less anxious to consume their products!

Insofar as Group A paid the taxes, and Group B sold bonds to the Treasury, the A taxpayers would find their real income—and wealth—position depleted. The erstwhile bondholders would now own money with which to bid up the prices of other bond issues, lowering interest rates and thereby aiding investment. But this would overlook the buying lapse from Group A, reeling under the stiff tax blow. The outlook would hardly be promising for the market economy before a long period of recuperation.

Where the bond redemption hits banking institutions, the operation would wipe out a corresponding amount of money. Thus as commercial banks owned about $110 billion of government securities (December 1980), demand deposits would instantly crash. A catastrophic 28 percent money deflation would occur; the money deflation would be calamitous for production and jobs in the exchange economy by hiking interest rates precipitately.

It is artificial in the extreme to conjecture a serious venture in debt repayment without further information on associated supporting measures. By itself, the devastating monetary blow would be as disastrous as that in the Great Depression. Stoics who casually prescribe the bitter pill do not have any real perception of the poisonous extract in their medicine; it usually manifests itself in a fanatic ill-suited self-destructive credo.

DEBT BURDEN?

It is possible to be obsessed with the "debt burden." As there is about $550 billion in government bonds held by the public, this implies that the government is in hock for this sum, or looked at the other way individuals and corporations can proudly claim that they *own* $550 billion in government bonds. They feel *wealthier* by this sum.

It is not a case of all debt and nothing positive: a debt to one is an asset to another. If someone owes, someone else owns. Likewise, when the government pays $80 billion in interest charges, then someone else—the owners of the bonds—counts the same $80 billion as income.

Table 9.1 indicates the ownership of government bonds as of January 1980. A total of $185 billion was owned by government agencies, such as the social security fund and other financial arms of the United States government. Another $116 billion was owned by the Federal Reserve. Some $97 billion was owned by commercial banks. Another large portion of $71 billion was owned by state and local governments. Thus of

TABLE 9.1

Ownership of the Public Debt, as of January 1980 (in billions of dollars)

U.S. Govt. Agencies and Trust Funds	184.5
Federal Reserve System	116.3
Private Investors	546.9
Commercial Banks	97.1
Mutual Savings Banks	4.0
Insurance Companies	14.4
Other Companies	24.5
State and Local Governments	71.7
Total Gross Public Debt	$847.7

SOURCE: *Federal Reserve Bulletin*, April 1980, p. A32.

the $847 billion total, about $550 or 65 percent of the total is owned by private individuals and firms who usually pride themselves on their prudent investment policy in owning government bonds which are *certain* in interest, and *sure* of principal repayment on maturity.

SHIFTING THE BURDEN TO FUTURE GENERATIONS?

About $20 billion of the debt is a legacy of World War I, and another $20 billion was a product of the Great Depression. Another $240 billion materialized during World War II. The rest was incurred during the Korean and Vietnam wars, the enduring cold war of heavy defense outlays, and the floundering economic mismanagement of the 1970s.

There are many, in expressing alarm at the debt, who declare it assesses an interest levy and redemption burden on future generations. This is a vast oversimplification, for, as noted, future generations will pay interest charges and collect the interest receipts; of course there are (fairly nominal) administrative costs, and it is also a fact that the taxpayers do not overlap entirely with the interest-gathering bondholders, so that there is a distributive aspect in the payment-receipt discrepancy.

But certainly the "burden" of the two world wars, or the Great Depression, was borne by those who lived, and died, at those times. The deeper "burden" could hardly be shifted forward to later generations. One could argue that borrowing was probably the least chaotic political means of raising the war revenues, and that military victory gave us the best chance to maintain freedom and our democratic way of life. On this vision the deficits conferred a priceless intangible *blessing*, rather than a burden, on future generations.

The condemnation really insults the intelligence of our heirs; in effect, the notion claims that past generations were smart enough to *escape* a burden, and to deflect it forward, and that the "future" legatees are so stupid as to be unable to work the same trick! This slanders their competence.

To allay debt, we must stop the deficits. To do so, we must tax more and spend less, in mutable combination. Circumstances will decide which measures spell prudent public policy. With President Reagan the pendulum should swing to a tax and expenditure slash. The promised balanced budget date has been deferred recently, according to the guesses of his economic advisers, to about 1985. Only in time will we know the validity of the estimate.

The overwhelming truth is this: we are where we are in time, and in debt magnitude. We can *blame* the past; we can *vent* our ire and *expel* our rage. After we stop the denunciation and pause for breath, we are still faced with the decision on managing our fiscal affairs. Reason does

CHART 9.2. Annual Percentage Change in Consumer Prices and Annual
Deficits since 1929

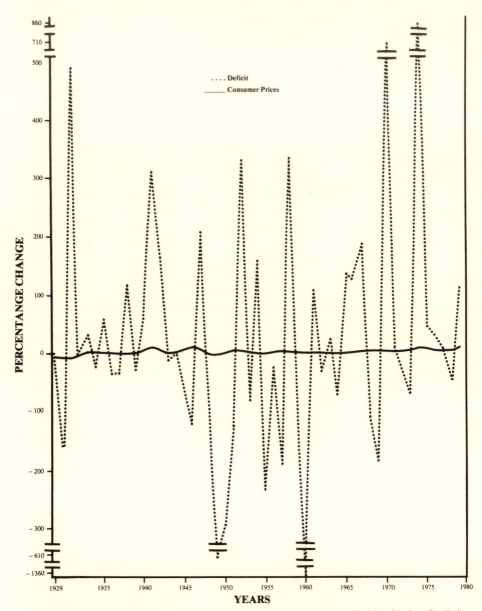

Source: *Statistical Abstracts of the United States*, 1972, 1979; *Handbook of Labor Statistics,*
1978.

138

CHART 9.3. Deficits to GNP, 1929-1980

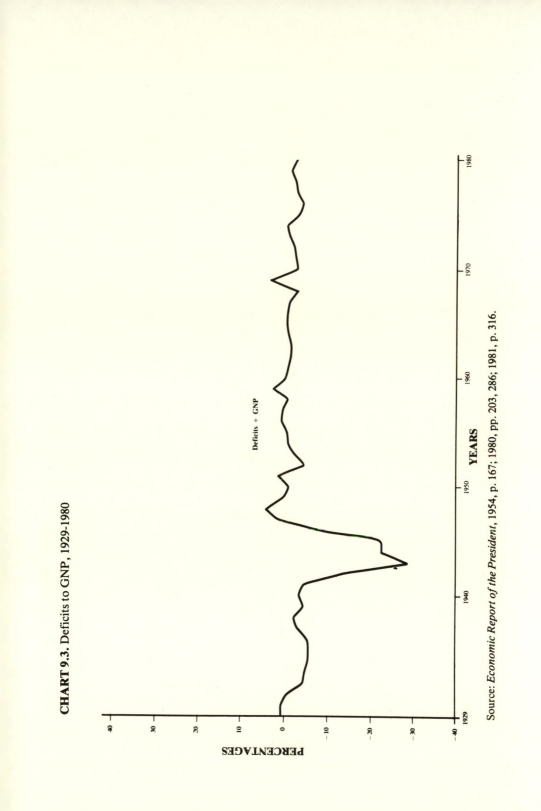

Source: *Economic Report of the President*, 1954, p. 167; 1980, pp. 203, 286; 1981, p. 316.

CHART 9.4. Federal Deficits to Government Expenditures, 1929-1980

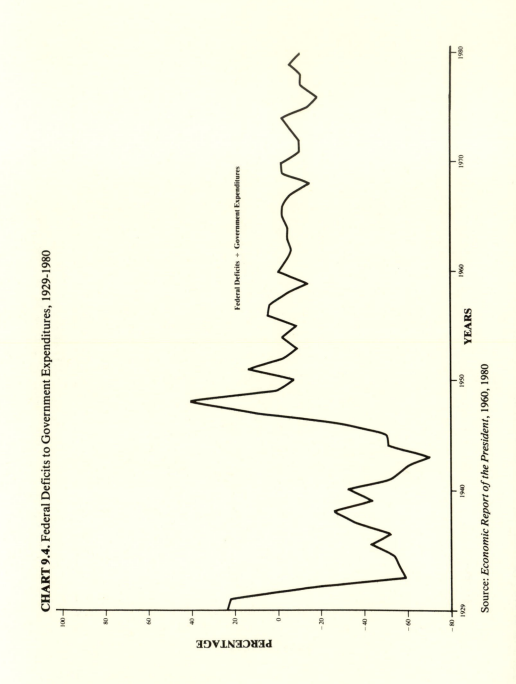

Source: *Economic Report of the President, 1960, 1980*

not suggest that the debt magnitude is alarming, for the ratio of debt to GNP is only about one-third (or less) of what it was after World War II, and the interest drain is quite manageable, by any criterion. In 1945 the national debt of $252 billion exceeded the GNP of $212 billion, in ratio of 1.18 to 1. For 1981 it should be about 1 to 3, for GNP will approximate $3 trillion and the debt $1 trillion. Despite the egregious magnitudes, the debt size is relatively smaller. Matching the 1945 ratios the debt would be over $3 trillion.

DEFICITS CAUSING INFLATION? A NEGATIVE VERDICT

Inveighing against deficits adds nothing to the inflation analysis; deficits are wholly a residual resultant of outlay-expenditure policy. The only valid inflation argument that might be entered on deficits as a price maker would follow insofar as they foster an increase in the money supply. But, as remarked, this identifies with the monetary theory of "more money chasing goods."

As to the national debt being the inflation *cause*, the proposition represents wholesale confusion. Debts are eased during inflation; inflation relieves the debt burden. Debt is largely irrelevant to the price binge. For those who allege that the possession of government debt makes borrowing by bondholders easier, this argument, too, merges with the monetary theories of inflation.

THE RELATIVE SIZE OF DEFICITS

Al Smith, a great governor of New York, defeated in the presidential race in 1928 by Herbert Hoover, used to say jauntily and triumphantly: "Let's look at the record!" Casey Stengel, the dazzling and rambling baseball manager, would say in the same vein, "You can look it up."

Chart 9.2 contains the path of consumer prices and the annual federal deficit since 1929. Obviously, there is hardly a trace of correlation between the two; in years of even sharp deficits, prices scarcely moved— until the mad pace of the 1970s.

Chart 9.3 discloses the annual budget out-turn with an occasional surplus as a percentage of GNP, on the presumption that we cannot know whether the deficit is big or small unless we compare it with something. Chart 9.4, on the other hand, compares the annual federal deficit (or surplus) to federal outlays. What appears in *both* charts is that the deficit has *not* been growing, either relative to GNP or to government outlays. That the absolute magnitudes are large is undeniable. But under inflation *all* dollar magnitudes have swollen so that mere size has optical but lacks causal significance.

Despite the enormous deficits for that time, the price level in the 1930s edged nowhere in particular, sharply down at the beginning of the decade, up near the close. The 1940s reflected the war, with its price controls to 1946. The 1950s evidenced hardly any inflation, by today's standards, despite some hefty peacetime deficits. The 1960s showed practically no annual price change until 1968, and even then only meager jumps by the 1970s experience. Again, deficit after deficit. The 1970s showed the deficits, several big ones absolutely, but with prices exploding as they never did before.

Over most of the 50-year period, despite chronic deficits, the price level behaved reasonably well. During the *largest* relative deficit in our history, in 1933 when federal government borrowing amounted to about 55 percent of its expenditures, prices actually fell by about 12 percent. Deficits are thus hardly the inflation demon despite the political crescendo which excels mainly in fear-mongering and thought evasion.

On the 1933 basis, with federal expenditures for fiscal 1981 in the $655 billion range, a comparable deficit today would be about $800 billion! The projected deficit looms at about $50 billion. Nonetheless, despite the "paltry" size by historic tests, inflation will continue to gush at the highest rates in modern history.

So much for the inductive evidence on deficits and inflation. The bluster of deficit doomsday prophets collapses when tested by empirical relations.

NOT ENOUGH SAVINGS?

Often it is asserted that the deficits "eat up" savings, or absorb them, and deny them to "profitable" business use. This, too, is an old wives' tale.

To set this to rest it is enough to invoke the major national income relationship, inculcated since Keynes wrote on the subject during the Great Depression. The equation is:

(1) Gross National Product Equals Gross National Income.

Gross National Product (omitting exports and imports) breaks down to:

(2)   Consumption (C) + Investment (I)
                + Government Purchases of GNP Output (G).

Gross National Income, likewise, decomposes into:

(3)   Consumption (C) + Savings (S) + Taxes (T).
         (For simplicity we assume *all* taxes are on income.)

It follows, therefore, that as consumption is the same in (2) and (3), that:

(4) $I + G = S + T$ or $I + (G-T) = S$ or $I + D = S$,

where D denotes the government deficit.

Thus it *must* be, except on a very twisted logic, that savings, whether by individuals or by corporations, are always ample to cover *both* the total private investments *and* the government deficit. To assert otherwise is to engage in contorted logic. The economy *always* churns out sufficient savings to support both the actual private investment volume (that is, private capital formation) *and* the government deficit. If the deficit was nil, the savings total would identify solely with the investment aggregate. Otherwise, savings will still exist in abundance, to also absorb the deficit.

It could be argued, with more verisimilitude, that if G, meaning government market purchase of GNP, were smaller, then there could be *more* C and *more* I, or that we could build more plants and equipment to produce more goods in the future. This argument is valid. But to say that government has *impeded* investment growth is to be loose with the facts, for, through most of the years, beginning with either 1930 or 1950, we have invariably had excessive unemployment. Ostensibly, it was possible to produce both more C and more I goods, but private enterprise, for one reason or another, abjured the full employment promontary. That government narrowed the breach to prevent even higher unemployment in our economy hardly constitutes an instance of government "absorbing" savings that "would otherwise go to private enterprise." Too many of such misinformed assertions pass as currency, posing as wisdom in a now popular antigovernment wave. Foolish statements remain vacuous, regardless of the ideological banner under which they are unfurled.

CROWDING OUT OTHER BORROWERS?

Sometimes the spurious judgment of inadequate savings to finance the deficit melts into another shading of the opinion, to wit, that the government's recourse to loan markets "crowds out" other borrowers, making "capital scarce." Some put it more baldly, that there will not be enough "money" to go around.

These expressions court the danger of confusing "savings" with money supplies. The "crowding out" argument professes that if government borrows, it absorbs loanable funds, often loosely referred to as "capital," from private enterprise. Manifestly, on the proviso that the money stock is constant, the salient point is acceptable, that government borrowing competes with private entrants. Presumably, if it did not borrow, the private borrowers would be able to acquire loan-finance on better terms. With the government also in the market, it may be that the rate of interest will poke higher.

But the same inference could be drawn, to wit, that the demands of other borrowers are also too high! There is nothing so very special about government borrowing—except that its credit rating is second to none—that could not be said about private borrowing and the rate of interest. The disciples of the theory that the government borrowing forces up the rate of interest are also guilty of injecting two dubious assumptions of "other things unchanged" into their condemnation: (1) the assumption that without the government budget activities the economic situation would remain exactly the same. But this can*not* be so: if government housekeeping details shifted, the economic position would differ. Above all, there is implicit in the argument (2) the premise that the money supply stays the same, whether government borrows or not. This need not be so. Money aggregates rest mainly on Fed policy.

At best, the "crowding out" alarm is superficially profound in dreaming up a "maybe" happenstance. For (1) private borrowers are not "crowded out," although (2) the cost of borrowing to them "may be" somewhat higher, with some prospective borrowers dropping out along the wayside. But point (2) depends on Federal Reserve policy. "Crowding out" is not an economic imperative, despite the emotional contentions of those who labor the point.

Real crowding out, in the sense of denial of labor and natural resources to private enterprise, could occur by government expansion in a period of full employment. Periods of optimal activity on a full scale have not occurred, unfortunately, in the 1970s. Labor supplies have been redundant and expressed in the high unemployment rate. The consideration relegates the theory of "crowding out" to a mirage status.

10

Productivity, OPEC, Overregulation, And Markups

A range of other aspects of our inflation ordeal invites comment. Money-income growth has been stressed as the inflation maker, and improvements in average productivity cited as an inflation breaker, capable of mitigating the price climb.

Productivity perturbations are critical. If annual personal productivity could bound up by 8 percent, average real incomes could bounce ahead equivalently and yield a stable price trend. It is thus useful to consider some recent productivity facts, and assess prospects of any big leap in these figures. OPEC oil, government regulation, and mark-up phenomena also invoke comment. The topics round out the inflation analysis.

PRODUCTIVITY MAINSPRINGS

The mainsprings of productivity improvement are easy to isolate. They group naturally under three headings, namely: (1) betterment in human resources, (2) enhanced natural resources, and (3) technological gains through knowledge-breakthroughs and modernized capital equipment.

GAINS IN HUMAN RESOURCES

Surely, it cannot be that people today work longer hours to produce more goods than their grandparents! Obviously, this is not so; over the last 100 years the workweek has been cut nearly in half, and most of the backbreaking tasks of previous generations have been replaced by digging, lifting, hauling machinery.

When we ask whether people are innately "smarter" today, the evidence speaks plainly too, whether we look at literature, mathematics, music—even economics—or sports heroes and athletic records; it is not so certain that contemporaries display overwhelming superiority in brains or physical prowess. Undoubtedly, there is better training generally, but more obscurity surrounds the question of whether the indispensable ingredient of personal discipline is any stronger now, or as steadfast as it was. Any complacency that individuals are very much brighter today is literally to judge our parents and grandparents as backward. Casual evidence hardly sustains the conclusion. This is an overwhelming subject on which the evidence is underwhelming. For concreteness we might look elsewhere for the explanation of productivity gains, per capita.

BETTER NATURAL RESOURCES?

Material resources, such as coal, minerals, and oil, are certainly not in readier access than they were. We have to dig deeper, or look to more costly sites for them, whether it is oil in Alaska or offshore, or in distant lands. As to land fertility, the verdict is mixed, with chemical fertilizers versus well-worked land; fertilizer use itself points to costlier production. Obviously, there have been new mineral discoveries but generally in more remote areas entailing higher transport costs.

The subject is vast; a final impression would probably be that despite discoveries and technology we have also been dissolute in dissipating our inheritance so that future productivity gains are unlikely to emanate from "more and better," meaning more accessible and rewarding natural resources.

TECHNOLOGY AND CAPITAL EQUIPMENT

By elimination the inescapable conclusion is that the important productivity gains mainly inhere in improved technology, entailing more and better capital equipment. Science, and its applied technology, have given us the array of equipment that has worked the productivity miracles. It is the better tooled worker, with electrically powered equipment, that has fostered the giant economic strides forward. There is the simple statistic that in 1930 about 30 percent of our population were farm dwellers; today, the figure is about 5 percent. And yet we have more food and fiber per person.

Consider something as simple as a farm truck. In backward countries, to travel to town 20 miles away for seed and supplies might take a few days by a team of oxen. By jeep, the turnaround time today may take two or three hours. Any number of comparable examples might be cited, as on the mountains of dirt moved by a bulldozer compared to the number of workers required to perform the chore with shovels.

More and better equipment scores the productivity gains. This is the obvious story of our material progress. Abundance is the offspring of technology. In this result the future is unlikely to differ from the past.

RECENT PRODUCTIVITY FACTS

Some recent productivity trends appear in Table 10.1.

From any angle, the productivity facts make appalling and disturbing reading for the years since the middle 1960s. For 1974 and 1979, per employee productivity actually declined, serving to elevate the price level by accelerating the impact of the money income escalation. The *difference* between output per hour (when the change is positive) and compensation per hour yields unit labor costs; when productivity slumps, the two sums must be added together. Manifestly, per capita productivity is the vessel for carrying along personal gains in real income.

PRODUCTIVITY AND INFLATION

Compensation has thus badly outpaced productivity, and thus fanned the inflation fire. The nagging productivity questions are: (1) what is the probable near-future productivity trend and (2) what is the right mix of policies to restore the productivity creep to a more benign performance?

Productivity does have a tendency to dwindle under slow growth or recession when firms cut output in greater degree than their release of valuable and key personnel staff; this seems to fit 1979-1980 when anticipations of brief recession were rife. Thus in an ensuing recovery a reasonable productivity upbeat should occur. But big gains are likely to prove elusive. Big advances do not come easily, as observed earlier. Energy facts are an impediment.

Stunning new technological developments alone, in engineering and in the laboratories, can change the pessimistic assessment. But even on an optimistic gauge the growth must take time; the trends are slow to break, and slow to be interrupted. Meanwhile, the tax laws, for one thing, can do something to encourage industrial research and facilitate plant modernization through accelerated depreciation tactics and lower corporate

TABLE 10.1

Labor Productivity Growth, 1948-1979 (Percent Change Per Annum)

	1948-1955	1955-1965	1965-1973	1973-1978	1978 IV-1979 IV
Private Business Sector	2.5	2.4	1.6	0.8	-2.0
Nonfarm	2.4	2.5	1.6	0.9	-2.2
Manufacturing	3.2	2.8	2.4	1.5	—
Nonmanufacturing	2.1	2.2	1.2	0.5	—

SOURCE: *Economic Report* (1980), p. 85.

profit levies. Otherwise, there seems to be no great magic available to come to our rescue.

The deeper moral is that a tighter incomes policy must be run to abort inflation insofar as productivity improvements cling to the abysmal 1970s patterns. Income tautness can be lessened when the productivity tide runs stronger. Despite the cheery sloganeering of supply side economics, most of the specifics, when purified of public relations hokum, come down to: (1) a business tax cut and (2) a denunciation of overregulation. Neither "remedy" is likely to work even minor miracles despite the enthusiastic and vociferous lobbies that promote their objectives.

GOVERNMENT OVERREGULATION

Recent political sport has been to decry regulatory zeal and to blame our inflationary distress on it. For example, when confronted with the directives of the Occupational Safety and Health Administration (OSHA), business spokesmen will generally admit its good intentions but then deplore regulatory overkill as the problem.

To evaluate government regulation would require a huge staff and culminate in a massive (unread) study. Some of the estimates floating around set the extra cost of regulation at about $100 billion, more or less, of the industrial production bill. Even at $200 billion, just to make a point, the sum amounts to about 10 percent of the gross business product. If all the regulatory agencies were eliminated, it *might* reduce business costs by a corresponding sum. Question: what would we do for an encore after torpedoing regulation? There would still be the need to confront the annual money wage and productivity pace.

Imposition, or removal, of regulatory tactics represents a one-shot, or once-and-for-all, change. It is not the stuff of which a persistent inflation is made. Inflation is not apt to be altered by one-shot charges despite the vast confusion on the subject.*

*The literature on regulation is vast and dates at least from Adam Smith in 1776. In recent years, Dr. Murray L. Weidenbaum, now chairman of the Reagan Council of Economic Advisers, has been a leading critic of government overreach. See his "Government Power and Business Performances," in *The United States in the 1980s*, edited by Peter Quignan and Alvin Rabushka (Hoover Institution, Stanford University, 1980). Also "The New Regulation," *Journal of Post Keynesian Economics*, Spring 1980, with replies by M. Ulmer and Daniel R. Fusfeld. A good compilation of agencies is provided by *The Directory of Federal Regulatory Agencies*, Center for the Study of American Business, Washington University, St. Louis, Missouri, 2d ed., 1980.

REGULATORY COST

Almost any figure put on regulatory cost will be badly inaccurate despite the spurious air of precision in a ball-park estimate of $100 billion, say. There is, of course, the bureaucratic measure of the agency budget. But then, for enforcement, there are Justice Department lawyers and the courts, generally excluded. Too, when the directive requires reporting by business firms it may be possible to tally personnel involved *directly*. But if a directive imposes a change in chemicals used, or their disposal, or in packaging, or in modifying health and safety features of a plant, or in altered shipping or transport relations, or in suppressing certain products, there can be no serious static cost measure of regulation. Most numbers are just numbers. They tote the visible costs, but perforce, they are unable usually to substantiate the invisible and suppressed cost tolls.

This is not solely to be critical of the mock answers to an inherently unanswerable query, but to alert us to the vagueness of the subject. The estimates resemble those of an accountant giving precise cost sums to products produced jointly: If numbers are wanted, if they will be paid for—or serve political needs—they will be concocted. But they can hardly classify as a barometric measurement.

ABOLISH REGULATIONS?

Do we want all regulatory curbs abolished? Very few of us are so zealous as to advocate a wholesale dismantlement. There have been too many recent health hazards in disposing of chemical wastes, for example, at Love Canal or the James River Kepone disaster. Too many lakes and waterways have been polluted, and too much of the air has been fouled, for most of us to accept the reckless attitude of many business firms legally unshackled from responsibility for damages inflicted on society by intemperate cost-savings practices which disdain any wider public interest.

Few of us, for example, would want our milk, meats, or food distributed without some assurance of compliance with health inspection standards. And even when we fault the bureaucratic procrastination of the Food and Drug Administration, the thalidomide disaster of the not too distant past provided a bitter lesson in the dangers of pharmaceutical laxity.

Some OSHA directives mandate various capital investments, including outlays for sanitation, safety, and health safeguards. Removing them would scarcely cut business costs severely. If regulatory costs amount to about 5 percent of the total, an irreducible minimum might come to about 2 percent—these are mere guesses. And not all of the total will consist of annual *recurring* expenses despite the incessant expostulational blather.

Regulatory opposition is thus apt to exaggerate costs. But there are obvious benefits in having safer work conditions and healthier employees, in preventing ecological disasters and oil spills, in making water purer, and having live fish in our streams rather than dead specimens. Thus, in meek defense of regulation a business firm must be envisaged as producing not only a good, but also a "bad," by way of industrial or environmental damage. Unbridled private self-interest, Adam Smith would attest, does not always coincide harmoniously with public or social interest. The harm inflicted on others—nowadays described as "externalities" by economists—can be egregious and unsavory aspects of undiluted laissez-faire.

Hitherto our flawed national income accounting has counted the "good," and shut its eyes to the "bad." Regulation, thus, is not a total deadweight cost when it succeeds in making life more humane for present or future generations.

Whatever our view on the proper part to be played by government, the attacks on regulation are a negative vindication of democracy—it is alive and kicking. However vocal the fervor over more versus less government intrusion, and the episodic swing of the pendulum here and there, the dialogue bears only vaguely on our inflation impasse. Regulation, mostly, as in other instances alluded to, entails "once-over" changes and lacks the determined and tenacious inflation substance.

OPEC AND IMPORTS: HUNTING FOREIGN SCAPEGOATS?

Politicians, to a public anxious to see foreign conspirators, castigate OPEC for our price level calamity. Nixon, Ford, and Carter all leaped at the chance to transfer culpability for their wretched, even weird, price-level performance.

There is much to fault in OPEC and its political oil malfeasance that menaces the economies of the Western world. But OPEC is only a junior accomplice in our inflation. On the price level—relative oil prices apart—*all* of their vile acts could be parried, or negated, by a rational national policy. OPEC can even rebut, with minor plausibility, that its own extortions were attributable to our fabulous inflation blunders.

Indeed, on the latter score OPEC's contention is that its higher oil prices were justified because: (1) prices of imported industrial products had escalated and (2) the foreign exchange value of the dollar had fallen and, with oil prices stipulated in dollars, they amassed fewer German marks or Japanese yen, or other currencies in exchange for petro-dollars in buying world imports.

And so controversy ran in a circle, with each country announcing "our inflation was caused by your inflation." Curiously, each country, and the United States is no exception, claimed that it imported inflation. Everyone alleged that inflation was manufactured abroad. The price explosion became a unique phenomenon: everybody imported it; nobody exported it!

Unfortunately, this "explanation" fails to explain. If prices are constant or falling abroad, a trading partner may get some price help from abroad. If import prices are soaring, the domestic situation will be exacerbated. In the former event, there can be a somewhat more lax application of the relation between money incomes and productivity. But with import prices exploding, a country must rely more on its own devices to overcome the price swell. In golf, a fair game can beat a poor game. A better performance is required against a scratch player.

The United States is economically awesome enough to forego the luxury of whining that it is at the mercy of world storms, or buffeted about by external turbulence, unable to extricate or insulate itself. Protective shields are available.

THE MINOR IMPACTS OF IMPORTS

To cinch the point we consider the relative size of imports and of OPEC, in our aggregate GNP, inclusive of import content. Usual GNP data are properly stated *net* of imports. Yet our marketed domestic output, as purchased by final buyers, obviously contains much import content. A tin of coffee holds imported coffee beans, maybe some imported tin, and domestic inputs of labor and capital for processing, delivery, advertising, and retailing. Chocolate bars embody imported cocoa, and domestic labor and nonlabor inputs as the sweet filters down to the consumer. Thus, the gross GNP, inclusive of imports, constitutes the final output value of the marketplace. The inclusive gross totals appear in Table 10.2 for some recent years.

Manifestly, OPEC oil and imports generally are vastly exaggerated overall; they have only a minor capacity to affect our price level. The domestic content of the inclusive GNP is over 90 cents in every $1 of goods sold here or exported by us. Obviously, it follows that the United States price level is made at home; our price destiny lies in our own hands, rather than being subject to the whim of foreign countries. It is ours to make or break—or brake or joyride.

According to the table, if import prices doubled, and even assuming our import quantities remained the same, the foreign content would jump from 7.9 cents (in 1979) to 16 cents in every $1 of sales. Our price level would "surge" from $1 to $1.08, or escalate a meager 8 percent or so, a

TABLE 10.2

GNP, Including Imports, Total Merchandise Imports, and Imports from OPEC, 1965-1979 (in billions of dollars)

	GNP, INCLUDING MERCHANDISE IMPORTS (1)	MERCHANDISE IMPORTS, TOTAL (2)	MERCHANDISE IMPORTS FROM OPEC (3)	PERCENT (2) ÷ (1) (4)	(3) ÷ (1) (5)
1973	$1,377.1	$ 70.5	$ 5.1	5.1	0.3
1974	1,516.5	103.6	17.2	6.8	1.1
1975	1,626.8	98.0	18.9	6.0	1.6
1976	1,826.3	124.1	27.4	6.8	1.5
1977	2,051.7	151.2	35.8	7.4	1.7
1978	2,303.4	175.8	33.3	7.6	1.4
1979*	2,572.0	203.5	41.5	7.9	1.6

*Preliminary.

SOURCE: *Council of Economic Advisers*, 1980, pp. 203, 319.

long way from the catastrophic 100 percent upheaval abroad. Actually, other than for OPEC, in many of our trading partners prices have risen annually by less than 10 percent.

The evidence, then, is formidable that it is a bald fabrication to allege that our inflation is imported; it is an indigenous variety. The most stringent assumptions were used to buttress this conclusion, namely, (1) that our import volume would stay rigid despite enormous leaps in import prices relative to domestic substitutes and (2) that despite more rampant and decisive inflation abroad, the foreign exchange value of the dollar would not improve. Both assumptions, which are contrary to fact, reinforce the assessment of the exaggerated influence imputed to energy and import prices generally in our inflation turmoil.

WILL THE FOREIGN PRICE RISE
RAISE PRICES OF COMPETING IMPORTS?

A more subtle argument is that a rise in the price of imports will be emulated by higher prices for competitive domestic items. Some prices undoubtedly will reverberate. But if this happened on a vast scale, signifying a domestic price rise independent of money-wage and labor-productivity phenomena, it would compel a rise in the average price markup. This phenomenon is not revealed in the data and the bogey may be discounted. (We discuss this below.)

OPEC AND OIL

Although a surprisingly minimal price-level bite of oil imports from OPEC is revealed in the foregoing table, this particular import situation begs greater elaboration, for it is so much in the news.

Everyone who drives an automobile uses energy directly, from the gas pump; we also buy heating oil or use electricity or equipment driven by oil. The fuel appears explicit or hidden as a cost in a long and multiphased capital and consumer good (or service) chain having many complicated loops and asserting diverse feedbacks.

Too often, we overlook the fact that in buying energy at each stage it is *not* the well-head price alone that matters. Even at the well-head oil has *some* labor and capital components; thereafter, in the oil distribution there are tacked on the labor, capital, and profit charges at each and every stage, including the local filling station. Thus, an OPEC price hike of 10 to 15 percent may translate to about 2 percent at the pump. (Even doubling the latter figure, as a markup tack-on, reveals government hyperbole in assigning OPEC as the subversive inflation villain.)

This is not an apologetic to exonerate OPEC extortion, but to put some perspective on the matter. Suppose we take the total cost of the barrels of oil consumed in the United States from *all* sources, domestic and foreign, in 1979. The near 5 billion barrels cost about $100 billion. Assume the price was lowered to one-tenth the value, thus to $10 billion. This stupendous turnabout would drop the GNP by about 4 percent. Our price level would be down by about 10 percent. Our price level has risen by some 150 percent since 1968. Despite the over tenfold OPEC increase, gasoline pump prices are now about three-and-a-half times their 1968 number.

OPEC exactions have far-reaching political and economic ramifications for the United States and the rest of the world. But it is a monumental instance of billowing political smoke before our eyes for politicians to indulge the fantasy that a dismemberment of OPEC would end our stagflation plight.

NEUTRALIZING THE OPEC PRICE GOUGE

Considering that OPEC and well-head oil prices account for only 5 to 10 percent of our appalling inflation since 1968, on the inflation story a Winston Churchill might conclude that "never has so much been made of so little"!

The enormous rise in oil prices, concentrated as they were since the 1973 autumn Yom Kippur war, has certainly done nothing to restrain our price blitz. Nonetheless, once import prices rise we have to keep a firmer lid on wage and salary hikes in order to steady the price level; this would have been the rational response to OPEC exactions. If incomes mounted less rapidly, gasoline prices would not have gone haywire to exert rippling effects through the economy. But to assign energy prices as at the center of the inflationary excrescence defies reason and touches off a fishing foray for a school of red herrings that never saw water. The tirades against OPEC, and OPEC alone, divert us from penetrating the core of our inflation and unemployment tangle. OPEC is a menace on several grounds. It is a nefarious cartel. Breaking it, as we should, will not end the stagflation malaise.

IMPORTS, OIL, AND THE PRICE LEVEL

Imports overall, and oil imports in particular, play a spear carrier's part in our price level saga; they are not at the bottom of our price chaos despite scapegoat rumblings to the contrary. OPEC can make our situation worse, unless we neutralize its self-serving acts by invoking an even tighter incomes' noose fitted to average productivity gains. Falling overseas prices allow more laxity in our incomes posture. Inflationary flares abroad require tighter income hampers at home.

If Archimedes could, with a lever long enough, lift the world, the equivalent economic proposition would be: hold money incomes in tow and we can establish any price level we want.

MARKUP CONSTANCY

Frequent reference has been made to the price markup and its substantial year-to-year and long-run constancy. Also, it is estimated that in our business sector, the markup hovers about 1.9. Interpreted, it means that for every $1 of unit labor costs, prices, on average, tend to be $1.90.

Given $1 of labor costs per unit of production, as market prices tend to veer close to $1.90, the extra 90 cents captured in the marketplace is destined to cover depreciation allowances, rents, interest payments, corporate property taxes, sales taxes, corporate profits and corporate profits taxes, corporate charitable grants, and so on.

In particular industries the markup oscillates markedly over time. In steel, railroads, airline fares, oil, computers, telephones, electric utilities, manufacturing generally, mining, farming, the individual sector markups have literally dashed all over the board, up and down in a baffling, frenzied, and erratic pattern. In individual industries the fluctuations probably mimic the wild oscillation of the Dow Jones stock market averages. Nonetheless, for the economy in toto the *average* movement has exhibited remarkable fixity, with upticks serving to counter-balance the more frequent slide down.

The overall mark-up constancy remains perhaps the major unsolved and far too little noticed, mystery of economics; what is ever more amazing, it is one which has escaped general detection. Research into the subject has been narrow; there seems to be a stark and inchoate refusal to examine the subject. Studies dealing with the relation can almost be counted on one hand despite the general facts being known for over 40 years. Apparently the subject, through silence and default, has become taboo while other topics are debated ad nauseam. Labor's income share, which is the reciprocal of the markup, has gone largely unattended despite its pristine importance.

More than its substantial constancy, the interesting conundrum is: why did the markup become stuck near 2, or our gross business product wage share set at near one-half? In the United Kingdom the markup is closer to 1.5; in Canada, near 2.2. Apparently, the structural importance of agriculture and industry has something to do with the size. But we shall never know until we delve into the subject and develop a theory of the relationship.

Nonetheless, without an explanation of the wage share determinants, the markup "near-constancy" remains the most important empirical "law" of economics. We are entitled to presume that since it has been reasonably constant for so long, it will stay put over the near future, so that we can use the empirical finding in our predictive work. It enables us, for example, to predict the course of the price level merely from the performance of unit labor costs. To maintain a stable price level entails alignment of the average wage-salary trend in good pace with the labor productivity series.

SUBSTANTIAL ALTERATIONS IN THE MARKUP?

There is perennial fuming over excess profit margins or markups for inflation.* Others, affronted by the exorbitant profit fortunes of the energy companies, of Exxon, Mobil, Texaco, and the others, in recent years, castigate the "obscene" magnitudes and generalize from them. Judgments become vehement in an advocacy of either more competition or government monitoring to slash profit margins to police inflation.

Clearly, forcing the markup from 1.9 to *below* 1 would carry the wage bill *above* sales receipts, imposing universal losses! Obviously this can never occur—for it violates market economy precepts. It cannot even occur in even the most benign socialist system, for it would deny collectivist firms their depreciation allowances. In our own economy, to cover employee compensation and depreciation magnitudes the markup would have to approximate 1.2.

But this would provide no margin for other legitimate business costs such as interest on borrowings, rents, property taxes, and sales taxes. Further, the market economy requires the lure of profits to entice production. The inference is that markups can at most be suppressed fractionally, after arduous and tumultuous efforts. The assist against inflation would be piddling so long as unit labor costs shoot ahead.

Moreover, when we ponder a mark-up cut, it also partakes of the nature of a "once-over" switch. When markups are urged to an irreducible minimum, surveillance of the money-wage-productivity nexus becomes even more germane in order to secure price stability, for mark-up dissents would be at an end.

Permanent insulation against inflation can thus hardly be achieved by an attack on markups. Implementing a strong assault would engender internecine economic warfare and widespread protests of excessive government zeal. After the acrimony and tumult ceased, the inflation

---

*This must not be interpreted to mean that I am pleased, or displeased, with the markup. As a consumer and salary earner, I would surely like it lower. The comments merely report the facts. It is too easy, in doing so, to be accused of "cheering them." If I report an illness or death, it cannot be interpreted as an approval of the fact.

ordeal would still be ongoing unless employee pay was tightly packaged to conform to productivity wraps.

REDISTRIBUTIVE POLICIES

Nevertheless, by antitrust policy, *something* can undoubtedly be done about markups, although probably on a limited scale. The ratio has been falling since 1950, albeit slowly: so far as the recent price binge goes, the mark-up decline since 1950 should have yielded a price-level slash of about 12 percent!

For those who are anxious to redistribute income from higher to lower income recipients, and if this is ever entertained seriously as a national policy in action which goes beyond rhetoric, it is likely to compel income shifts within the wage-salary sector, from the top of the employee heap to those down below. For in an economy where wage-salary income, and owners of Mom and Pop operations, amount to about 80 percent of the total, most of the yearning for a more equitable income division must come from a different apportionment of four-fifths of the economic pie.

Profits for non-financial corporations, after corporate taxes, set at about 8.6 percent of the net income total (1980 data). Before taxes they were about 13 percent.* The data suggest there is a limit in "profits" to divide in an enterprise economy. Viability of the market system would undoubtedly be threatened, and the system could come to a standstill.

As the general markup has held so firm over the last 80 years, it is unlikely to be altered swiftly by any new policies; the markup has held despite the introduction of the corporate income tax, the entry into the motorized age, the near trebling of population, two great world wars, the revolution in industrial technology and in communications, transportation, and in the ascending countervailing power of big labor, big business, and big government. Given this history we can surmise that the mark-up phenomenon will hold at roughly its present levels.

The greater wisdom, therefore, as against witless valor, is to stay reasonably reconciled with the facts, and to make at least uneasy peace with them. Ineluctably, then, money wage and productivity facts remain the two blades that hack the price level swath.

Chart 10.1 shows the mark-up course. From the evidence available, the ensuing profit margins cannot be assailed as *the* inflation maker. Since 1950—and earlier—the mark-up forces would have meant *falling* prices, with the tendency overcome by the mismatch of money wages and productivity. In the most recent years, despite the prominent profit orgy of oil companies, the mark-up path has mainly edged sidewise.

Economic Report (1981), p. 246.

CHART 10.1. Average Markup, 1950–1978

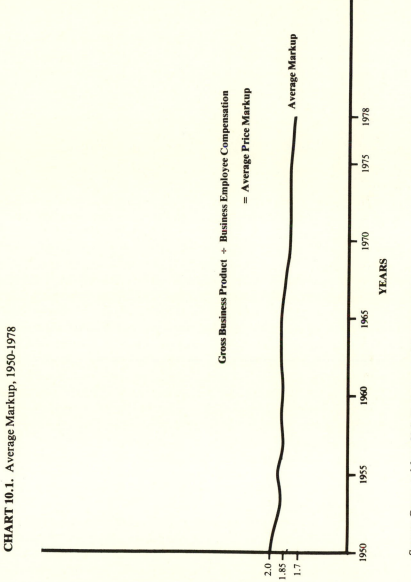

Gross Business Product ÷ Business Employee Compensation

= Average Price Markup

Average Markup

MARKUP (LOGARITHMIC SCALE)

2.0
1.85
1.7

1950 1955 1960 1965 1970 1975 1978

YEARS

Source: Computed from U.S. Department of Commerce Data

159

PART III

ENDING THE STAGFLATION MALAISE

Earlier chapters concentrated on the causes and pseudo-causes of inflation, emphasizing the misalignment of money incomes and real output, and especially recognizing that average labor productivity was being outpaced by the spurt in money wages and salaries.

It was also abundantly insisted that government budgets, OPEC oil, and overregulation were mainly small and temporary carriers of the price assault. In addition, Fed monetary policy was shown as unable to contain the inflationary disorder; instead, whenever it cracked the whip, its "cure" spelled unemployment. Yet it has been unable to block the price blitz while dumping us in the stagflation swamp.

There is then a critical policy gap involving a need for a direct mechanism to establish the pay-productivity alignment without the unemployment toll. Required is a method to gear money incomes to productivity in a manner that can be reconciled with the operations of the market economy. It can be done, and without a severe institutional wrench, by the adoption of TIP—a tax-based incomes policy.

Before describing TIP, the more commonplace price and wage controls invite an airing, with a ventilation of their shortcomings which dim their survival prospects in our enterprise economy. Controls may be described as a nuts-and-bolts approach to our problem: The approach concentrates on pieces of the picture to some neglect of the full panorama. It is as one with assessments, which emphasize farm prices, or food prices, or prices in certain industries, sectors, or firms. What we should seek, however, is a general principle covering phenomena affecting *all* prices. Pay increases constitute this broad gauge, for they simultaneously comprise most of cost and demand magnitudes.

11

PRICE AND WAGE CONTROLS: A DIM FUTURE IN A MARKET ECONOMY

Considering the oppressive burden of our stagflation malaise, there is an ever-ready chorus chanting an invocation for price and wage controls. Unfortunately, their adoption would not be an effective solution; they would inject a new set of problems, and we would hasten to dismantle them. Advocates have been deaf to a decade of technical discussion on more feasible alternatives. We can eradicate the inflation scourge, but controls are not the best design for a market economy.

We consider the case *against* controls. In doing so, it might be conceded that, lacking alternatives, controls might be adjudged superior to undiluted sadistic fiscal and monetary remedies. It is also possible to support controls for a brief interlude while we debate more feasible options which make only a modest institutional departure from our traditional market ways. That controls are endurable for a brief period is another way of stating that our economy can temporarily stand practically any impediment.

Though the categories are neither mutually exclusive nor exhaustive, we shall consider administrative, political, legal, bureaucratic, enforcement, and economic features of price and wage controls. Some may find the objections overdrawn. But as Harry Truman once said of his "give 'em hell" campaign oratory against the Republicans, he didn't have to lie about their record, for the truth was bad enough!

ADMINISTRATIVE AND POLITICAL ASPECTS

Administratively, there is first the need to organize the control agency, and to decide whether the price and wage boards should be centralized or separated. Because of the varied decision criteria, some severance is usually condoned, with the units wrapped together at the top for policy coordination. Quickly the nettlesome questions arise of whether dividends or profits should be policed, or whether rents should be included. Ultimately, the answers turn in the affirmative because of the political equity overtones in these matters.

Initially, and in incessant exacerbation, the organization of the agency comes under siege as disputes arise over "proper" representation of business, labor, consumer, agricultural interests—and with lobbies for farmers usually winning an exemption for farm prices. There is conflict over the political complexion of the agency, how the minority party and today, how political minorities should be represented. Should the governing policy group consist of 3, 5, 6, 7, 9 . . . members, terms of office, of reporting, executive and legislative oversight, and so forth. Should there be an ultimate price and wage czar, or are all board members separate and equal in vote and decision making?

Most of these newspaper issues are resolved, after early battles and bruised vanities. But they lend themselves to incessant bickering, with each disaffected group publicizing its outrage and grievance, and seeking some fancied advantage to protect or promote its interests. Spillover to the political area is guaranteed and furious displays of rhetoric are fascinating, often diverting attention from the serious purposes of the agency.

OF THEATRICAL CONFLICT IN IMPLEMENTATION

Manifestly, cost is entailed in creating still another regulatory agency with sweeping and exacting powers over the economy. Immediately, there is a scurrying for expert staff—where "victory" belongs to the quickest—to prepare informational memoranda, and specify options for the official hierarchy charged with governing the multitudinous prices and wages that comprise the economic network.

The larger mission will find that in the court of public opinion its fortunes will depend on whether its mandate is designed to *control* inflation, and thereby effectively to *sustain* it, or to *stop* it. To stop inflation requires income alignment with economy-wide productivity developments. Normally, as politically-oriented control boards function and have aims to survive—which can be better promoted by not affronting any major group in their public constituency—the tender temporizing is likely to lean to a "gradual" containment of inflation. Practically, this will mean approving wage scales to bring the price binge down from a previous 12 percent range to 10 and then 8 or 9 percent per annum. Thus the control board will invariably report slow progress, *and will mostly serve as an inflation vehicle*, not a stop mechanism. Timorous advisers abound to counsel this self-serving recipe as "economically reasonable policy." The argument, when dissected, is invariably to support a policy to ravage only those who have been ravished already by the inflation. Of course, the timid approach carries the euphemism of a gradual plan of "moderation." Memoranda, steeped in sophisms, will point to the "dislocations" if inflation is precipitously stopped.

Basic decisions are bound to provoke personal conflicts, which will be magnified in the press, as each participant jockeys for public support. Labor members will urge permissiveness in wages while pleading for rigid clamps on prices; others will advocate equally incompatible goals. Business leaders, for example, will adopt a contrary tack. Compromise is predictable, after headlines, huffiness, threats of walkouts by disaffected members, and political battles in Congress on behalf of affected constituencies.

In the torrent of words, new and novel only in the calendar dates of newspaper headlines and media frenzy, there will be predictable deflection from the original solitary and solidifying goal, namely, to *stop* inflation. For students of human drama there will be plenty of farce and posturing but for adherents who want to stop inflation, it will be a painful human comedy to witness.

THE HEADLINES CONTEST: TWO HUMAN LAWS

The contest for media attention is bound to be diverting, if sorrowful to observe, as board members, suddenly plucked from obscurity are pandered to by the media which thrive on human conflicts, especially over bread and butter issues whose essence is universally comprehensible. Phenomena which in themselves are inconsequential suddenly loom as portentous, as if civilization itself hangs in the balance. The public fanfare gives the participants in the debate an importance hardly transcended by the threat of nuclear warfare! A huge distraction is set in motion, with the human circus submerging from the truly novel, intricate, and serious issues of our age.

Implicit are two human laws: (1) Paltry issues edge out big ones. Everyone understands a rise in the price of bacon of 5 cents. Few of us can evaluate the merits of SALT, or the safety of nuclear power, or the need for a neutron bomb or cruise missiles. So, by virtue of our technical ignorance, and the equally uninformed media people preferring light fare, we debate the unimportant: the price of bacon, maraschino cherries, or flat toothpicks. A Gresham's Law of public discussion asserts itself: controvery over easy, unimportant matters drives out a focus on hard, important topics.

Then (2) members of the control commission smell political fame and personal fortune in their elevated status to public prominence. Promoting their own image by garnering media attention comes fast to most people. Key control board figures become disenchanted when a day passes without their name making page 1 news. Rather than viewing the mission as devoted to the untidy matter of curbing inflation, it becomes confused with an exaggerated politicizing of their personal accomplishments—or window-dressing their lack of major success by glorifying trivial actions by hyped press releases.

BUREAUCRATIZATION

In tiers below the upper-echelon mandarins charged with implementing the mission are the lower-level lackeys rendering logistical support. In the pecking order are: (1) upper-level advisers to polish the informational and position papers to brief the ruling hierarchy. If there are plural boards, as for wages and prices, dividends, rents, and so forth, duplication in eight versions, say, comes with the territory. Then there are (2) supporting specialist staffs concerned with specific industries or labor markets for "studies" meticulously destined mainly to fill file cabinets of their superiors; the "research" may occasionally be hastily consulted for generating informational tidbits in the event of emergency excitement. At work at the grindstone will be a secondary legion, accumulating outdated or incomplete data on industries or component firms.

Then there will be (3) the need for an army of "chicken" inspectors, or indispensable snoopers, to ferret out regulatory noncompliance. These posts will attract lower officious clerical police skills to report and summon violators of the agency directives. Hearing boards to weigh the snoopers' findings have to be organized.

Next come (4) the lawyers, or the ultimate and most sartorially elegant band in the army of enforcers. Among both enforcers and defense organizers, there are apt to be a preponderance of Captain Queeg mentalities, single-minded in tracking down the "missing plate of strawberries"; the heinous crime often consists of some tradesman selling a loaf of bread to a willing buyer at 67 cents rather than, say, an ordained 65 cents—and to a willing buyer!

Disdained is the fact that the transaction is consensual, and that the seller is unwilling, or finds it impossible, to sell at 65 cents, for to abide the lower price would entail loss and jeopardize business survival: breaking the bureaucratic directive is the dastardly crime, to be dealt with severely! Punishment must never fit the crime—Gilbert and Sullivan to the contrary, notwithstanding.

So we breed a new class of "criminals." Rather than laws to purge our system of consensual "crimes," the price directives enlarge them on a huge scale. The perversion of democratic government becomes the rule, and tyrannical methods ride high in the saddle as the bureaucratic mind observes the letter of the law while discarding the spirit of a free society.

Contemplating the Herculean nature of the task, probably no fewer than 100,000 bureaucrats, directly and indirectly, will be required as a not undue estimate for the control mission. To visualize the minutiae of the policing task, try to count the number of items in a supermarket, a department store, Sears Roebuck, or a hardware shop!

We have not even mentioned the arduous task of monitoring *quality* changes: is an auto with more plastics, or ashtrays, or air vents, the same as a prior model with more steel? Or is clothing having fewer buttons, less wool, and cheaper synthetics identical to the previous "style"? Prices which omit a quality stipulation are about equivalent to no price control at all. Shoddy and inferior materials substituted for quality merchandise play some hoax on the buyer confronted with "fixed" prices.

In any event, an agency with 100,000 employees at an average pay of $20,000 (excluding "fringes") entails some $2 billion. This makes no allowance for supplies, office space, telephones, necessary travel, and so on. Probably, with overhead, $5 billion would be a current realistic minimum bill for administering price and wage controls.

BUSINESS COSTS

This is to count only the obvious government costs, omitting legal costs such as work for an expanded judiciary and perhaps bailiffs and penal facilities. We leave this as too vague for conjecture at this time. But there are business compliance and reporting costs. To provide price and cost information to the control agency business firms will probably require specialized accounting personnel in the controlled firms. A *guess* might put the reporting costs at about one-fifth of the government toll. These must contribute to *raising* business costs and prices, and must be injected as part of the bill for price and wage controls.

Omitted so far are legal expenses, which can be enormous, considering the fancy fees of legal talent.

LEGAL HISTRIONICS

Price and wage controls erect, above all, a stage for lawyers to demonstrate forensic talents in defending price violators with a proclivity for diluting trivial issues with gravity and to display a formidable propensity for dilatory tactics. And the price comes high for the lavish legal fees come as costs to the business firm, to pass on ultimately to the consumer.

Obviously, constitutional infringements color almost any control legislation. Debatable points wend their way upward to Supreme Court adjudication. Even on lesser directives which escape hearing by the high court, controversy and quarrel over agency verdicts also carry a cost tag, not to mention fines, or over legal indictments for price violations. Delays will abound as lawyers plead for more time to prepare their case, and to muster their cast of competing "expert" witnesses. By the time a peremptory decision is rendered, many of the charges will be obsolete. Meanwhile, in booking the economic "crimes," court calendars will be clogged as judges assume the mantle as arbiters of economic "transgressions" by a new breed of consensual criminals whose offense stems from a willing buyer and a seller agreeing to violate an illogical directive.

How harsh can the penalties be? If they are criminal penalties, the jails are likely to overflow with a new "criminal" class. If the penalties are civil, pecuniary, they are bound to be insignificant to the large corporation, and oppressive to small businessmen. Happy resolution is likely to be rare.

To minimize court challenges, the control mechanism will have to be porous and lax, signifying some frivolity; the controls will lapse by mutual evasion. If they are Draconic, they are likely to arouse monumental protests, and become unpopular as the tangle becomes a legal nightmare. Apparently, there is always a generation gap on controls; each age turns to them; apparently each age must learn that the courtroom is not the proper place to arbitrate consensual transactions in each of which the national stake is apt to be quite nominal.

DELAY

Easily the most uneconomic aspect of courtroom hearings is that they promote inordinate delay in implementing an economic decision. If a firm feels it must charge higher prices or otherwise jeopardize its operation, delay enters at each phase, robbing buyer and seller of time and flexibility. There is the need to request approval by the control board, to await its invariable "study" and to endure its sonorous hearing, and then have it thrown into the courts if the agency verdict is negative. Entering the matter in a semi-judicial and then a courtroom squabble evades the necessary immediate economic resolution. The decision, to be meaningful to a firm, must be rendered almost immediately; it is in the nature of a legal test to stall and delay. Time, in these instances, is rightfully described as costly. A legal contest lacks the speed virtues of market resolution which inherently evokes mutual agreement. Judgment by directive, on the other hand, underwrites inflexibility and a dictatorial arbitrament.

ECONOMIC ASPECTS

The delay from phrasing to promulgating a legally binding directive is costly for the firms involved because the only meaningful directives are those which affect them adversely; directives which approve of what would be done anyway is a remarkably redundant control.

Decision-making authority becomes centered in a Washington bureaucracy, remote from *all* the facts, and away from firms intimately involved with the issue. As the game is played, firms become as helpless as fathers at birth in processes that concern them vitally, with their economic fortunes only partially protected by hearings—if these precede the directives—or by court appeals after the event. With economic power being preempted by the control agency, only by happenstance will it duplicate the unfettered decision of the firm; if it does so generally, the controls are superfluous indeed.

THE UNECONOMIC NATURE OF CONTROLS

Note that a price-control agency, which has an anti-inflation mission, operates by restraints on *individual* prices. To block a price-level escalation it inevitably interferes with *relative* price formation. It intends to control the totality but throws its wrench into the *relative* mechanism. Palpably it is capable of throwing interrelated parts out of kilter.

If cost and demand circumstances never changed—perhaps we could restore the Middle Ages—the invocation of controls might impel scant controversy: a "just price" society could be implemented. This wholly ignores the dynamics of the economy. Prices are a reasonably fast and flexible signal of a change in cost or demand conditions, and an impulse of dynamics signifying that past information about the market has become obsolete. In demand-oriented markets, as for raw materials and farm products, higher *relative* prices provide a cushion to slacken demand pressures, and thereby perform the dual function: (1) cutting back demand to match the limited supplies, averting rationing through coupons or queuing, as in totalitarian countries, and (2) signaling producers to expand production. Forestalling the higher price aborts the system by inhibiting the provision of supplies that are imminently called for by the market and are thus an uneconomic act.

In cost-oriented markets firms set prices according to movements in costs they face, for materials and for labor, and according to the dictates of the imperfectly competitive forces operating in the sector. The firm is in better command of the facts than a government agency remote from breaking events. Yet under price controls the firm is compelled either to secure approval before making a price move, or to appeal to a less-experienced judgment of a board of functionaries in lieu of expressing its own strategic plan.

It is in (1), where, at the going prices, demands exceed supplies, that black-market "under-the-counter" payments, or seller discrimination in disgorging goods only to favored buyers, arise. It is in this respect that disdain and disrespect for law is engendered. If law-abiding producers predominate, the economic system will report shortages, and unofficial queuing, and rationing with "lucky" buyers reselling at illegal prices. In this phase controls operate at their worst in frustrating efficiency.

When compliance becomes excessively costly, evasion of the regulations is likely to occur by firms willing to skirt the letter of the law. Quality deterioration will set in through shading previous content, with the violation discernible only to experts. Many of the switches can be subtle and defended as "normal" market practices "unrelated" to the regulatory zeal on pricing, as the substitution of a "bit" more vinyl for leather, or dispensing with a "few" hand stitches or buttons, or having a bit less steel in the car. How to prove that all these variations are cost saving corners rather than attuned to the market as legitimate or stylistic innovations? The alternative is to "freeze" styles and content. But this imposes an obviously unwholesome rigidity.

One can go on at length to analyze the uneconomic side of price controls. Enough has been said to indicate that when they are stringent enough to affect firms, formidable enforcement problems will ensue. They will become more costly to administer, incite acrimonious controversy, and impede the enterprise system by provoking political turmoil. On the other hand, we can be sure that if they operated smoothly without business protest and agitation they would be ineffective.

WAGE CONTROLS

Attempts to mandate gains in money wages are bound to evoke a new set of controversies. Just as with prices, after a control board announces a preconceived pay increase it will be bombarded with claims for exemptions. Insofar as the aim is to tolerate some price-level increase, the directive will stipulate, on average, that wage claims *transcend* the productivity norm. This will build inflation into the control mechanism, by administrative design.

For example, if the objective is to hold the price line to a 6 percent burst, and if productivity gains average out to 2 percent, then an annual wage increment of 8 percent can be a standard norm. Consistency and compatibility are prerequisite in setting price *and* pay scales. This, too, is likely to touch off harsh debate and cantankerous grandstanding by board members at the highest levels, and by their congressional allies. Selection of the norms possesses all of the ingredients of a drama for political aggrandizement.

Inherently, a pay board will be faced with three painful sources of contention which can jeopardize its functioning: (1) Claims for increases in pay beyond the *average* pay boost, on grounds of equity, by labor groups contending they were left behind in the pay scramble at the time when the regulations were instituted. This often justified plea will be hard to resist, especially on recognition of "princes and paupers" in the labor groupings where some sectors have been obvious laggards in the pay race.Unfortunately in this imperfect world, as one group's "equity" is another's "inequity," fair compromise is for another world.

Then (2) there will be industries with a need to attract workers for skilled, or arduous, or disagreeable tasks, or to relocate geographically. To resolve these questions is the very purpose of the price system and a flexible wage structure—exemptions will obviously be in order. How substantial should the discrepancies be? Whatever is done, after "study," hearings, and procrastination in decision making can snowball into new claims based on legal and philosophical purity but mostly exaggerated economic content.

And (3) there will be vocal protests to exempt executive personnel from the rules, because of greater individuality, differentiation, and status. This will be a frequent bone of contention, controversial beyond the numbers or skills involved, because of the articulate press releases that will be mounted, and the political ideology enlisted. Special pleas of the power elite will be hard to resist.

Firms will undoubtedly curtsy to the letter of the law adopted on executive pay while they circumvent the intent. Evasion will come by enlarging noncash perquisites, making them more commonplace in the pay bargain. Trips, entertainment, vacations, cars, can all be cited.

STRIKES?

Strikes for pay transcending some general norm would surely occur: a walk-out took place by John Lewis's "coal miners" even in the midst of

World War II. The pay board would thus have to resolve its attitude toward strikes, whether it would cave in and abrogate its pay rules, or adhere to them. Either way, the economic process would end up being more politicized, with crushing pressures to "do something," and then finding that however it intervened—or abstained—about half of the electorate would be alienated. A small storm could quickly blow into a hurricane, especially when issues are fairly simple and clear and able to arouse a hard stand in public opinion. Strikes might become rife if the control board is perceived as vulnerable to pressure.

CONTROLS: A TEMPORARY EXPEDIENT AND A PERMANENT SORE

The best case for controls is for use as a *temporary* expedient, either to stop a rampant inflation or to calm the economy while other measures are being debated. For a brief period they have merit; for a longer time they are a dubious venture, and very unlikely to endure as they accumulate a variety of barnacles incompatible with our enterprise economy. They expose too clearly the exercise of a noxious and inflexible bureaucratic power. On the best face, if they succeed quickly there will be agitation that they are superfluous, and their very success will stir a clamor for their dismantlement, thereby to prepare the stage for the next round in the inflation orgy. Because our problem is persistent, they offer little promise for permanent relief.

Controls operate through political denunciation, harassment, civil and criminal penalties, and general interference in private contractual price, purchase, or hire agreements. They do not set general rules under which the economic play runs, but instead enter unwisely into details in the vital matters of price, quality of output, or rates of pay. In insisting on poking into these matters there is a rigidity in action in situations where there is the need for flexibility to roll with the complexities of the market, and to resolve the numerous contingencies occasioned by the diversity of trans-actions. Decisions resemble too much the centralized systems of collectivist governments, and they allow too little scope for compromise by the interplay of self-interests. Controls impose solutions that appeal to mandated rules which may not accord with market interests; the directives may satisfy a bureaucratic eccentricity inconsistent with designs of people animated by utterly independent motives.

However much we fault privately administered, oligopoly, monopoly, or rigid prices in the marketplace, the *un*regulated outcome is apt to be a model of discretion, sensitivity, and alacrity compared to the directives of most any control board. Involved are the old conundrums of private property versus socialism, centralization versus decentralized economies. In the United States the verdict was rendered long ago, and it has been reenforced overwhelmingly for decentralized decision making, with respect for individuality and even a quest for frivolous originality being venerable economic traits. So be it. In this environment, price and wage controls will always be an anachronism. To adopt them would ensure only a short-lived career.

SOCIALISM?

Many will find this assessment unpersuasive. They want the private property and socialism issues contested, and the pros and cons of centralized and decentralized decision making staked out once more, and evaluated. To do so would require a far different kind of book, and a wholly separate analysis. In the end, however, ideology and judgment will determine perspective. Reasonableness and candor also suggest that it is impossible to render a judgment to fit all times and places.

For our country today the debate is a vast sideshow. Our issue is *inflation*, and how to *stop* it. For those who want to reshape our system, a stronger case can be made for controls to entrench power in Washington. But this kind of ramble deflects our concern with stopping inflation to one of reconstructing our economic system. It is thus a gigantic digression reserved mainly for intellectuals and designed to provoke an ideological battle in which only the citizen, with perhaps impeccable curiosity in never-never economics, is totally interested. In the irrelevant diversion, our inflation ordeal is likely to be overlooked.

To eradicate inflation *within our market framework* we must seek a method that is compatible with the enterprise system, and harmonious with our traditions of freedom. Price and wage controls conflict with these principles, and they are not likely to be countenanced by the market economy except in an emergency as a temporary stopgap.

RELATIVE PRICES AND THE PRICE LEVEL

Inflation represents the up-tick of *all* prices on average. Some may hold firm, others go down, some go up by 2 percent, others explode by 20 percent. The price index records the *average* upswing. *Relative* prices, however, obviously vary under inflation: not all prices show the same percentage movement. It is the *relative* price moves that signal particular demand and cost pressures.

Controls, as is implicit in all these pages, are, by definition, concerned with *individual* prices—they focus on the links in the price chain rather than the swelling of the whole chain itself.

It is this fascination with price links rather than with the whole average bloat that imparts a distorted perspective to price controls. We want the *relative* price system to operate; it is the absolute swell that we want to stop. By concentrating on individual links, price controls start from a wrong premise and end up in imposing an obnoxious and most dispensable heavy bureaucratic hand in combating inflation.

Controls are concerned with inflation parts rather than the whole problem. The perturbing and deranging aspects should be borne in mind as we proceed to outline TIP.

12

TIP As An Inflation Suppressant

Recoiling from price and wage controls as impairing choice, conciliation, and freedom, and moving the economy closer to centralized intervention than public opinion is likely to tolerate, it behooves us to seek another way out of our inflation impasse.* The method must be compatible with our enterprise system, infringing on it at most only peripherally.

It happens that there are ways to rehabilitate the economy, and protect it from the stagflation rot, with only nominal modifications in ongoing producing, hiring, and transactions decisions. Entailed would be an innovative harmonious twist in our corporate tax structure.

TAXES AS INCENTIVES AND DETERRENTS

Essentially, there are just two ways of accomplishing all the indispensable and disagreeable tasks that must be performed to get goods and services to the consumer; their application, to make the work lot more tolerable, borders almost on getting us to laugh through our tears. The two methods are: (1) coercive techniques and (2) economic incentive and deterrent methods. The shopworn metaphor invokes the image of the "carrot and the stick."

*Aside from the original TIP proposal by Wallich-Weintraub, important contributions to this discussion come from the works of the late Arthur Okun, James Tobin, A. P. Lerner, David Colander, and particularly Laurence Seidman.

Coercion marks the prison system, or the army, or a totalitarian regime, or feudalism. In each instance, with varying mixtures of sadism and sympathy, people are commanded to do a task, "or else"—with the alternative being a more dire fate. Penalties are bestowed by the warden, or overseer, with each authoritarian layer occupying a vulnerable place on the ladder subject to the dictates of upper echelons of the hierarchical structure.

It is just such arbitrary abuse of physical power and tyrannical subjugation of humans that our consensual market system averts. Thus in the evolutionary march to a freer and fairer way, discarding the divine right of kings which has been replaced in totalitarian regimes by a divine self-perpetuating elite, market exchange has developed. As Adam Smith long ago observed, its stimuli reside in the play of self-interest. "It is not to the benevolence of the butcher, the baker, the brewer that we look for our evening meal; it is to their self-interest." It is a complex game in which "you do this for me, and I do that for you." Give me a sum of money so that I can buy something I want, and I will hand over the goods or service you want.

Our economy thus operates through the lure of pecuniary incentives, or deterrents, rather than by physical coercion and some begrudging reward, as to a slave or prisoner. Incentives and deterrents are inherent in the price system. Producers, as businessmen, compare prices to unit costs. Insofar as the ratios are favorable, they will exercise labor hire decisions, produce, and contract for the sale of goods. Unfavorable price-cost ratios will lead to withdrawal from production.

Price-cost ratios are thus the "carrots and sticks" that drive our economy; they are the prizes held out in the market game, and quantify the victories achieved; losses are the defeats that stigmatize failures. In other terms, the market condones a search for profitable ventures and conditions an aversion to projects that promise losses.

CORPORATE TAXES: AN INCENTIVE-DETERRENT MECHANISM

The corporate income tax—and the personal income tax to a lesser degree—exemplify the incentive-deterrent mechanism. For example, in promoting the Kemp-Roth bill adapted by President Reagan, its sponsors stress the *incentive* aspects of a corporate tax reduction; presumably, high tax rates discourage plant modernization programs so lower tax rates are advocated. Also, accelerated depreciation provisions are pushed to permit, say, a firm to write off the capital cost of equipment in five years rather than ten, and thereby to make the initial investment recovery tax-free, in half the time.

The point need not be labored: as tax aspects bulk large, business firms today scarcely take an innovative step involving huge investment sums without consulting their tax advisers. They well appreciate the incentive-deterrent aspect of taxes.

A CHANGED CONCEPTION OF THE TAX SYSTEM

Although the profundity is lost on the authors, the Kemp-Roth bill reveals a "revolution" in the thinking of the Republican party. The bill framers will be amazed to see their handiwork defined in these "radical" terms.

Once upon a time, a balanced budget was the solitary objective of "prudent" fiscal policy. In an earlier age it would even have been thought that government should first seek to collect "frugal" revenues, and then spend them parsimoniously, with the revenue side carrying top priority. Later, there came the recognition that there could first be borrowing, and thereafter expenditure, with taxes levied on the higher income that would evolve. With the taxes, the prior loan finance could be repaid. Thus a balanced budget could be obtained, although the sequence of events would be reversed: governments would first decide on their expenditures, and then proceed to collect the revenues. Rather than cut the size to the cloth, the size would determine the amount of cloth to be acquired.

With the advent of Keynes and the impact of his work in the 1930s, it was discerned more widely that the balanced budget dogma was obsolete* and that, by taxing less and spending more, governments could contribute to an upswing in jobs and production. By switching the process, they could put a lid on an economy steaming too fast. The ideas were widely embraced, with even Richard Nixon in 1973 declaring "he was a Keynesian now," when he embarked on fiscal stimulation on these lines. Eisenhower had also adopted the precepts. Keynes' fiscal doctrines, it is correct to note, had supplanted an earlier thought of a budget that was intended to be balanced over the longer term of a business cycle, where surpluses in prosperity counterbalanced deficits in recession and depression phases. (The latter, a balanced budget precept, rejected the fiscal year as the appropriate time span.)

Logic compels that we progress to consider taxes not only as a mode of amassing revenues, but to assist in imparting ample incentives and deter-

---

*Lest this view appear shocking and heretical, it is even embraced, for example, by the very conservative Milton Friedman. See his "Deficits and Inflation," *Newsweek* (February 23, 1981), p. 70.

rents to economic conduct. Government revenues and expenditures constitute gigantic levers to nudge the economy in desirable directions, and to deflect it from objectionable orbits. "Steering" is a proper function of sound social policy, and the tools to do the job adhere in the tax and expenditure mechanism, with their incentive-deterrent features. In his own way, President Reagan *has* adopted this proposition implicitly while denouncing it explicitly.*

This is a fundamental doctrine that we must learn to implement consciously. Actually, governments have always acted on the premise, albeit in limited fashion, in imposing sumptuary taxes to discourage the consumption of whiskey or alcoholic beverages generally, or in imposing heavy cigarette taxes to make smoking more prohibitive, or in levying exorbitant gasoline taxes whereby European countries seek to discourage oil imports. Subsidies operate the other way.

The principle is unexceptionable. The tax mechanism can surely be enlisted as a weapon to thwart inflation. What must dominate our thought is to treat our tax system as a fiscal lever devoted to induce socially desirable price-level behavior and to face up to its corollary, to deter unsavory behavior.

TIP: A TAX-BASED INCOMES POLICY

This is the philosophic genesis of TIP, an acronym for a tax-based incomes policy.** Analytically, TIP applies the underlying principle of income gearing, intending the alignment of *average* rates of pay increase to the annual average economy-wide rate of productivity increment.

THE TIP PROPOSAL

Briefly, TIP contemplates levying an extra corporate income tax on firms who raise their average pay scales by more than, say, 5 percent per annum. To defeat inflation, the stipulated norm would probably, in 1979 or 1980, have had to be in the neighborhood of nil, or 1 or 2 percent per annum pay boosts; nonetheless, for illustrative purposes the 5 percent figure is retained in the following elaboration.

With the current corporate income tax levy approximately 45 percent, TIP would impose, say, an extra 3 to 5 percent tax onus on firms which

*See my article on "The Reagan Regress," *New Leader*, March 9, 1981.

**TIP is also known as the Wallich-Weintraub TIP, for it was developed by the present author in collaboration with Dr. Henry Wallich, then a Yale professor and now a Federal Reserve Board Governor. See my *Capitalism's Inflation and Unemployment Crisis* (Reading, Mass.: Addison Wesley, 1978). Also for the original articles, see my *Keynes, Keynesians, and Monetarists* (Philadelphia, University of Pennsylvania Press, 1978).

puncture the norm by lifting their *average* pay scale (including managerial and executive incomes) above 5 percent. The extra tax bite can be made progressive, with a moderate penalty for minor transgressions, say, a pay hike over 5 but under 7 percent, and an extra penalty thereafter to a ceiling of perhaps 10 percent.

The calculations for the firm would be elementary. Suppose TIP was adopted in 1982. From its corporate income tax form, the firm (or accounting unit) would have to list:

1. total wages and salaries for 1981, from its corporate tax form,
2. total number of employees (from social security or W-2 forms), and
3. divide (1) by (2) to compute the average pay level.

Then, for 1982:

4. total wages and salaries for 1982,
5. total number of employees, and
6. divide, to derive the average pay level.

Finally, (7) if the *average* pay increase in 1982 exceeded 5 percent, the firm would be subject to the stipulated tax penalty. Otherwise, the firm would be unaffected. (A bonus 2 percent—a very limited incentive— could be attached for compliance or for average pay hikes of not less than 3 and not more than 5 percent.)

This is the essence of the TIP proposal. The computations are elementary and they do not cause any undue filing complexity. Just 7 extra lines on the corporate income tax form are required, perhaps listed on a separate page for easy auditing review.

TIP LIMITATIONS AND SUPPLEMENTS

The TIP penalty would not have to be directed at each and every firm. Limiting TIP to the 1,000 largest corporations, measured in terms of total sales or total employment, would encompass about 55 percent (or a bit more) of gross business product output. Extending coverage to about 2,500 firms, the sweep would hit about 85 percent of business output.

Thus TIP would involve about 2,500 firms, and affect large-scale firms employing upward of 25,000 employees. Also, TIP does *not* fix the wages and salaries of each and every employee, or restrict their pay boost to 5 percent. Many individuals could get increases well in excess of 5 percent, though others would then have to abide less, or expose the firm to an extra tax bite.

Some analysts may want to widen the net, say to firms employing 10,000 employees, or in an alternate definition, firms with annual sales of $200,000,000 or more. On some legislative designs the latter figure may be dropped as "low" as $50 or $25 million. (My own preference would be to cover only 2,500 firms, and to resist a larger control net.)

Gearing the average pay increment to productivity in the largest firms would block out the general pattern for pay boosts through the economy. There is no need to extend TIP to small shops and firms which act, not as wage pace setters, but followers in pay scales once the big bargaining negotiations are completed in industries dominated by big business.

TIP SUPPLEMENTS

Suppose TIP was adopted, and firms sought to hold to a 5 percent annual pay increment, and this was roundly rejected by unions. Suppose unions walked out, to strike the plants. Conceivably, the firm would have to submit or face bankruptcy because of the cessation of its cash flow. A firm in this position would seem to be a victim of double damnation, namely, either going bankrupt or submitting to the union and puncturing the norm, and paying higher taxes to boot.

To protect firms bargaining in good faith, and obeying the noninflation mandate, it should be possible to institute government loan guarantees to ensure the firm of enough loan finance to meet fixed charges to avoid insolvency. Manifestly, the provision would have to be hedged to prevent collusion between union and firm abusing the law. But finance availability to the largest firms would serve ample notice on the unions that they are not dealing with a weakened firm on the verge of collapse and compelled to yield to a strike threat.

TIP could also be supplemented so that National Labor Relations Board certification is withdrawn from any union which strikes despite an offer by firms of a pay advance within the 5 percent guideline. This would place some "ceiling" on firms with which labor bargains, and it would curb intemperate strikes where union conduct was conducive to inflation, and thus uneconomic and antisocial. In states which grant food stamps or unemployment compensation to strikers, this government largesse which underwrites strike action could be halted.

In melioration, these last provisions could be relaxed in cases where unions could prove that their membership pay scale, on average, was 20 percent or more *below* other industries. This would counter criticism on the score of inequities, and of manifest pay discrepancies between business sectors. For these cases, the norm might be relaxed by *no more than* 1 or 2 percent per annum. It is impossible to correct all historical inequities in one swoop without rearing a new wave of discriminatory instances.

Others may devise better TIP supplements to enforce its implementation. The basic TIP is amply flexible in allowing a multitude of supporting measures to render its main ingredients effective.

TIP AND A CORPORATE TAX CUT

Superficially, TIP injects a tax penalty on firms. This misinterprets its purpose: its objective is *not* to collect taxes, but to deter uneconomic conduct. If its invocation collects important sums, it would be judged an abysmal failure.

A good analogy compares TIP to a posted city speed limit, where local ordinances confine autos, say, to 35 miles per hour. The purpose is to stop suicidal road conduct, especially driving which menaces the life and limbs of others. If substantial revenue is collected, it is evidence that the speed ordinance is being roundly violated and failing in its purpose. Ideal enforcement would occur where a watchful patrol detected absolutely no speeders and no fines flowed into the town's coffers.

Ideal TIP observance would likewise yield no revenue. Any revenue collected would attest to some breakdown in the program. If a huge amount of revenue was collected, TIP would deserve instant revocation and interment for its inadequacy as an inflation deterrent. It is not, to reiterate, a revenue measure. A speed limit which seeks to collect spectacular revenues should post a 1 or 2 mph maximum in order to trap everybody as a speeder!

Nonetheless, despite the best of legislative intentions, TIP is likely to amass *some* revenue. To offset it, the normal 45 percent corporate tax rate can be precipitately cut—say, to 40 or 42 percent—so that the total corporate tax take remained constant. Nobody could then allege, with any veracity, that TIP would "erode"—in the cliché of financial journalism—corporate venture capital. It would not.

Enactment of TIP could carry even a deeper cut in the corporate income tax. For as TIP succeeded in downing the inflation rate, the Federal Reserve Board could make use of its instruments of monetary policy toward fostering jobs, especially through lower mortgage interest rates, thereby facilitating housing starts and business investment. The "multiplier" effects would carry GNP higher and then, through the increasing Treasury tax revenues, lower unemployment payments and rising personal and corporate income tax collections, the outcome would warrant substantial tax cuts. The federal budget could even be trimmed to a balance.

Corporate venture capital would be enhanced under TIP, and Fed monetary policy would be free to work for full employment. Our industry and economy would be the beneficiary. Growth would be fostered.

CHANGING THE TAX BASE

Implicitly, the last remarks reveal the real nature of TIP; it is *not* a tax measure, though it is designed to alter the base on which the corporate tax is computed. A lower tax rate would be imposed to stand as a corporate income tax, and a *possible*, or *potential* surtax would be levied on the average pay position, depending on the degree to which firms guided their corporate affairs to establish a less inflationary climate. Philosophically, the corporate income tax is levied for its revenue potential. TIP would be imposed in the ardent hope that its yield would be nil. Objectives are diametrically opposite.

UNION AND BUSINESS BARGAINING BEHAVIOR

TIP would undoubtedly affect bargaining postures and strategy. But any grievance that may be conjured is more fancied than real. *Some* change in methods, tactics, or settlement size is incumbent if the market economy is to escape from the strains that have trapped it in the anguish of inflation and the frustrations of unemployment.

BUSINESS BARGAINING

Business firms would apprehend quickly the need for restraint in their pay awards to a 5 percent formula, if this figure were established as the norm. Presently, an obvious reason prevails for grants in the 10 percent range; firms expect that their competitors will make the concession so they tend to acquiesce early, rather than to evoke a costly strike which will carry ultimate submission, irreparable ill-will, and higher prices under the new cost structure.

Under TIP, firms will expect other firms to settle in the 5 percent range under penalty of higher operating costs *and* a higher tax bracket. Thus each firm's mutual reenforcing conduct will be such as to condone the 5 percent framework. Too, with supplements to sustain TIP, firms can be confident that their chances of winning the 5 percent settlement in any strike are vastly improved. The norm could be generally realized.

UNION STRATEGY: PUNCTURING THE AVERAGE

Rationally, countries do not go to war unless there is a chance to win. Likewise, unions would be irrational to strike unless their victory holds good prospects of success, despite cases where membership anger compels symbolic walkouts whose outcome is doomed. Apart from such pathological cases where nothing very sensible can be said, unions will perceive that they cannot push an exaggerated bargaining posture beyond a 5 percent norm.

Actually, they *can* acquire more, perhaps carve out a 6 or 7 percent gain. But if this award is granted, and the firms want to check their tax impost, the firms will have to hold clerical, managerial, and executive pay increases below 5 percent in order to keep the *average* pay hike at the norm.

Collective bargaining could then be directed into a more fitting groove, namely, as a dispute over *relative* income positions. As matters stand now, unions win 10 percent more, and the same "victory" is quickly transmitted to nonunionized, and executive and managerial employees. As the pay gains become universal, the income shares or relative income distribution remain nearly frozen, while the pay "gain" erupts in inflationary smoke with the imbalances between groups perpetuated.

Unions could do much to make bargaining a true dispute over *relative* incomes under TIP. And this is a more rational objective than the current practice of collective bargaining acting as a spear carrier mainly for inflation.

UNION LIMITATIONS?

TIP does mandate some restraint on bargaining for pay gains (which also include fringe benefits). Manifestly, it implies some infringement on labor and management conduct. Beyond the (slightly) inflexible ceiling, all would be as before in negotiating concerns with work conditions, seniority, and other grievances. No limitation on the rights of association, or the right to present a united front to employers on other issues, is contemplated. Accusations of a restoration of "sweatshop" conditions, or the inhumane conditions which gave too much validity to the protests of the early socialists in capitalism's embryonic days, and imparted credibility to the denunciations of Karl Marx in his condemnation of the conditions of 150 years back, would fall wide of the mark; the demogoguery would be perceived as a rhetorical distortion in attacking TIP.

Unions are already subject to restraints, on the number of marching pickets, on secondary picketing and boycotting, on criminal trespass, and violent behavior. TIP would impose a new limitation adopted in the social interest, and certainly a restraint for forging *labor* benefits. For on a successful TIP—and if it does restrain money income it will be successful —we would be relieved of inflation, and all that it portends, while the economy could run a full employment track, with jobs for all. Pension rights would be insulated from the ravages of inflation, and a better start could be made at ironing out the gross disparities in income distribution.

Only the most powerful unions could protest the result. For the "princes" of the labor movement, as in construction, trucking, steel, autos, have often held the economy at ransom, fueling inflation and fostering unemployment. TIP would inject more equity into labor practices as it focused collective bargaining disputes not on *absolute* pay hikes which become generalized, and thus inflationary, but turned the focus to shape opinion on *relative* income shares.

UNION BARGAINING MYOPIA

Even without TIP it is possible to indict union bargaining practices today as an exercise in myopia which succeeds mainly in achieving illusory gains—except at the expense of other union members or nonunionized workers.

Consider the typical collective bargaining routine. After the usual drawing of hard lines, and public posturing by unions and management, a settlement is ultimately reached. Suppose it is seen as a good settlement by the union, say a 12 percent pay boost carved out for its members. Pursue the development after the announcement, jubilation, and glee at the "victory."

Quickly, it is a Pyrrhic triumph as other workers at the particular plant or industry obtain much the same *percentage* hike. That is, if the average union production-line employees go up from $15,000 to $16,500, the same type of increment will extend, before long, to the clerical staff. Supervisors and managerial people earning $35,000 will poke through to about $40,000, and executives in the $200,000 range, moaning over their "obligations," will scoot up to $250,000. At the end of it, the *relative* position of the union people will show scant improvement, or even deterioration. Apparently, though data are hard to come by, it seems that while union pay scales in recent years have been spurting ahead by about 10 percent, executive pay has been surging forward by closer to 17 percent. And the list of perquisites is pyramiding.

TIP would be far more equitable. As it aims at the *average* pay hike within firms, it is doubtful that firms could practice topside discrimination whereby upper echelon pay gains vastly outstrip incomes at the lower end of the scale.

EROSION IN INFLATION SMOKE

The blurred vision inherent in contemporary union bargaining practices arises at the next step: not only do all other employees in the firm or industry share the gains, and stay the union relative income standing, but the firms affected by the higher wage cost hike their prices. The pay-price spiral erupts in earnest.

At work then is a multistep ladder, with each group climbing and shoving prices up at the last step. As prices rise in the industry, say in autos, then part of the union gains are whittled away as its members buy cars. Ordinarily, employees in any one industry spend only a small fraction of their income to buy the goods they help make, so that only a mite of their real income is immediately bartered away. But the price facts impair the real income of all other workers, or employees in other industries. Thereafter, as the same process unwinds in other negotiations, the price perturbations in steel, transport, retail shops, or electrical supplies, and so on constitute a general price-level upheaval, or a wave more or less synchronized as all firms and all industries act in imperfect unison to protect their profit margins and fortify their exposed cost flanks.

THE PROFIT MARGIN MYOPIA

Unions can thus be faulted for ignoring the full ramifications of their "victories" on only squeezing profit margins temporarily before their pay gains erupt in higher prices. The more the unions report spectacular success in the size of pay gains, the more absurd the pattern becomes as prices rise when firms reply in lock-step to revive their profit margins. Inevitably, the pay escalation is thereupon dissipated in an inflation fire. Flares occur in industries vulnerable to pay grabs, with their protective price action implying a nibbling away of the pay gain. As the pay pattern fans out to other firms and industries, everyone is affected by the inflation. Workers originally pleased over their pay "gains" find the advantage short-lived, and always below what they anticipated. The more devastating real income loss is suffered by workers whose pay gains are slower, and who eke out less than the average gain, and thus fall below the average price rise.

Even apart from TIP unions must learn to cope with spiraling prices in firms with which they make their pay agreements: unions have been badly derelict in this respect. Moreover, to improve their *relative* income position—which is what really counts—they will have to do something to erect roadblocks in pay hikes of upper-income echelons who garner far greater absolute—and relative—income leaps in a mismatch of pay jumps for union employees.

TIP would contribute something to a resolution of the latter phenomenon, which entails nothing short of correcting the *relative* income scale. By maintaining a stable price level, TIP would ensure that pay gains are not aborted in inflation, disappointing the sanguine expectations after a successful bargaining outcome. A 5 percent money income gain would translate into a 5 percent real income gain, and not into something less. Presently, even a 10 percent money income "victory" terminates in a nil, or a 1 or 2 percent real improvement, while it wreaks stagflation havoc on the economy.

TIP-CAP

The TIP proposal revolves about aligning pay increases to *economy-wide* productivity improvements. Historically, as noted several times, the technical advances have been of the order of 2 to 3 percent per annum—say 2.5 percent. In the 1970s they were a meager 1 percent, and *negative* in 1974, 1979, and 1980.

Some may see the TIP norm as distinctly unfair and insist instead that pay increases be geared to the productivity enhancement *within the firm*, in order to provide a direct incentive to improve efficiency and to remunerate employees in firms displaying stellar feats. Adopting an in-firm approach would be an egregious error which would institutionalize discriminatory pay scales of epic proportions. A simple illustration can make the point.

Suppose there are twin brothers, perfectly alike in terms of ability, according to all available measures. One, say, gets a job in the local garage pumping gas, and the other secures work at the local airport, pumping gas into airplanes. Initially, each is hired at $200 per week. Suppose productivity generally improves by 10 percent per annum at the airport. Suppose it is at a standstill at the local garage. After six years, because of new handling equipment, the airport employee's pay will jump to about $400, while the garage pay will remain at $200! In another six years, $800 for one and $200 for the other. Exactly quadruple pay will go for identical work and skill. Discrimination will be rife.

In essentials, this would occur if pay is geared to industry or firm productivity, rather than to economy-wide performance. Rationally, in industries which show above-average productivity gains, unit costs will fall and prices should *decrease*. In firms where productivity lags, unit costs and prices should *rise*. This is how an optimal price order would behave, for, in an above average productivity situation, technology is rendering the product easier to produce, so more of it can be made available to consumers. Price should be lowered, to encourage larger market purchase. Where productivity lapses, or advances slowly, we are being signalled that these products have become *relatively* harder to produce; their prices should reflect the relative obstacles to production: prices should advance.

Thus *economy-wide* productivity is the right criterion for determining *average* pay increases. This would sustain an optimal price performance. Policy should be designed to facilitate the right price signals, and not to impede them. Economy would be impaired if every time there was a superior productivity performance as a result of technology, money wages rose to maintain unit costs constant: the cost-push would impede a price fall, and retard technological abundance. More limited productivity concepts would yield discriminatory pay and deny us the virtues of technological triumphs.

TIP-CAP

Some gesture could be made to superior productivity drives within the firm through a mild variant of TIP. For example, if the economy-wide productivity enhancement touched 3 percent, for a firm which reported a 9 percent vault in average output, some part of the 3 and 9 differential, maybe one-third, might be granted as an extra pay bonus in computing the pay norm for that firm. Thus, if the stipulated figure for pay hikes was 5 percent, another 3 percent could be tacked on, to achieve average pay increases of 8 percent without any TIP penalty. The "extra" would reward superior achievment.

To qualify for the "bonus" a firm would have to compute its average sales, or output, per employee for, say 1981, and then for 1982. To ensure that the gain reflected productivity and not merely inflation, the figures for 1982 would have to be corrected for prices. Then, if the economy-wide improvement implicit in the 5 percent pay norm was 3 percent, the firm might enter one-third of its extra productivity increase as a bonus in computing its pay norm before being subject to TIP penalties.

The complexity is a minor one; all that is required is to divide the total output value, or sales, by the number of employees. Thereafter, to correct for inflation, an index of prices is applied. The result is a corrected average product—CAP, to implement a TIP-CAP program.

By this device the general objective of TIP could be preserved, along with a special bonus incentive to stimulate productivity. If only about 2,500 firms are involved, the accounting aspects are not formidable, despite this attempt to transmit simple calculations verbally. The computation hardly transcends grade school arithmetic.

DUBIOUS ECONOMIC OBJECTIONS

Two fairly shallow objections to TIP have surfaced so far, both of which misconstrue the proposal. Of course, there are objections from those who oppose any new idea in defending monetary and fiscal policy despite their stagflation havoc for over a decade. Many of the critics are on record as against the 20th century, even though we stand on the threshold of the 21st.

A superficial view is that TIP imposes a "unique" and solitary pay increase that cannot work in the diverse circumstances of American industry. This is a monstrous blatant confusion even when uttered in high quarters. Surely, fixing a norm of, say 5 percent, is scarcely the same as fixing an *absolute* pay increase. A 5 percent increase on $100 is $5, on $200 it is $10, and so on. This criticism is bewildering in betraying innocence of elementary-grade school arithmetic.

Above all, as TIP or TIP-CAP is confined to the largest firms there is absolutely *no* attempt made, despite rambling professions to the contrary, to fix the absolute (or even the percentage) increase for *any* employee, or for *any group* of employees. The object of TIP is to deal with the *average* percentage movement, or the pay pace of the entire bloc of employees, not with any individual runner in the pack. The merit of TIP is that it allows flexibility, rather than mandating what any individual or group is to earn. It is a hoax to charge TIP with fixing individual pay when its entire emphasis is on a very broad *average* gain in very large firms.

Can dissenters from TIP who use this line of argument contend that it is possible to raise *all* pay scales by more than the productivity increment, and still stabilize the price level? If they know how, they should specify how it can come about, to enlighten all of us, rather than hide behind the skirts of an illogical objection. True, there can be a modest shift from profit margins, but this can be only meager indeed, and can at most be a temporary palliative. The objection can thus be put aside, for it reveals arithmetical deficiencies and a misapprehension in thought.

MORE SERIOUS OBJECTIONS

More serious is the following contention. Suppose a firm inflates its executives' pay, say, from an average of $500,000 to $1,000,000. Not able to depress the norm of 5 percent offered to lower-level employees, and wanting to escape the extra TIP penalty, presumably it will hire a lot of low-skilled, low-priced labor to evade the surtax by clipping its average pay level.

To this, two points in rebuttal may be made. First, during periods of high unemployment such "excess labor hire" is not entirely wasteful, perhaps less so than the waste in unemployment; the social cost of the "excess" hire is reduced by the decline in unemployment compensation. In a deep depression such as the one in the 1930s, the result might even have some unsuspected economic virtue.

Analytically, going beyond this casual defense of "uneconomic hire," it follows that any firm pursuing the policy would be irrationally myopic. For in subsequent years, when executive pay is not the object of corporate largesse, the firm would be the victim of higher labor costs, and lower profits. If it dismissed the excess labor, it would have to face a TIP penalty.

In long-run profit maximization precepts, therefore, the prospect of excess labor hire of the lowest skilled ranks to evade the tax becomes a less promising escape route.* Even if something of the sort happens it is unlikely to bulk large in the macro-economy. Any irrationalities through this channel, measured against the costs of inflation and the $50 to $200 billion per annum real loss in GNP through unemployment, must count as minor. Too often, those who make this mythical argument assume that we have an economy which automatically grinds out full employment, with optimal resource allocation; thereafter the TIP opponents adjudge any preferred proposal by comparing it to an optimal stagflation-free economy rather than to the actual economy in which we live. Policies judged weak by the one test can become very commendable on a more realistic comparison.

A far more serious contention is that TIP would impede capital formation intended to uplift technology through the complementary hire of more skilled employees. For example, a firm may contemplate replacing its billing clerks, payroll people, and filing personnel by computer specialists, engaging one $20,000 employee, say, to supplant three $10,000 people.

Some might profess that the retardation of technological unemployment would alone *commend* TIP. But this limitation can be rejected; if seriously entertained it would consign our people to lower living standards than those attainable with technological advance.

The argument is flawed, however; any capital retardation is likely to be minor, almost trivial. At most, only in the *first* year of the innovation will the firm be subject to the penalty tax imposed by TIP. Thereafter, once the more skilled staff is in place, the same large-size pay jumps would not be imminent.

Yet even this concession to the argument is superfluous inasmuch as TIP is confined in application to only the very largest firms, with employees numbering over 25,000 or so. Firms of this size will seldom consummate a technological revolution on such a scale as to displace instantly so many of its employees: hence, the criticism is likely to be misdirected. Only in very strange cases would the upgrading be so extensive as to change the mix of skills dramatically and drastically.

In cases where it did occur, and with TIP restricted to the big firms, exemptions for upgrading of skills by submitting evidence of enormous capital investment could be entertained. On several occasions "certificates

---

*This point has been made by Laurence Seidman.

of necessity" have been used by the Internal Revenue Service to qualify firms for special tax treatment of their investment activities. TIP, likewise, could be waived, perhaps within a 1 to 5 percentage point limit, to cover these instances.

Criticism of TIP for "impeding technological advance" is an overdrawn objection which can be vastly exaggerated. The defect can be repaired.

SAFETY-VALVE ASPECTS

The opinion that TIP enforces an *identical* pay hike for everybody was judged fallacious, for it was based on a misrepresentation of the notion.

A supreme merit of TIP is that, like all good legislation, it provides a "safety valve" or "escape clause" compatible with a democratic order. For example, in laws designed to prevent traffic speeding, all of us can violate the posted limits, in cognizance that we will have to pay a fine, or forfeit our driver's license. Yet circumstances exist, such as an accident involving a trip to the hospital, or other emergency instances, when we are willing to accept the penalty with equanimity, on a personal cost-benefit appraisal. Even in murder cases our justice system organizes trial procedures to consider mitigating circumstances!

The concept is true of TIP. Firms may violate its mandates, recognizing the presence of the tax piper. TIP has this flexibility, allowing firms to puncture its ceilings, but at a cost. In contrast to price and wage controls, there is no harassment, no denunciation, no disapprobation for immoral and reprehensible conduct. In short, no muss, no fuss. Just a definite tax penalty.

In this respect TIP passes the test of good and wholesome democratic legislation. Moreover, it is compatible with our democratic ways, entailing *at worst* some increase in corporate tax rates. The greater likelihood, however, is that TIP would *reduce* corporate taxes, and substantially so.

ADMINISTRATIVE VIRTUES

In its administrative dimensions TIP vastly overshadows any other proposal conceived so far as a remedy to stop the skyrocketing of money incomes that spell inflation.

As noted earlier, the TIP computations would entail 7 new lines on the corporate income tax form. With TIP-CAP, the total information would take about another 6 lines.

It should be easily within the competence of an auditor in the IRS to examine about two such forms per day, even allowing for numerous coffee breaks. At ten forms per week, this would add up to 500 per annum. For 2,500 firms it would entail about five additional auditors in the Internal Revenue Service. At $25,000 per annum, the government cost would come to $125,000 per annum. Magnifying this fourfold, to $1,000,000, or even upping the figure to $10,000,000 to allow for overruns, it is still a paltry sum, for the big prize at the end of the trail is an annual GNP increase of $50 billion to $250 *billion*.

This is a stupendous trade-off, spending so little with a highly certain prospect of winning so much. Above all, if TIP were an abject failure—and from what we know of the deterrent effect of taxes, it could hardly be a loser—it could be abandoned, for it does not rear a large vested bureaucracy with a commitment to its survival. If TIP were dismantled, the handful of employees could very easily be absorbed in other government bureaus; there would not be a personnel army to resist and to sustain it.

Compared to the 100,000 to 200,000 employees needed for price and wage controls, TIP comes out as a super-bargain. Its cost is nominal; its job reasons for a bureaucratic domicile are nil. Its focus is on the main problem, targeted to a relatively small handful of firms; its mission would alienate public rancor on inflation while its operation would not raise congressional hackles for epic battles in conducting its well-defined mission.

Tremendous economic gains are waiting to be plucked, namely, conquering inflation and attaining full employment by enabling the Federal Reserve to submerge its inflation fears and instead, to go ahead to lubricate the economy with the financial resources for funding jobs for all under a stable price level.

Adversaries must not be permitted to misrepresent TIP. It is *not* anti-union. It is *not* anti-business. *It is anti-inflation, and pro-full employment*.

A NOTE ON COLLECTIVE BARGAINING

Deserving of special attention are some remarks in this chapter which indict collective bargaining for being obsolete. The brief contends 1) that unions *neglect*, within their firms or industry, the transmission of equal (or greater) pay gains for nonunionized employees, and thus a widening of absolute pay discrepancies which contribute to a more lopsided income distribution, 2) the oversight in the price boosts in their own firms and industries, and 3) the price spiral extending outward to other business sectors.

These issues transcend TIP. The union movement will in the large fail of its objectives on real income gains and distributive equity unless a new vision is installed. Otherwise unions will thrash and tread water in the stagflation sea while our economy writhes in distress.

13

TIP VARIANTS AND SUPPLEMENTS

To round out the discussion, some alternate TIP conceptions and features are appraised. Reward, as against penalty, TIPs have more political appeal, but their luster dims in the complex operational drawbacks.* The threat of the "stick" is less ponderous administratively than the sweet smell of a "carrot."

A TIP ON PRICES AND PERSONAL INCOMES?

It might seem odd that a penalty TIP on price increases has not been projected. But several factors render this superfluous or futile. First, on the conceptual model of the *modus operandi* of the economy, it would prove superfluous. Recall, our image of the economic system posited an outpayment of money wages as costs, and income, and the return tide of consumer purchases; the wage-salary incomes were the bread cast upon the economic waters. On this logic by tying income payments to productivity, prices would stay stable. In addition, mark-up constancy would ensure that profits would be normal and reasonable, with the income ceiling clamping a protective lid, prohibiting an exorbitant outcome.

*I find it amazing, in the light of their obvious negative features, that the Carter economic advisers continued to be fascinated with the idea, devoting substantial space to it in the *Economic Report* (1981), pp. 57-58, 84-98. For a criticism, see my article on "A Thalidomide TIP," *Journal of Post Keynesian Economics* (Spring 1981).

If profits somehow became outrageous, it would always be possible to invoke the corporate income tax system to sweep in the extra fluff: a profit inflation could be a piece of cake instantly devoured by a tax bite. So if TIP did somehow spur a profit eruption, it could be eliminated forthwith. Certainly, an advocacy of escalating money wages, in the event of a high profits turnout, would only kick up prices and knock profits further, both absolutely and perhaps relatively.

Analogously, the nigh insuperable obstacle to a TIP schema for prices is that it would engender a hapless bureaucratic snarl, as a near kin of price controls. Almost every large firm produces literally *hundreds* of products: what particular steel price would be subjected to TIP? What auto price, with what accessories, what size, and what model? What price for General Electric or Westinghouse appliances, or Xerox or IBM models? And if some way was found to specify the particular models to be priced, how would a TIP handle quality changes in composition, size, or other product attribute?

Quality aspects, and product variations, thus make a TIP on prices sheerly impossible to enforce. The best that could be done would be to place a TIP on profit *margins*. That is, firms might be penalized for exceeding their "average" markup experience for the last three years, or five years, or some other compromise. But then, the TIP would provoke a series of strategic games played out by the firm, for example, profit margins being raised in years when profit prospects are slim, and thus any TIP penalty was small, and margins held constant, or reduced, to evade the tax when profit prospects were promising.

Probably the best solution would be the use of a reward TIP, which *lowered* corporate tax rates whenever firms abated their markups or profit margins. Reflection, however, suggests that a slack in profit margins as large as 10 percent would trim the price level by 1 percent. Simultaneously, to accomplish it the corporate tax rate would have to be hacked by about 10 percentage points, from 45 to 35 percent. This would entail a substantial revenue loss, to be made up by higher personal income taxes, for a meager price improvement. Note, too, the gain via price relief would be largely digested by the higher personal taxes.*

To drive the price level down by 5 to 7 percent would thus involve a *complete* abolition of the corporate income tax, and substitution of higher personal income levies. Still, the price respite would be brief, for, after the corporate income tax was dismantled, the nagging query would erupt: what do we do for an encore after wages persist in an escalation unaligned to productivity?

*The calculations are elaborated in my *Capitalism's Inflation and Unemployment Crisis* (Reading, Mass.: Addison-Wesley, 1978), chapter 7.

Chipping away at corporate income tax rates to trim profit margins thus ranks high as a one-time shot, without a lasting impact on the churning inflation emanating from wages and salaries outracing productivity.

A PERSONAL INCOME TAX TIP

Reasons abound for rejecting a TIP on personal incomes; the omission of the proposal till now was not inadvertent.

It would be extremely cumbersome administratively, stretching to about 100 million taxpayers. It would require a bureaucratic legion, say, to check income increases over 5 percent either to impose penalties, or to cope with the mountainous claims for tax rewards for lower pay bounties. How would we handle people on first jobs? What exactly is a *first* job? How deal with promotions? How trace the income pay movements of people shifting jobs, or enjoying perquisites in lieu of money income?

Obviously, a TIP program on personal incomes would complicate an already intricate tax code. A personal income TIP would be feasible, with all its drawbacks, only in bringing to a quick halt an experience like the German hyperinflation of 1923 when prices skyrocketed by trillions and trillions percent per annum. The personal income TIP loses its rationale, in the maze of administrative complexities, in the steady cantering inflation that plagues us.

REENFORCING TIP

TIP, by itself, would be a strong ally in slowing the pay escalator that translates into prices. To do a more thorough job in shutting the money income door, reenforcement could be secured by measures directed at industries outside the TIP net which traps only the largest firms.

CONSTRUCTION: REPEAL OF THE DAVIS-BACON ACT

Pay scales in the construction industry have generally been the bell-cow in the money-income acceleration over the last 30 years; the only surprise is that we seem shocked that home prices have zoomed. It should not require 12 graduate courses in economics, with arcane discussion of money supplies, or government largesse, to apprehend that new home prices are inexorably destined to jump nearly fivefold when average wages in home-building mount from about $5,000 in 1950, for example, to about $25,000 in 1980. Only a tortuous logic of evasion strives to explain the price facts on new houses in terms other than construction costs of on-site labor, and the price of building materials which are guided by roughly the same wage facts.

As most construction firms are small, they would be untouched by TIP, at least directly. Yet because of the overwhelming price tag carried by the industry, something would have to be done to mitigate the construction price ascent. For example, the government spends over $100 billion, directly and indirectly, on new construction. Under the Davis-Bacon Act, contractors on projects financed in whole or part by government are subject to a clause stipulating the payment of "prevailing wages." The phrase is interpreted to mean the highest pay scale in approximately a 50-mile radius of the work site. Thus the government *insists* on paying top dollar for its construction, and for whatever edifices it assists, however meager its participation. The act is a Great Depression legacy which aimed at that time to raise pay standards.

The repeal of this anachronism is overdue. It would immediately restore more competitive bidding for government contracts.

Davis-Bacon should be replaced by a clause mandating that pay rates should not rise, from the *prevailing* construction wage scales, by more than 5 percent per annum over the life of the contract. Currently, and too often, labor lobbies, along with contractors, for the congressional authorization of construction projects that spell jobs for its members. Once the contracts are awarded, or when approval is imminent, there are strikes for higher pay, perhaps recompensed by cost-plus contractual stipulations. Effectively, there is "benign collusion" in a raid on the public purse.

It is known also that a criminal element dominates the leadership of several construction unions; a stronger enforcement effort by the Justice Department to weed out the nefarious individuals, often insensitive to labor's welfare, would keep pay scales from jumping inordinately. Over the years, labor defenders have been prone to close their eyes to the parade of hardened criminals and corrupt union officials serving prison terms for *anti*-labor activities.

TRUCKING

Trucking is another industry, important in the aggregate although dominated by smaller firms, that would escape TIP. Its teamster union has long had leaders, from Dave Beck to James Hoffa, who have gone to jail; and there is widespread suspicion that other leaders are candidates for incarceration for unsavory practices, including the frittering away of union pension funds in easy loans to gambling casinos or other enterprises on the criminal fringe.

The teamsters have often set the bargaining pattern, and its members are the princes of the labor movement; its leaders wield enormous political power in the "invisible" government where politicians are bought. It should be possible to deny government transportation contracts to any trucking firm which violates an average annual 5 percent pay boost. This would help to hold pay hikes to reasonable norms. Alternately, trucking firms doing over $5 million in business, or having over 50 employees, might be made subject to TIP.

This would widen the scope of TIP. Nonetheless, in any serious program it would be necessary to make special provision for construction and trucking because, in the nature of things, the firms are small but the total number of employees are large. Both occupations have generally been conspicuous in igniting inflationary pay standards.

TIP could be initiated without special coverage for construction and trucking. But if their emerging pay grants threatened the price fabric by their disdain of the 5 percent norm, supplementary control measures would be in order.

CONTRACT AUTHORIZATION INCOMES POLICY (CAIP)

Through government contracts it would be possible to extend the scope of TIP and simultaneously work the miracle of curbing cost overruns on government procurement, especially by the military and its industrial complex. Success would block raids on the public purse for gross private enrichment.

Very many government military contracts are negotiated on a "cost-plus" basis. Obviously, under the terms of the agreement there is little private incentive to protect the public interest by containing costs. Consequently, not only are pay scales lavish, but the top echelon rewards itself generously in what amounts to a no-risk enterprise, where most of the performance specifications for the military hardware are dictated, down to the last detail, by the Defense Department. This personal aggrandizement at the public trough could be brought to a halt by a TIP provision on average pay grants. Thus TIP-CAIP, with CAIP signifying a "contract authorization incomes policy," inserted prominently into procurement contracts, would pay for itself handsomely in containing the federal budget.

Many of the defense contractors would already be subject to TIP, for the military complex is a veritable "Who's Who" of our largest firms. Insofar as they are already subject to TIP, or TIP-CAP, the CAIP approach would impose no extra burden. Lesser firms, however, could be made subject to the same pay restraint.

GOVERNMENT EMPLOYEES

TIP would be assisted enormously by including government employees under a parallel control mechanism. For example, all federal employees might be limited to a 5 percent average annual increase and, to ensure that their pay did not lag private scales, at the end of every two or three years a review would provide adjustments to prevailing market pay scales. If this led, in the interim, to a practice of excessive promotions to evade the restraint, each Cabinet agency or independent bureau might be restricted to an overall average 5 percent pay ceiling, distributed by top management discretion, subject to federal union negotiation.

State and local governments could be covered by the same framework through the various grants made by the federal government; they could be conditioned to adhere to the noninflationary pay norm.

FARMERS, PROFESSIONAL PERSONNEL, AND SMALL BUSINESS

Farmers, and professional people such as doctors, dentists, lawyers, and music teachers, and small business people, could be exempt from any control or infringement on their income. The good reason is that their prices are largely *demand*-oriented. For example, if average money wages go up from $4,000 to $16,000, it should not cause amazement that doctors' fees rise from about $10 to $40 a visit, more or less. Similarly, as incomes go up it is inevitable that there is pressure on beef prices to rise from 50 cents per pound to $2. If most money incomes were held in alignment with productivity, the many demand-oriented prices would hew a close noninflationary line.

There is much substitution and imitation in these categories. If industrial wages rise far faster than farm incomes, people will leave the farms for the factories. If electronic workers show spectacular pay gains, then TV repairmen will have to earn corresponding sums; otherwise they would abandon their business for paid employment. Or if earnings jump inordinately in private small businesses, there would be an outflow from electronic factories to small service shops.

The host of small business firms and professional occupations, as well as farmers, could safely be omitted from TIP, or any analogous program devised to stop inflation.

REWARD TIPS

Stimulated by the Wallich-Weintraub penalty TIP, the late Arthur Okun ingeniously sought to turn TIP around by eschewing the stick for the carrot, with an enhanced politically appealing Reward TIP.* Briefly, the major drawback to a bonus TIP is that when a bounty is to be dispensed for good behavior, then (in the Jimmy Durante refrain) everyone wants to join the act. Administratively, it becomes an unwieldy jungle.

In a penalty TIP, individuals or firms will *prefer* to stay out, or to be overlooked. For rewards, they insist in joining in the fun. Unfortunately, when rewards are to be roundly granted, they must inevitably be small and meager. As an illustration, reverting to the earlier speed limit analogy, we can either fine violators of the posted speed limit or we could donate incentive rewards to those who abide the law. If rewards are to be given, and claimants are numerous and benefits are slim, they will fail to accomplish their purpose; generous bounties will prove onerous to finance.

Suppose a 2 or 3 percent TIP tax cut was handed only to large firms who abided the 5 percent pay norm. The hue and cry over discrimination would make it politic for the carrot to be dangled before all firms, rather than confined to only large firms. Statistics reveal that there are over 13 *million* firms in the United States. Administratively, to verify tax returns properly would be a costly and unwieldy bureaucratic task, compared to a penalty TIP on 2,500 firms.

This is ample motive to preclude a reward TIP. Consider labor's reaction to a reward TIP: the union protest would be that firms are being paid to "hold down wages." If the tax rebate rose for a zero pay increase, and thereafter fell on a progressive formula for a 2, 3, or 4 percent pay boost, labor would charge that the law was designed to "exploit labor," by making it financially virtuous to underpay workers.

Conversely, a penalty TIP would be punitive on the firms, and would make them ambivalent in tax calculations about forcing pay hikes below 5 percent. A "slave labor" indictment would roll off and be seen as partisan nonsense, for at a 5 percent pace, average pay would double about every 14 years. Also, if unions opposed a penalty TIP it would be the first time that they assumed a stance in opposition to a tax on corporations. Tactically, and administratively, merits adhere to the Wallich-Weintraub penalty TIP compared to a bonus TIP.

REAL WAGE INSURANCE

To induce workers, particularly unionized employees, to moderate pay demands Arthur Okun also devised a tax deduction, of about $150 at the time, for unions accepting contracts abiding pay increases in the 6 percent

*Somewhat earlier I had made a similar suggestion to cope with the 1974 slumpflation. See "A Tax Cut for Wage Restraint," *Challenge*, January 1974.

range. A similar measure was recommended by the Carter administration in the 1979 budget, but defeated soundly in a Congress widely uninformed on its vital intent.

The Carter version, as sent forward, had bald defects, especially in its limitation to union employees. There is no reason in equity for two individuals, one a union member and the other nonunion, both receiving the same starting pay and pay increment, to be treated differently under the tax laws. This discriminatory aspect was an unnecessary concession to union membership. Secondly, the lure of a $150 tax rebate for complying with the plea for moderation was paltry; a bellicose union leadership would shun the "peanuts" for an assault on employers for a far higher pay gain, say 10 or 12 percent, to overshadow the nominal tax bait.

COMBINING CARROTS AND STICKS

Yet the Okun principle remains valid, if slightly modified. *Everybody* who found their income from wages and salaries, and also from other sources, rising by less than 5 percent might be granted a tax deduction in the $300 range. This would be tantamount to a 2 percent pay increase on $15,000 per annum, or slightly more inasmuch as the credit is computed *after* taxes. This might do *something* to mitigate union pay demands, by perhaps 1 or 2 percent.

Combining this "reward" as a quid pro quo for income restraint, coupled with the Wallich-Weintraub penalty TIP on the largest 2,500 corporations, supplemented with TIP-CAP, and supported by the repeal of Davis-Bacon, and by CAIP, our inflation nightmare could be *ended*. We could dispense with the elusive and evasive 3 percent goal for 1988, proclaimed by former President Carter in his never-never-land economics. His 1988 goal would never have been reached under the then prevailing policies.

Inflation can be conquered, and in under a year, with a drive to full employment as a reality and not a dream. For without inflation worries to rationalize its job-depressing maneuvers, the Federal Reserve could use its monetary influence to guide the economy to jobs for all.

An economic boom to revitalize America is within reach. To grasp the opportunities will require new, innovative, and imaginative policies. Their origin is apparent for the power to tax is not only a "power to destroy" but a means to build by deft and benign influences on the market system. President Reagan, in declaring that "the taxing power . . . must not be used to regulate the economy or bring about social change," in his first address to Congress in which he proposed just such a use of tax reduction to stimulate the economy and to drop inflation, was not only baldly contradictory but also spelled out a narrow perception of the function of government and its budget levels.* The Reagan budget vision is clouded. Its precise function *is* to influence the economy in auspicious ways.

*President Reagan, "Message on Economic Recovery," *New York Times*, February 19, 1981.

EPILOGUE: ON GOOD-BYE
TO *THE ECONOMICS OF DERISION*

The theme of this book is somber, alarming, and disheartening, for the gist of it is that on present policies we are doomed to a future of inflation and unemployment. The judgment is not altered after an appraisal of the Reagan policies. There will be scant respite from an enduring stagflation malaise unless we shuck the shop-worn monetary recipes and Pangloss attitudes that all is well in the private sector, despite the remarkable and debilitating disarray in labor markets for over twelve years now. Nationally, we have basked in the economics of derision, embracing it as a loving parent hugs a child.

The economy will not improve despite maybe occasional splashes under current therapies; there is only darkness and not light in the tunnel ahead, unless we mend our ways with innovative measures, with TIP as the prime candidate to subdue inflation and lift us out of the unemployment mire. Federal expenditure austerity and tax abatement are not nearly enough. New policies on the pay-productivity front will alone permit us to master our economic destiny, opening the road to full employment, stable prices, and steady growth. Once market prices are brought to book, monetary policy could help secure the economic heights within our reach.

This is the optimistic overtone of these pages. But the breakaway will take courage, brains, and audacity; we will have to defuse a series of minor obfuscations and release the congressional handcuffs and slip the mental straitjacket about unfettered collective bargaining purveyed by the conventional myths as ample for our age. Our practice still clings tenaciously to archaic, sadistic monetary and McKinley budget policies. There is a befuddling conviction that has taken deep root in the land, to wit, that what has continually failed must, despite logic and evidence, ultimately succeed if only it is pursued long enough—even if the patient dies under its prolongation. The enterprise sector was not an undiluted triumph in its glory days. It has faltered in recent decades. Mere invocations will not suffice to yield modern miracles. A closed and confused mind on the money-income nexus and Fed money policies has been a key article of faith of those indoctrinated in the economics of derision.

Rationally, optimism over what we might do must animate anyone with a thought on economic amelioration, just as it incites pessimism on appraising what we have done and what we continue to do as captives of outmoded economic doctrine. The glory-road of steady prices and jobs for all can be traveled; but our leaders will have to grasp some stern facts of life, above all to parry opposition from groups congenitally opposed to the approach of the 21st century, let alone a new practice. Some politician, some day, will be startled to meet an enthusiastic constituency by echoing Adlai Stevenson, in his exhilarating 1952 presidential campaign call: "Better to lose an election than to deceive the American people."

TIP, to any potential political leader who embraced it, could be given a pure political orientation, for it is *not* antilabor, *nor* is it antibusiness. It is consistently *pro*-full employment, inherently *pro*-growth, and incessantly *anti*-inflation. These objectives lie within the ideological purview of both political parties and all major constituencies.

It is thus no accident that John Anderson endorsed the general TIP theory during the 1980 presidential campaign. Also, in former President Carter's August 28, 1980 message announcing, with appropriate fanfare, his Economic Revitalization Program (ERP)—a mini-New Deal to placate Senator Edward Kennedy—there was an undeveloped, fairly obscure paragraph tucked away reciting a TIP in 1981, if reelected.*

THE HUMPTY-DUMPTY ECONOMICS

Analytically, our consistent dissent has been over the Humpty-Dumpty economics of derision pursued by Nixon-Ford-Carter. President Reagan seems to be driven by an ideological aloofness based mostly on tenacious faith. It cannot survive as permanent policy. Regardless of political

*The same point was made by Treasury Secretary Miller, *New York Times*, October 11, 1980. Unfortunately, the thoughts were muddled in the mischievous version of TIP elaborated in the final Carter *Economic Report* (1981), pp. 57-88. As remarked earlier (p. 193), I regard this as "A Thalidomide TIP."

incumbency—and incompetency—the tactics constitute the legacy of price-level wisdom imparted by the 7 maids with 7 brooms sweeping the 7 seas at the Federal Reserve Board. (We are apt to suffer many reruns under a Ronald Reagan presidency.) The critique is a melancholy, and a marvelously nonpartisan indictment, applicable to Republicans and Democrats alike as both see unflagging novelty in reactivating the monetary buzz-saw to stop inflation. Invariably, when the recovery road is being run, the Fed, in season and out, becomes alarmed and starts its bashing to squash the price menace by tight money. Once the production and job upturn is arrested—with inflation *unabated* despite their unfailing subtle boasts of their heroics—and the economy "recessed" as much as is politically tolerable, the Fed undertakes to reverse its motion to restore the economy.

It is a game of first dumping Humpty, and then assembling the pieces to a previous posture—or more like pouring a broken egg back into the shell by reversing a TV film clip. In the last ten years, on at least four occasions, 1972, 1975, 1977, and 1980, steps were taken to "rev" up the economy after the Fed had undermined it earlier. Somehow, public officials never weary of a destroy-to-revive fantasy; they indulge it as a mark of economic "statesmanship," despite the injury inflicted on our people. The Fed antics could inspire a Gilbert and Sullivan parody, complete with dancing clowns, on how chronic ill-health acts as a miraculous curative balm. It is possible to indict the Fed follies as tedious, gross, corny, crude, sadistic, relentless, and downright scary for the future of capitalism.

Although a child should penetrate its irrational features, adults remain beguiled by the prevailing monetary wisdom, especially when it is articulated by assorted Wall Street mystics, who support academic mandarins, and befog media people who disseminate the brew as among the eternal verities in veiled and clipped remarks which pretend it has a sane base. So we go on prancing in a mad derisive dance, of toppling our economy in order to revive it! Judging by the hysterical historical record, the Fed's performance has been an egregious flop. The old follies should be taken off the stage, put in mothballs, and carted to the same wing where old magic, based on sublime illusion, is warehoused.

THE KEMP-ROTH SPOOF

The Senate in 1980 actually had passed a bill to cut personal and corporate incomes taxes by $40 billion, in a flirtatious compromise with the Kemp-Roth proposal. The House did not act on the pre-Reagan jaunt. The measure followed the Republican convention call of Ronald Reagan to cut taxes, decrease expenditures, increase military expenditures—and balance the budget! Simultaneously, Paul Volcker, Fed chairman, declared his opposition to a tax cut.

On February 18, 1981, President Reagan called for a 10 percent individual tax cut in each of the next three years. If enacted, a classic confrontation is shaping up. Just as the tax cut should be stimulating to the economy, the Fed, even at the bottom of the 1980 recession, is tolerating long-term interest rates, to the *best* borrowers, in the 15 to 20 percent plus range. Once again, one hand of the government is negating the flourishes of the other hand. Many in Congress who support the tax cut even applaud the Fed's tight money maneuvers! President Reagan promised to honor a full scope for the Fed.

Either this is political hokum or political absurdity. Either way, the unedifying spectacle attests to maladroitness in current economic policy. Our only reward for the Fed's unrelieved policies will be more inflation, higher interest rates, and a prolongation of the recession; still we will have to endure Fed boasts of its valiant interminable fight against inflation. Rarely does it occur to the Fed heroes that they are wielding the wrong weapons from the wrong armory, and on the wrong front. Mild alleviation on prices may come from future-jam tomorrow—government budget cuts and regulatory dismantlement; one can suspect that this will mean a job downturn except in the military complex.

These sad and counterproductive events occur in our great country at this late date. Yet there is a slight ray of hope in the current chaotic legerdemain. Though in tax policy we have the army advancing, and in the Fed's posturing we have it retreating, one step forward and one plus backward, the Kemp-Roth sponsors tender their bill as a recipe for righting the economy, particularly in monotonous chants about supply side economics, to raise productivity by the tax cut fostering plant modernization. Their optimism is never tempered by the prospect of the Fed, through still tighter money, neutralizing the tax inducements to invest. They are blithely and blindly uncognizant of the fact that this and other recessions are made at the Fed.

Even barring obstructionist Fed tactics, the productivity assistance of Kemp-Roth will be minuscule, and deferred, and thus mythical in the here-and-now; by 1990 it may make a slight difference!

There is one grand quarterback dodge by Congressman Kemp that deserves mention. He constantly harks back to the Kennedy tax-cut success as warrant for his own digressions. He fails even to mention that Kennedy invoked price and wage *Guideposts* so that prices were literally constant and the Fed was free to sustain interest rates in the 5 to 7 percent range, and secondly that government expenditures in money and real terms escalated under Kennedy. Without these supporting facts the Kemp analogy is an unadulterated spoof, and a supreme trifling with the facts.

But the philosophy motivating Kemp-Roth finally recognizes that the budget objective should be less concerned with achieving an illusory prospective balance and more devoted to nudging the economy in a desired direction. Despite the Kemp-Roth merchandising of their bill as a cure for all our ills, their recognition of an economic objective represents a grand advance beyond transcending the immediate vision of the sponsors. (Their remarks on surging treasury revenues which will balance the budget, based on Laffer curves, can be disregarded as mainly huckstering for their pet.)

Kemp-Roth thus holds a parallel to TIP; its legislative genesis is based on the same precept, to wit, to use the tax mechanism to aid recovery. Kemp-Roth and TIP, in this respect, are brothers under the skin. But TIP puts the priority in the proper perspective in its concern with inflation and its money income source.

THE FUTURE

Jimmy Carter named a "target" date of 1988 to brake inflation at 3 percent.* Some "target" that! It would condemn us to eight more harsh years of the price ordeal. President Reagan appears to put the date about 1984. Fortunately, Carter's term has expired. Nonetheless, on Reagan policies we are likely to be apprised of a deferral to 1986 and then moved forward again. Persistence in the same addiction to monetary and budgetary shibboleths, and the Bourbon capacity never to unlearn, leaves our economic fate sealed to an unknown date. Economic opaqueness appears, too often, to be an instant qualification for high office.

We can stop inflation. Not in 1986 or 1988 but now, meaning within less than a year. We can have practically full employment. We can once more resume the growth path. There is no need to postpone our growth for a never-never future date.

To reach the better day we will have to drop old dogmas and supplant timid officials who only fear obstacles and never seize opportunities; befuddled by fuddy-duddy thinking, they are impervious to a new thought as they see a grandeur that never was in the enterprise system; it had booms and big drops too often. Rather than try to improve on a con-

Economic Report (1980), p. 10.

structive idea, they magnify small hampers rather than seek means to surmount them. The tactics are reminiscent of too many professional economists who prefer living, and dying, in discussing a problem rather than in resolving the issue. A great man, General George Marshall, was fond of saying that "for new policies you need new people." There is a long list of people in high government circles who qualify for reassignment.

It bears repeating that the Carter economic policy that traces back to October 1978 with the appointment of Alfred Kahn, was *never* a policy to *stop* inflation. It *was* a policy to *sustain* it at approximately 7 percent, with error only possible on the upside. Of course, we have had miscalculations aplenty, and thus double-digit inflation. Any resemblance of the 1978 policy to TIP, despite some penalty features, is wholly fictitious.

Margaret Thatcher, prime minister of Great Britain in 1981, has quite unintentionally demolished the old monetary myths which she extravagantly propagated before and since assuming office. Her unbridled faith in the monetarist nostrums, which scorned incomes policy, has since accomplished a price explosion of 20 percent per annum as pay grants settled in about the same range. Before her sojourn prices, which had escalated by 25 percent per annum, had been tethered down toward 9 percent under the Labour Party pay curbs. British unemployment in year-end 1980 registered 10 percent, the highest since 1936. Even Herbert Hoover's score was not as grotesque; prices fell during his incumbency at the outset of the Great Depression.

Nixon, Ford, Carter, Thatcher—there are others in other countries— have performed an extraordinary, if not exemplary, feat in eclipsing the economic fiascos that were once indelibly attached to Hoover's name. The current crew of "leaders" might yet immortalize him as a great economic leader, rather than a colossal blunderer. On Reagan, who is changing the course of government, the verdict can only come later. But though he may report initial successes, an ultimate triumph, if one hazards an estimate, is dubious.

Can we not read a page from the British follies and monetarist horrors? If our own record is not plain enough to discern, there is a litmus test in the United Kingdom.

It should be possible to learn *something*. Politicians over time can detect a new idea. But first, our economic education will have to be completed. The economics of derision, built on the quicksands of monetary policy and a myopic and calloused disdain of the money income-labor productivity nexus, will have to be purged from our administrative manuals. Solemn officials with repressive economic impulses will have to be supplanted by visionary people dedicated to surmounting economic obstacles, rather than congenitally devoted to erecting them.

A REAGAN POSTSCRIPT

There is one small qualification that may be entered as a postscript. President Reagan, in following the Kemp-Roth tax creed, may enjoy some triumph in creating jobs. But this will mean price pressures on goods directly, and, if truly successful, it will generate indirect pressures via wage hikes. His expenditure cuts will wipe out jobs on programs dependent on these outlays. Taken all together, it will largely wash out as a standoff. If he is more successful than present programs and magnitudes suggest, there is always the depressing Federal Reserve presence for higher interest rates to thwart any impulse toward exultation.

Reagan may, however, be lucky. Fortune can smile on him for a time. He may profit by the distress in autos and steel, and be the beneficiary of lower wage settlements as a *back-door* incomes policy of pay restraint. He is also limiting government employees to a 4.8 percent hike. Inflation relief, however, will be spotty and short lived, especially if through import limitations the auto industry recovers reasonably well. There will be a need for a TIP in our future.

We should not condone job miseries to stop inflation.

INDEX

214 / Index

About the Author

SIDNEY WEINTRAUB is Professor of Economics at the University of Pennsylvania and coeditor of the Journal of Post Keynesian Economics. He has lectured extensively throughout the world and has been a consultant to numerous government agencies. His seventeen books include:

Price Theory (1949)
Income and Employment Analysis (1951)
An Approach to the Theory of Income Distribution (1958)
Forest Service Price and Appraisal Policies (1958)
A General Theory of the Price Level (1959)
Classical Keynesianism, Monetary Theory, and the Price Level (1961)
Some Aspects of Wage Theory and Policy (1963)
Intermediate Price Theory (1964)
Growth Without Inflation in India (1965)
A Keynesian Theory of Employment Growth and Income Distribution (1966)
Keynes and the Monetarists (1973)
Income Inequality (Editor, 1973)
Incomes Policy for Full Employment Without Inflation in Canada (1976)
Modern Economic Thought (Editor, 1976)
Capitalism's Inflation and Unemployment Crisis (1978)
Keynes, Keynesians, and Monetarists (1978)